Consuming Germany in the Cold War

Leisure, Consumption and Culture

General Editor: Rudy Koshar, *University of Wisconsin at Madison*

Leisure regimes in Europe (and North America) in the last two centuries have brought far-reaching changes in consumption patterns and consumer cultures. The past twenty years have seen the evolution of scholarship on consumption from a wide range of disciplines, but historical research on the subject is unevenly developed for late modern Europe, just as the historiography of leisure practices is limited to certain periods and places. This series encourages scholarship on how leisure and consumer culture evolved with respect to an array of identities. It relates leisure and consumption to the symbolic systems with which tourists, shoppers, fans, spectators, and hobbyists have created meaning, and to the structures of power that have shaped such consumer behaviour. It treats consumption in general and leisure practices in particular as complex processes involving knowledge, negotiation, and the active formation of individual and collective selves.

Titles previously published in this series

German Travel Cultures
Rudy Koshar

Commercial Cultures
Edited by **Peter Jackson, Michelle Lowe, Daniel Miller and Frank Mort**

The Politics of Consumption: Material Culture and Citizenship in Europe and America
Edited by **Martin Daunton and Matthew Hilton**

Histories of Leisure
Edited by **Rudy Koshar**

Museums and Modernity: Art Galleries and the Making of Modern Culture
Nick Prior

Water, Leisure and Culture: European Historical Perspectives
Edited by **Susan C. Anderson and Bruce H. Tabb**

Consuming Germany in the Cold War

Edited by
David F. Crew

Oxford • New York

First published in 2003 by
Berg
Editorial offices:
1st Floor, Angel Court, 81 St Clements Street, Oxford, OX4 1AW, UK
838 Broadway, Third Floor, New York, NY 10003-4812, USA

Berg is the imprint of Oxford International Publishers Ltd.

Library of Congress Cataloging-in-Publication Data
Consuming Germany and the Cold War / edited by David F. Crew.
p. cm. – (Leisure, consumption, and culture)
Includes bibliographical references and index.
ISBN 1-85973-766-8 – ISBN 1-85973-771-4 (pbk.)
1. Consumption (Economics)–Germany (East) 2. Consumption (Economics)–Germany (West) 3. Consumer behavior–Germany (East) 4. Consumer behavior–Germany (West) I. Crew, David F., 1946- II. Series.

HC290.795.C6C66 2003
339.4'7'094309045–dc21

2003010058

British Library Cataloguing-in-Publication Data
A catalogue record for this book is available from the British Library.

ISBN 1 85973 766 8 (Cloth)
1 85973 771 4 (Paper)

Typeset by JS Typesetting Ltd, Wellingborough, Northamptonshire
Printed in the United Kingdom by Biddles Ltd, Guildford and King's Lynn

www.bergpublishers.com

Contents

Acknowledgements

The idea for this book emerged from a panel at the German Studies Association Annual Meeting in Houston, Texas, October 5–8, 2000. Being asked to serve as the commentator on the three papers in this session by Katherine Pence, Judd Stitziel and S. Jonathan Wiesen gave me the chance to think seriously about the importance of consumption in East and West Germany after 1945. Post-panel conversations with Kathy, Judd, Jonathan and the chair of the session, Shelley Baranowski, convinced me that here was a subject that deserved a collection of essays. At Berg, Kathyrn Earle's early enthusiasm for this project encouraged me to develop a book proposal quicker than I might otherwise have done. Thanks are due also to Eli Rubin, Jeff Schutts and Robert Stephens for agreeing to add their contributions to the original three essays by Katherine Pence, Judd Stitziel and Jonathan Wiesen. Kathleen May and Ian Critchley have made the process of moving this book from manuscript to print as streamlined and painless as possible. Rudy Koshar, the general editor of the series in which this book appears, deserves special mention for his careful reading of the original manuscript and for his timely assistance at a critical point in this project's history.

David F. Crew,
Austin, Texas,
April, 2003

Notes on Contributors

David Crew is Professor of History at the University of Texas at Austin. His most recent book is a study of the Weimar welfare state and its interactions with citizens, *Germans on Welfare: From Weimar to Hitler* (Oxford, 1998). He is also the editor of *Nazism and German Society 1933–45* (London, 1994). He is now working on his next book, *Nazism's Afterlife: The History of German Memory, 1945 to the Present.*

Katherine Pence is Assistant Professor of History at Baruch College, CUNY in New York City. She has published a number of articles, the most recent of which is "'You as a woman will understand': Consumption, Gender, and the Relationship between State and Citizenry in the GDR's June 17, 1953 Crisis" in *German History* (2001). Her forthcoming book examines gender, consumption and Cold War politics in East and West Germany in the late 1940s and 1950s. Pence completed her PhD at the University of Michigan, taught at Adrian College in Michigan, and was a James Bryant Conant Fellow at Harvard University before moving to New York.

Eli Rubin received a B.A. from Swarthmore College in 1997 and an M.A. from the University of Wisconsin-Madison in 2001. He returned from a year and a half as a Social Science Research Council Berlin Program for Advanced German and European Studies visiting fellow, and is currently working on a dissertation at UW-Madison on Plastic Consumer Goods and Everyday Life in the German Democratic Republic.

Jeff Schutts will defend his dissertation, entitled "Coca-Colonization, 'refreshing' Americanization, or Nazi Volksgetränk? The History of Coca-Cola in Germany, 1929–1961," in 2003. Capitalizing on his training at Georgetown University's interdisciplinary BMW Center for German and European Studies, his examination of the Coke case study employs a historian's discipline, the sensitivities of a cultural theorist, and the pragmatism of political economists in order to illuminate the genesis of global consumer culture, the dynamics of so-called Americanization, and the role of corporate capitalism within the Third Reich. Complementing this work on cultural transfer and transnational relations, Schutts is developing a new project on the role of dissent in the military that will examine the interactions between the European peace movement and anti-war GIs stationed in Germany.

Living in Vancouver, Canada, while completing his dissertation, Schutts has been employed as a sessional lecturer at the University of British Columbia, Kwantlen University-College, Douglas College, and Western Washington University. Assisting his wife, Michelle Mason, he also has produced a television documentary on an international veterans' reconciliation project in Vietnam, The Friendship Village (Cypress Park Productions, 2002). He can be contacted by email: *schuttsj@georgetown.edu*.

Robert Stephens is Assistant Professor in the Department of History at Virginia Polytechnic and State University. His research focuses on youth cultures in postwar Germany, and he is currently completing a manuscript on drug consumption and youth culture in the Federal Republic after the Second World War.

Judd Stitziel has taught as Visiting Assistant Professor at Cornell University and Wesleyan University and is currently an independent scholar. He received a B.A. from Yale University and an M.A. and Ph.D. from The Johns Hopkins University. One of his forthcoming articles on consumer culture and politics in the GDR is "Konsumpolitik zwischen 'Sortimentslücken' und 'Überplanbeständen' in der DDR der 1950er Jahre," in *Die DDR vor dem Mauerbau: Politik und Gesellschaft*, edited by Dierk Hoffmann, Michael Schwartz, and Hermann Wentker (Munich: Oldenbourg). He also is revising his doctoral dissertation, "Fashioning Socialism: Clothing, Politics, and Consumer Culture in East Germany, 1948–1971," for publication.

S. Jonathan Wiesen is Assistant Professor of History at Southern Illinois University at Carbondale. He is the author of *West German Industry and the Challenge of the Nazi Past, 1945–1955* (Chapel Hill, 2001) and articles on postwar memory, National Socialism, and German business. He is currently writing a history of public relations during the Third Reich and is also at work on a larger project about fears of "the masses" in Modern Germany.

List of Abbreviations

AiF	Amt für industrielle Formgestaltung
ARD	Arbeits gemeinschaft der öffentlich-rechtlichen Rundfunkanstalten Deutschlands (working-group of public service broadcasters in the Federal Republic of Germany)
BA	Bundesarchiv
BA-BL	Bundesarchiv, Abteilungen Berlin, Berlin-Lichterfelde
BAK	Bundesarchiv Koblenz
BAP	Bundesarchiv Potsdam
CCCA	Coca-Cola Company Archives
CDU	Christlich-Demokratische Union (Christian Democratic Union)
DAMW	Deutsches Amt für Material- und Warenprüfung (later Deutsches Amt für Meßwesen und Warenprüfung)
DDR	Deutsche Demokratische Republik
DEFA	Deutsche Film-Aktiengesellschaft
DFD	Demokratischer Frauenbund Deutschlands (Democratic Women's League of Germany)
DGB	Deutscher Gewerkschaftsbund (German Trade Union Federation)
DIA	Deutsche Industrie-Ausstellung (Germany Industry Exhibition)
FDGB	Demokratischer Frauenbund Deutschlands
FDJ	Freie Deutsche Jugend
FRG	Federal Republic of Germany
GATPO	German-American Trade Promotion Office
GDR	German Democratic Republic
KWAF	Kultur- und Werbegeschichtliche Archiv Freiburg
LAB	Landesarchiv Berlin
NES	New Economic System
SAPMO-BA	Stifttung Archiv der Parteien und Massenorganisationen der DDR im Bundesarchiv
SED	Sozialistische Einheitspartei Deutschlands
SMAD	Sowjetische Militäradministration in Deutschland
SPD	Sozialdemokratische Partei Deutschlands (Social Democratic Party of Germany)
USIA	United States Information Agency

VEB	Volkseigener Betrieb
VVB	Vereinigung Volkseigener Betriebe
ZfG	Zentralinstitut für Gestaltung

1

Consuming Germany in the Cold War: Consumption and National Identity in East and West Germany, 1949–1989, An Introduction

David F. Crew

Since the fall of the Berlin Wall, the history of East Germany has rapidly developed into an important new growth area for research. Unprecedented access to East German archives that were virtually off-limits to Westerners for four decades has made it possible for historians to correct misconceptions and to fill in long vacant spaces in our understanding of the GDR. Our narratives of East German history should soon be as detailed as those already constructed for the Federal Republic.[1] But will these remain two largely separate story lines? Or will it be possible to talk about the ways in which the histories of both East and West Germany have been shaped by their real relationships and mutual imaginings? And will this be an unequal story in which West Germany (real and imagined) turns out to have been much more important for East Germany than vice versa?[2]

From the moment of their creation in 1949, East and West Germany competed with one another for legitimacy in the eyes of their own and each other's citizens. This competition was fought out on several different terrains. One of the most important was the relationship of the two successor states to the Nazi past. East Germany insisted that, unlike West Germany, it had radically extinguished all vestiges of Nazism on its soil. The Federal Republic claimed that, like Nazism, East German communism was simply another form of totalitarianism. Most ordinary East and West Germans were also preoccupied with the recent past. Their memories, however, were not of Nazi atrocities and genocide, of perpetrators and their victims, but of the suffering to which ordinary Germans had been subjected during and immediately after the war: hunger, homelessness, mass rape, flight, deportation, and forced labor.[3] The pain of these recent experiences of war was reinforced by many Germans' memories of hunger and deprivation during the First World War, the postwar inflation, and the world economic depression after 1929. The combination of Hitler's "economic miracle" (the result of the rearmament boom in the mid/late 1930s) and the first deliriously successful years of the Second World War had tantalized many Aryan Germans with the dream of a brilliant national future. But the brevity of this period of prosperity (gained by plundering occupied Europe) made the experience of postwar deprivation and suffering all the more bitter. Sitting in the ruins of the "Third Reich," most Germans only wanted to know which of the two postwar German states would be able to banish the reality and the memory of wartime hardships more quickly, more thoroughly. Consumption and the quality of everyday life rapidly emerged as important battlefields upon which the East–West conflict would be fought out.[4]

West Germany was the first to achieve this particular form of "overcoming the past." Michael Wildt concludes that by the late 1950s in the Federal Republic,

> The memory of hunger, ever-present in the minds of the older generation, was disappearing. The stores overflowing with goods and the abundant displays in the butcher-shop windows – all demonstrated not just a transient dream of prosperity, but permanent affluence . . . the need for frugality was receding, along with structural restrictions of the past and the cultural limitations of an older way of life.[5]

The less dramatic pace of economic revival in East Germany left the traces of Germany's wartime deprivation closer to the surface of everyday life. Rationing of some food items continued until 1958.[6] Well into the 1960s, shortages could assume a symbolic significance greater than their immediate material consequences. In 1965, for example, an East German woman who was trying to organize a wedding celebration was told she could have one piece of butter and one bottle of condensed milk for 30–35 guests. She found this allotment absurd because "We are no longer in the year 1946, when we literally had nothing. I believe that our Republic is rich enough to put more at our disposal for such occasions."[7] Another East German accepted the fact that oranges, nuts, and imported apples, all of which required scarce foreign currency, were in short supply but he simply could not understand why there were no potatoes: "After all, it is no longer 1945."[8]

Certainly no one (except perhaps students and senior citizens) went hungry in the GDR. The prices of basic necessities such as bread, milk, and meat were fixed by the state at relatively low levels, and wages continued to rise. The problem, as Jeffrey Kopstein puts it, "for the East German consumer was generally not a lack of marks but a lack of products on which to spend them."[9] Even during the "golden" years of the GDR (the 1960s and early 1970s[10]), consumers could not count on a steady and predictable flow of the TVs, cars, and washing machines they desired at prices they could afford. Yet, at the same time, the GDR's planned economy produced large amounts of goods that could not be sold because of their inferior quality (pullovers with one sleeve longer than the other, for example), or because they were priced too high (especially when compared to similar West German goods). These items had to be stockpiled in warehouses or off-loaded at bargain prices.[11] Warehouses full of unwanted goods made the issue of shortages all the more irritating.

Ina Merkel has, however, cautioned against constructing a one-dimensional narrative of the East German economy which is a simple story of failure. She argues that East Germany should not be seen as just a shabby imitation of Western consumer society but rather "one attempt among many others to find solutions for similar problems."[12] Yet it would be wrong to argue that a separate and distinctly "socialist" regime of consumption developed over the course of the forty years of the GDR's existence. East Germany was never able to disentangle itself from the influence of the West German capitalist economy. For most of the period from 1949 to 1989, the standard by which East Germans judged their material existence was not their own previous deprivation in 1945 or 1946 but the real and imagined quality of life across the border in West Germany. Before 1961 when the Berlin Wall was constructed, East Germans could still travel to the West, especially to West Berlin, where simply by looking in department store windows they could compare the results of West Germany's "economic miracle" with their own state's version of postwar economic recovery. After the wall put an abrupt end to this cross-border traffic, East Germans still had daily access to images of West German consumer society via the Western television broadcasts that reached almost every area of the GDR. When they opened any one of the millions of gift packages sent by relatives and friends in West Germany, East Germans could make direct comparisons between their own material culture and the living standards of citizens in the Federal Republic.[13] East German pensioners, one of the few categories of GDR citizens still allowed to travel to the West, also provided up-to-date information on West German consumer goods.[14] These opportunities for constant comparison between the everyday realities of East German socialism and West German capitalism helped to corrode the legitimacy of the East German state. By the 1970s, at the latest, East Germans were well aware that the regime's bombastic promise, made at the Fifth Party Congress in 1958, that the GDR would soon "overtake the West" had become completely hollow. For most East German citizens, West German consumer society set the standards which East Germany repeatedly failed to meet.[15]

The relationship between the two Germanies involved concrete economic interactions as well as the imaginings and longings of East German consumers. The construction of the Berlin Wall in 1961 stopped the flow of people between East and West but not the movement of goods. East Germany was never able to do without Western imports and it became increasingly hungry for the hard currency its exports could earn in the West.[16] After Erich Honecker came to power in 1971, the involvement of the capitalist West in the East German economy continued to expand, assuming ever more pathological forms. Unable to finance increased consumption and social services from its own production, the GDR began to run up huge foreign-trade deficits. Borrowing from the West to bridge this gap set off a destructive spiral; to service its mounting foreign debt, the GDR emphasized production for export, which in turn deprived domestic consumers of goods and made investment in the domestic consumer industry more difficult. The only way that the Honecker regime could offer East German consumers many of the products they desired was to increase Western imports. These Western goods were sold only for West German currency in the *Intershops* which had originally been set up to supply diplomats, tourists and other foreigners living in or visiting the GDR. The massive expansion of the *Intershops* under Honecker did bring in significant amounts of hard currency but also created new social divisions between those with and those without access to foreign money.[17] The "place of residence of your aunt" (i.e., whether or not you had relatives in the West from whom you could get West German currency) was now as important as many other forms of social and economic difference.

The East German leadership did not commit the resources to the consumer-goods industry that would have been required to make an independent "socialist consumer society" possible, because political imperatives pulled the East German economy in too many different directions at the same time. East German industry was expected to achieve independence from the West, to contribute some of its production to the rearmament decreed by the Russians, yet at the same time to devote more of its productive capacities to consumer goods. These competing claims could at times assume bizarre manifestations – a factory that produced turbines, generators, and boilers for power plants also became the sole supplier of electric razors in the GDR.[18]

Yet, even if the regime had devoted greater resources to the consumer-goods industry, it is not clear that East Germany would have been able to surmount the contradictions and weaknesses that were intrinsic to the GDR's planned economy.[19] The planned economy was supposed to be superior to the capitalist market economy because it would allocate resources efficiently and produce only for "real" needs. Yet, the plan's emphasis on quantity gave the producers of consumer goods little reason to care about quality.[20] To make sure they met the quota required by the plan, producers might concentrate on goods (such as short-sleeved pullovers) which required fewer materials and less work, regardless of whether these items could actually be sold. Methods of determining prices and the GDR's dependence on poor raw materials from the Soviet Union added to the weaknesses of the planned economy.

The East German regime did attempt to address these problems. In 1963, for example, SED leaders introduced a program of significant reforms, the New Economic System. Within the framework of an economy that remained centrally planned and state-controlled, the New Economic System (NES, 1963–70) created space for more decentralized and flexible decision-making, workers were given new material incentives, and profit became an important measure of performance with the result that "enterprises had to manufacture products of a quality which could be sold and to keep a close eye on production costs."[21] These reforms seemed promising. Then the political climate in the Soviet bloc changed. The Prague Spring of 1968 combined with political developments in Poland to convince East Germany's Soviet masters that they could no longer afford to tolerate such experiments. Economic reform seemed to carry with it the danger of political changes which would challenge Moscow's hold on the Eastern bloc. The fate of the NES demonstrated quite clearly that in the "political economy" of socialism, economic policy would ultimately be subordinated to the political interests of the people in power. By 1970, the New Economic System had been shelved.

Schooled in orthodox Marxism and with memories of the Great Depression still fresh in their minds, the SED leadership was never fully comfortable with definitions of popular needs that went beyond the more fundamental items of daily consumption.[22] However, as East Germans began to formulate new "needs" and expectations (encouraged to no small degree by the ever-present example of the West German consumer economy) the SED could not afford simply to ignore consumer "demand." Yet even after Honecker's declaration of the regime's greater commitment to improving the quality of East German life, SED consumer policy continued to be "a dangerous game of testing, over and over again, what the population would put up with."[23] Bread, milk, housing, and public transportation were provided cheaply, their prices kept artificially low by the state. Goods considered to be "luxuries" – cars, TVs, refrigerators – were not produced in ample quantities, and prices were kept artificially high, in part to subsidize the low prices of "basic" goods but also to drain off so-called "excess" purchasing power. Jonathan Zatlin observes, for example, that "[i]n 1989, the average monthly income was around 800 East German marks. A roll cost 5 pfennigs and a haircut 1.90 marks, but the cheapest two-stroke Trabant [automobile] cost 12,000 marks. The cheapest version of the last Wartburg [car] which came with a four-stroke engine, cost 30,200 marks."[24]

Although East German consumers were also producers, they experienced the contradictions and inadequacies of SED consumer policy most intensely not in the factories and agricultural cooperatives where they worked but in the stores and supermarkets where they tried, but often failed, to find the goods they wanted. East German consumers had to learn how to wait on lists and in lines. (The wait for a new car actually increased from an average of eight years in the 1970s to twelve years in the mid-1980s).[25] East Germans learned to buy what was available, not what they wanted. They could always trade what they had for something else later.[26] East German consumers also learned to hoard – Merkel describes one of her friends who kept three complete Trabant exhaust systems in his basement because he was sure that when he needed a replacement for his old exhaust, it would not be available. Being a successful East German consumer meant above all finding ways around the system. Cultivating connections to people with access to scarce resources through gifts and bribes was vitally important (i.e., Vitamin B for *Beziehungen*, "connections"). In the border village of Kella, for example, a good relationship with the director of the cement factory, or with the local plumber, mason, or carpenter assured access to scarce building materials allocated by the state. These connections were often more important than money: "You could earn lots of money, but if you didn't have connections, you were a poor swine."[27] East German consumers were fortunate if they had relatives in the West who could send them Western products as gifts or buy them eastern products through the specially created East German "gift service." If East Germans had access to West German currency, they could also buy West German products in the special *Intershops*. [28] The *Delikat- und Exquisitläden* sold quality East German goods for extraordinarily high prices in East German marks.[29] East Germans who could not afford to buy Western goods, could always dream (and be frustrated by these dreams) about Western consumer affluence as they saw it reflected in West German television. East Germans fetishized West German products, even going so far as to display unopened boxes of Western soap and hair products in their bathrooms.[30] But even the acquisition of scarce East German goods could create a special symbolic value which made these items marks of distinction. Telephones were, for example, regarded as trophies "demonstrating success . . . in the battle against the snail's pace of the bureaucracy."[31] On the other hand, what should perhaps have been a distinctive element of a socialist regime of consumption, namely cheap, subsidized public transport, housing, and basic foodstuffs, seem simply to have been taken for granted until after they were gone, after 1989.

Consumption and the Legitimacy of the State

The important decisions concerning the production and distribution of consumer goods in East Germany were made by the political leaders, not by the market or by individual businesses. Because the relationship between politics and consumption was more direct and transparent in the GDR than in the Federal Republic, the dissatisfactions of consumers could and did easily translate into criticisms of the state.[32] But, after the 1953 uprising, these grievances did not seriously threaten the political power of the SED until the very end of the GDR. East Germans grumbled constantly about the deficiencies of "actually existing socialism" but their complaining did not escalate into organized political opposition. Yet, the SED's failure to keep pace with West German consumer society did eventually exact an enormous political cost – the end of the GDR. When the final crisis came in 1989, years of dissatisfaction and frustration with everyday material life had already deprived the GDR of that minimum of political legitimacy it would have required to survive as a separate and independent state, even in a radically reformed and democratized version. Most East Germans had little difficulty choosing between the abstract promises of a new "socialism with a human face" and the immediate benefits (the costs were not quite so apparent right away) of "actually existing" West German capitalism.

In West Germany, the success of the emerging postwar consumer economy granted legitimacy to the new democratic state. Erica Carter argues that traditional forms of patriotism and national identification, irretrievably tainted by Nazism and the Second World War, were no longer available to aid in the process of physically and morally reconstructing Germany after 1945. In their place, however, the Federal Republic was able to substitute "consumerism as the source of core values for the nation."[33] In the 1950s, "the national economy [became] a fantasy object for collective identification,"[34] the "characteristic qualities of nationhood" were transposed onto the "social market economy as discursive formation,"[35] and the social market economy became a "displaced space of the nation."[36] The democratic aspirations of postwar Germany were focused upon the market rather than the state. The consumer "exercising free choice in a free market context came to figure as the very embodiment of the democratic free citizen."[37] Commitment to the market economy anchored West Germany firmly in the "Christian West," but did not result in a slavish imitation of American-style free-market capitalism. The "imagined community" of the social market economy was a compromise between "the liberal vision of Germany as a political community of free citizens and the conservative view of the German *Kulturnation* as third space between East and West, as cultural bastion against the barbaric East."[38]

The deeper political effects of the amazing success of the West German "economic miracle" were, however, quite ambiguous. West German prosperity certainly encouraged citizens of the Federal Republic, including many former Nazis, to tolerate, to accept, and eventually to embrace the new West German state. Yet Michael Wildt observes that "West Germans became democrats through consumption; they did not fight for democracy but rather struggled for prosperity"[39] and he warns that "West Germans did not . . . have to fight for . . . human rights, and they have not been tested in truly difficult times."[40]

In the 1950s and 1960s, despite its limitations and contradictions, the East German economy had managed to create a certain degree of material security for most of its citizens, however modest that achievement might appear by comparison with circumstances in the West. East Germany became the leading economy in the Soviet bloc, and East Germans felt that they were better off than most of their "socialist brother countries." By the 1980s, however, East Germany was tottering on the brink of disaster. This spiral into economic collapse, well before the wall came down, was to no small degree the result of the regime's continuing commitment to sacrosanct social programs that it increasingly could not afford. Honecker would not even consider scaling back his ambitious housing schemes, or raising the prices of basic necessities. Yet East German industry was becoming increasingly less productive, hence less able to help foot the bill. Hobbled by inadequate reinvestment policies which left factories with aging, worn-out machinery, worker productivity in the GDR had dropped to about only 30 percent of West German levels by the late 1980s. To avoid total bankruptcy, East German policy-makers desperately sought new sources of hard currency from the West. This meant expanding the production of goods that sold well abroad, seeking foreign loans and increasing the sale of expensive Western goods in the *Intershops*. But these measures also expanded the influence of Western capitalism and the role played by West German currency in East Germany. Perhaps most damaging to the legitimacy of the East German regime, however, was the resurgence of a black market in scarce consumer goods in the 1980s.[41] This new black market constructed an alternative realm of exchange which directly challenged socialist principles and undermined the state's alleged control of the economy. In the black market, prices were fixed according to supply and demand. Black-market commodities could be obtained with West German currency, with goods which could be bartered, and through social connections, but not with socialist money. The illegal black market distributed goods more effectively than the official economy but at the expense of the primitive egalitarianism which the regime had tried to enforce since 1949. The black market promoted new forms of social differentiation. East Germans now found themselves split between those who had access to Western currency with which to deal in the black market and those who did not. In this respect, the black market spread important elements of Western capitalism to the GDR before the opening of the Berlin Wall in 1989.

The Gender of Consumption

Gender was central to the construction and reproduction of West German consumer society. In the Federal Republic, women were not encouraged to work for wages outside the home.[42] West German women were expected to play an important role in the creation of consumer prosperity and in the "restitution to cultural order of the postwar nation, through their work as cultural producers of consumer lifestyles in the family home."[43] Erica Carter detects three major stages of postwar economic recovery between 1945 and 1960, each of which required different forms of female labor in the household: (1) subsistence economy, 1945–49, (2) market stabilization, 1949–57, and (3) accelerating market expansion, 1957–60. In the first phase, housework was quite simply strenuous physical labor in the bombed-out ruins of Germany's cities (hauling water, gathering or stealing wood and coal, "hamstering" for food in the countryside), tasks for which women had been well trained in the last disastrous years of the Third Reich when bombs and battles destroyed the material infrastructure of urban life. Housework continued to be physically demanding for at least a decade after the war, but in the early 1950s women's domestic labor began to assume a second function, what Carter calls the "primitive accumulation" of family savings for the vacuum cleaners, washing machines, refrigerators, radios, and automobiles that West German industry was now starting to manufacture. In the late 1950s, with the transition to consumerism (the third stage of postwar recovery) "the emphasis of housewifery shifted again from rational management of scarce resources to the creative production" of a modern consumer lifestyle.[44] Housework had now become a form of cultural production requiring "aesthetic creativity" and generating "aesthetic value and social meaning."[45] Carter acknowledges that each of these successive constructions of German women's roles could be regarded as oppressive; but she refuses to see this generation of postwar German women simply as victims. Arguing that it "was as consumers . . . that West Germans in the postwar period gained one form of access to citizenship," Carter insists that "the postwar generation of housewife-consumers must be viewed as the bearers of a specifically feminine form of historical agency: as active participants in . . . the reconstruction of the Federal Republic as social market economy."[46] Although postwar representations of women's roles as housewives "cemented a hierarchical gender division of labor,"[47] Carter thinks that women's desires and energies were managed, channeled and regulated, rather than simply suppressed.

East German women were expected to contribute to economic recovery and the construction of socialism as *both* workers and consumers. The project of "building socialism" in the GDR depended upon the wage labor of women as well as of men, but it also required women to consume "responsibly," to adopt "socialist consumption habits," and to teach them to their husbands and children. As East German women tried to juggle the competing demands of wage labor and housework, they found that the frustrations of life as a GDR consumer added to the weight of this "double burden." The ubiquitous queues that were a permanent feature of socialist consumer society consisted largely of women.[48] To deal with the chronic shortages produced by the command economy, women resorted to a variety of tactics, including finding ways to jump to the head of the line or the waiting list for scarce consumer goods, writing letters of complaint to the authorities or even fabricating certain scarce items themselves at home.[49] All of these activities claimed considerable time and energy which many East German women, who already combined working in a factory with taking care of their families, could ill afford.[50] East German women (and men) did manage to devote time, energy, and imagination to the aesthetic dimension of their everyday lives. Yet, the managing of scarcity which continued to constitute a large part of women's domestic labor in East Germany had little in common with the cultural production of aesthetic lifestyles that Erica Carter sees as West German women's emerging new domestic role in the 1960s.

The research on the GDR which has flourished since 1989 gives us a more detailed understanding of East German economy, society and culture than anyone could have imagined just a decade ago.[51] We now have a clear picture of the important phases of East German history, from the very beginning in 1949 to the precipitous end of the GDR in 1989. Although historians of the Federal Republic have certainly not neglected the post-Adenauer years (1963–1989), much of the recent research concentrates on the 1950s.[52] This appears to have been the decisive decade when West Germany put the devastation and deprivation of the Second World War firmly behind it and became the prosperous consumer society which has been the permanent foundation of West German identity ever since. However, Axel Schildt has recently demonstrated that the "golden 1950s" were a good deal more austere in West Germany than numerous TV shows, magazine articles, and coffee table books would have us believe.[53] Most of the 1950s were thrifty years. Families saved for the consumer durables lost in the war. Work continued to occupy a central place in most West Germans' everyday lives. The impressive annual industrial growth rates in the 1950s – 10 percent in most years – which gave the "economic miracle" its name required long hours of hard work. In the mid-1950s, the daily industrial work week averaged 50 hours. And until the late 1950s, most West Germans enjoyed their limited amounts of leisure time in the same ways as they had in the 1920s; reading, listening to radio, and frequent movie-going (some 817 million cinema visits in 1956, for example) until the "slipper cinema" (television) produced a nose-dive in film attendance at the end of the decade. Schildt concludes that the 1950s combined the final phase of a longer cultural history stretching back into the 1920s with a new stage of social modernization which became fully visible only after 1960.

When historians do begin to explore the 1960s, 1970s and 1980s as intensively as they have investigated the 1950s, several major questions should guide their research. How has West German consumer society changed since its relatively austere beginnings in the late 1950s? What major phases can be detected in the production and distribution of consumer goods in West Germany and how do these transitions relate to the political turning points of the Federal Republic? How have consumers appropriated and given their own meanings to the increasing range of consumer goods which the postwar "economic miracle" put on display and on offer? In what ways have West Germans' experiences as consumers produced expectations, behaviors, even personality structures which are noticeably different from those of East Germans? Questions about the relationships between state policies and consumption are central to any analysis of East Germany but have not attracted the same degree of attention in discussions of West German consumerism. In what ways should we bring the state back into the story of the West German "social market economy?"[54] Anti-consumerist ideologies emerged in West Germany with the 1968 student revolt and became firmly anchored in the Green environmental movement. Yet, historians have not explored the ways in which this radical questioning of West Germany's "economic miracle" affected the production of consumer goods and the behavior of consumers in the Federal Republic after 1968. Nor have historians paid much attention to the darker sides of West German affluence, aspects brutally revealed after 1989 to many East Germans who found that unification with the West meant unemployment and demoralization, not the consumer paradise they had expected. In the 1950s, Adenauer's Economics Minister, Ludwig Erhard, held out the promise of "prosperity for all."[55] But West German consumer society never included all West German citizens equally. The "economic miracle" also marginalized many of the non-Germans – Spanish, Portugese, Italians, Greeks, Turks – without whose imported labor as "guest workers" West German prosperity would have been impossible. Our understanding of West German consumer society can be deepened if we look at those within the Federal Republic who did not have access to the benefits of affluence, as well as at those who did.

Rebuilding the two Germanys after the Second World War required the fabrication of images of the future as well as the actual manufacture of industrial goods. This virtual labor of representation attempted to mobilize the support of ordinary Germans for the contrasting projects of national recovery in East and West Germany. Each of the two new German states was intent upon representing itself as the better Germany which offered a bright future to its citizens. These representational struggles were fought out in print and on the airwaves, but also in industrial and trade fairs and fashion shows. East Germany had the good fortune to inherit the site in Leipzig of the most important German Trade Fair. In Chapter 2 of this volume, Katherine Pence shows that in the late 1940s and 1950s, the *Leipziger Messe* was made into a showcase for the achievements of the new socialist regime. Here, the newest "socialist" products were first presented to East Germans and to foreign visitors. Not to be outdone, West Germany created a completely new venue for the exhibition of Western industrial products and consumer goods, the Hanover Trade Fair. Before the Berlin Wall went up in 1961, East and West Germans could visit both of these fairs and compare the progress each German postwar state had made in the national project of overcoming the material devastation caused by the Second World War. Although real products were on display in Leipzig and Hanover, these were representations of a reality that had not yet become part of ordinary East Germans' everyday lives. The products in the Hanover and Leipzig exhibition halls were promises of a better future that most East and West Germans would have to wait some years to experience. Pence's discussion of the reactions of East German women's consumer groups to the products exhibited at East and West German fairs gives an unusual insight into emerging consumer cultures in the DDR, and the intersection of consumer culture with postwar East German constructions of gender. It also shows how even at this early stage West German consumer goods were beginning to set the standard by which East German products were found lacking (with regard to design and quality) in the eyes of both West and East German consumers.

Judd Stitziel's discussion of fashion shows in the early GDR, in Chapter 3, explores the contradictions of attempting to create a distinctively "socialist fashion." "Fashion" was after all a term that in the Marxist lexicon was synonymous with "decadent" capitalism. "Fashion" signified luxury, excess, and artificial stimulation of consumer desire. It should have had no place in a socialist consumer culture. Yet, the East German regime believed that fashion shows were one way of demonstrating socialism's achievements to East German citizens and to the world at large. Quickly, however, it became apparent that even the top East German clothes designers were unable to develop an independent socialist style. East Berlin would never rival Paris as a center of haute couture. Moreover, the luxurious clothes exhibited in East German fashion shows were not to be found in most East German stores. The opulent displays of fashionable, Western-style clothing on fashion-show runways could not have been further removed from the everyday reality of poor-quality, yet, nonetheless scarce mass-produced garments.

Perhaps it was inevitable that the scarce products of East German "high fashion" would suffer from comparison with their Western European counterparts. But what about the larger range of mundane items such as buckets, pots, pans, furniture, and toys found in all East German households? In his contribution to this volume in Chapter 4, Eli Rubin shows that by fabricating a large range of such everyday products from a single material, plastic, the East German regime provided an important test of its ability to create an alternative socialist consumer society. Both East and West Germany manufactured plastic consumer goods but their meaning was quite different on each side of the Berlin Wall. Western consumers frequently continued to see plastic as a cheap and nasty substitute for wood or metal. The East German regime, on the other hand, publicly identified plastic consumer items with a specifically socialist vision of modernity. But did East German consumers embrace this official image of plastics? The East German plastics program did help to form a distinctive aesthetic of everyday life under East German "socialism." Ironically, the production difficulties experienced by the East German "chemistry program" made plastic products more highly valued in East than in West Germany because they were less readily available. Rubin's interviews with former citizens of the GDR indicate that many consumers thought plastic products were extremely modern and chic, although they did not necessarily view these symbols of modernity as specifically socialist. Those East German consumers who felt that plastic was an inferior, even *kitschy* substitute (*Ersatz*) for the real thing sought out alternatives made of older materials. But this set them apart from the mainstream. By altering the texture of everyday material life (the "order of things" as Rubin puts it), the production of plastic items encouraged East German consumers to develop cultural identities that were different in significant ways from those of their West German counterparts. Yet this was not the same as constructing a uniquely "socialist" consumer culture.

If East Germany found it difficult to create a distinctively socialist consumer society, it could at least claim to have more successfully resisted the dangerous inroads of "Americanization" than had the Federal Republic. Since the 1920s, Germans had envied American prosperity, yet feared its cultural consequences.[56] American mass-production methods produced a wealth of new goods but seemed also to promote cultural and spiritual emptiness. In German minds, American consumer society and popular culture were synonymous with the rise of the "masses" and the decline of high culture. Preserving a distinctive German national identity appeared to many commentators in both East and West Germany to require containment of American influence.[57] East Germany could claim to be doing a better job than the Federal Republic of defending "Germanness" against "Americanization," especially after the Berlin Wall was put up in 1961. Whereas the communist state authorities could simply prohibit American films and music in their part of divided Germany, the Federal Republic found it much more difficult to negotiate its postwar encounters with American popular culture.[58] Few commodities symbolized this tense relationship as vividly as Coca-Cola. Indeed, the soft drink gave its name to the anxieties many Europeans felt about postwar American influence. "Coca-Colonization" seemed the best description of a much wider range of American cultural imports which threatened to debase and denature European cultural traditions and to undermine the character and morals of the young. In France, Coca-Cola was even banned. It is ironic then, that Coca-Cola's sales figures skyrocketed in West Germany after the soft drink was reintroduced there in 1949. It had already been marketed in Germany from 1929 to 1942.) In Chapter 5 of this volume, Jeff Schutts shows, however, that the phenomenal postwar success of Coca-Cola in West Germany depended to no small degree on the company's ability to link the soft drink's image to distinctively German concerns – Coca-Cola quickly became a symbol of the new postwar prosperity created by the West German "economic miracle" (*Wirtschaftswunder).* At the same time, with their daily consumption of "ice cold bottles of Coke" millions of West

Germans gained access not to a transplanted American popular culture but to a new democratic, international, and cosmopolitan consumer identity. By drinking Coke, West Germans entered an imagined cultural space where they could distance themselves from the Nazi past without becoming surrogate Americans.

Jonathan Wiesen's Chapter 6, "Miracles for Sale: Consumer Displays and Advertising in Postwar West Germany", argues that the West German "economic miracle" was itself imagined, scripted, and staged well before it actually happened. The image of the "economic miracle" was marketed to West Germans in industrial exhibitions, trade fairs, and print advertising. The promise of prosperity was transmitted to West German consumers through "visual images of abundance" which would erase painful memories of war-induced deprivation. The project of representing the "economic miracle" as a metaphor for the West German future also involved recuperating alternative German pasts, in particular resuscitating memories of German quality work and technological superiority which would allow the slogan "Made in Germany" to be rescued from its recent association under the Nazis with tanks, gas chambers, and crematoria.

At some point, of course, image had to become reality or the symbolic capital gained from the work of representation that Wiesen describes would simply be squandered. By the late 1950s, West Germany was quite literally "delivering the goods" to consumers. Yet, the very success of the West German "economic miracle" could also become the focus of criticism. By the 1960s, as Robert Stephens argues in his Chapter 7 of this volume, a younger generation began to question and reject the obsession with consuming that appeared to have dulled the older generation's critical faculties and allowed them to evade any serious confrontation with the Nazi past. Stephens' discussion adds an important dimension to this volume by showing how the growing consumption of drugs by West German young people can be understood as a rejection of the rampant consumerism that seemed to have taken hold of West German society by the 1960s, yet also as an illicit version of the dominant consumer ideology. As an escape from the market economy, the drug trade nonetheless created new, if illegal, commercial networks and forms of consumption. The growing West German drug problem therefore points to a challenge faced in a more general sense by both East and West Germany: how to promote yet at the same time control consumption?

By exploring the ways in which East and West Germany have functioned as each other's "other" since 1949, the discussions in this volume suggest some of the possibilities for a new narrative of postwar German history. While taking full account of the very different paths pursued by East and West Germany since their establishment in 1949, this story line should also be able to demonstrate the importance of competition and connections between the two German successor states as well as the ways in which these relationships have changed since 1949.[59] In the 1950s, each German state defined itself in the mirror of an intense comparison with the "other Germany." To West Germany, the GDR was the sometimes feared, always despised Communist "other." To East Germany, the Federal Republic was the puppet of American imperialism.[60] Down to 1989, this mutual imagining continued to be important for both East and West Germany. But by the 1980s, West Germany had become a good deal more significant, in both real and imagined ways, for East Germany than vice versa.[61] West Germany provided the most important standard by which East Germans measured the quality of their material lives. Important elements of West German capitalism had already penetrated "actually existing socialism" in the East. [62] Until the very end of the Cold War, West German citizens may certainly have derived satisfaction from the knowledge that they could consume more and live better than their East German counterparts. After the 1960s, however, the citizens of the Federal Republic found more relevant reference points in Western Europe and the United States. The unequal relationship between West and East Germany has not disappeared simply because the two postwar Germanies now inhabit one nation state. The commentaries in this volume help us to see that the current tensions between the eastern and western regions of the new, united Germany are the legacy of forty years of rivalry between East and West as well as the result of East German encounters since 1989 with the realities of everyday life in the Federal Republic.[63]

Notes

1. Although this knowledge is still much more developed for the 1950s than for any subsequent period.

2. Christoph Klessmann, *Zwei Staaten, eine Nation: Deutsche Geschichte 1955–1970* (Göttingen: Vandenhoeck & Ruprecht, 1988), p. 14.

3. See for example Margarete Dörr, "*Wer die Zeit nicht miterlebt hat . . .*": *Frauenerfahrungen im Zweiten Weltkrieg und in den Jahren danach* (Frankfurt/New York: Campus Verlag, 1998), Volumes 2 and 3 and Robert G. Moeller, *War Stories: The Search for a Usable Past in the Federal Republic of Germany* (Berkeley/Los Angeles/London: University of California Press, 2001).

4. Katherine Pence, "'You as a Woman Will Understand': Consumption, Gender and the Relationship between State and Citizenry in the GDR's Crisis of 17 June 1953," in *German History: The Journal of the German History Society*, 19(2), 2001, pp. 220–1; Ina Merkel, "Consumer Culture in the GDR, or How the Struggle for Antimodernity Was Lost on the Battleground of Consumer Culture", in Susan Strasser, Charles McGovern, and Matthias Judt, eds. *Getting and Spending: European and American Consumer Societies in the Twentieth Century* (Washington D.C. German Historical Institute: Cambridge University Press, 1998), p. 282.

5. Michael Wildt, "Changes in Consumption as Social Practice in West Germany During the 1950s," in Strasser et al., Getting and Spending, p. 313. See also Michael Wildt, *Am Beginn der "Konsumgesellschaft:" Mangelerfahrung, Lebenshaltung, Wohlstandshoffnung in Westdeutschland in den fünfziger Jahren* (Hamburg: Ergebnisse Verlag, 1994).

6. Ina Merkel, "Der aufhaltsame Aufbruch in die Konsumgesellschaft," in Neue Gesellschaft für bildende Kunst, ed., *Wunderwirtschaft: DDR-Konsumkultur in den 60er Jahren* (Cologne/Weimar/Vienna: Böhlau Verlag, 1996), p. 8. Rationing of most consumer goods and many foodstuffs had ended by 1953.

7. Felix Mühlberg, "Wenn die Faust auf den Tisch schlägt: Eingaben als Strategie zur Bewältigung des Alltags," in Neue Gesellschaft, *Wunderwirtschaft*, p. 176.

8. Ibid., p. 180.

9. Jeffrey Kopstein, *The Politics of Economic Decline in East Germany, 1945–1989* (Chapel Hill and London: University of North Carolina Press, 1997), p. 186 and Annette Kaminsky, *Wohlstand, Schönheit,Glück: Kleine Konsumgeschichte der DDR* (Munich: Verlag C. H. Beck, 2001), pp. 133–5.

10. Elizabeth A. Ten Dyke, "Tulips in December: Space, Time and Consumption before and after the End of German Socialism," in *German History*, 19(2), 2001, pp. 257–8.

11. Leonore Ansorg, " 'Irgendwie war da eben kein System 'drin': Strukturwandel und Frauenerwerbstätigkeit in der Ost-Prignitz (1968–1989)," in Thomas Lindenberger (ed.), *Herrschaft und Eigen-Sinn in der Diktatur: Studien zur Gesellschaftsgeschichte der DDR* (Cologne/Weimar/Vienna: Böhlau Verlag, 1999), p. 82; Judd Stitziel, "Konsumpolitik zwischen 'Sortimentslücken' und 'Überplanbeständen' in der DDR der 1950er Jahre," in Die DDR vor dem Mauerbau: Politik und Gesellschaft [Schriftenreihe der Vierteljahrshefte für Zeitgeschichte, edited by the Institut für Zeitgeschichte München], eds Dierk Hoffmann, Michael Schwartz, and Hermann Wentker. Munich: Oldenbourg, forthcoming.

12. Ina Merkel, *Utopie und Bedürfnis: Die Geschichte der Konsumkultur in der DDR* (Cologne/Weimar/Vienna: Böhlau Verlag, 1999), p. 8.

13. Ina Dietzsch, "Deutsch-deutscher Gabentausch," in *Wunderwirtschaft*, pp. 204–214; Christian Härtel and Petra Kabus, eds., *Das Westpaket: Geschenksendung, keine Handelsware* (Berlin: Ch. Links, 2000).

14. The regime let pensioners travel to West Germany in the hope that they would decide to stay there and the GDR would no longer have to pay their pensions.

15. It is important to point out that the GDR and the West generally shared the same measures and symbols of prosperity and modernity. See for example Judd Stitziel's discussion in Chapter 3 of this volume of the place of *haute couture* in East Germany.

16. Patrice Poutrus shows, for example, that the attempt to make the East German food supply independent of the West by industrializing the production of chickens (the "Goldbroiler Program") could not have gotten off the ground without equipment and expertise imported from the capitalist West. See Patrice G. Poutrus, *Die Erfindung des Goldbroilers: Über den Zusammenhang zwischen Herrschaftssicherung und Konsumentwicklung in der DDR* (Cologne/Weimar/Vienna: Böhlau Verlag, 2002).

17. Jonathan R. Zatlin, "Consuming Ideology: Socialist Consumerism and the Intershops, 1970–1989," in Peter Hübner und Klaus Tenfelde (eds.), *Arbeiter in der SBZ-DDR* (Essen: Kartext-Verlag,1999), pp. 555–72.

18. Claudia Erdmann, "Graphitelektrode und Zierkeramik: Konsumgüterproduction in der DDR," in Dokumentationszentrum Alltagskultur der DDR e.V (ed.), *Fortschritt, Norm und Eigensinn: Erkundungen im Alltag der DDR* (Berlin: Ch. Links Verlag, 1999), p. 75.

19. See for example André Steiner, *Die DDR-Wirtschaftsreform der sechziger Jahre: Konflikt zwischen Effizienz- und Machtkalkül* (Berlin: Akademie, 1999) and János Kornai, *The Socialist System: The Political Economy of Communism* (Princeton: Princeton University Press, 1992).

20. Ansorg, " 'Irgendwie war da eben kein System 'drin'.," p. 82.

21. Mary Fulbrook, *The Divided Nation: A History of Germany 1918–1990* (New York: Oxford University Press, 1991), p. 203.

22. Jonathan R. Zatlin, "The Vehicle of Desire: The Trabant, the Wartburg, and the End of the GDR," in *German History*, 15(3), 1997, p. 363. and Susan E. Reid and David Crowley, *Style and Socialism.Modernity and Material Culture in Postwar Eastern Europe* (Oxford/New York: Berg, 2000), p. 10.

23. Ibid., p.159. Erich Honecker (1912–1994) succeeded Walter Ulbricht as First Secretary of the Central Committee of the SED in 1971 and served as chairman of the State Council of the DDR from 1976 to 1989.

24. Zatlin, "The Vehicle of Desire . . .," p. 367.

25. Kaminsky, *Wohlstand, Schönheit, Glück: Kleine Konsumgeschichte der DDR* (Munich: Verlag C. H. Beck, 2001), p.136. However, in this as in other areas of consumption, Berlin received preferential treatment. The average waiting period in Berlin in the 1980s was 132 months compared to 156 months in some other districts: Kaminsky, p. 150.

26. Ibid., p. 138.

27. Daphne Berdahl, *Where the World Ended: Re-Unification and Identity in the German Borderland* (Berkeley, Los Angeles and London: University of California Press, 1999), p. 118.

28. Zatlin, "Consuming Ideology."

29. The *Intershops* were founded soon after the construction of the Berlin Wall. East German citizens originally were forbidden from shopping in the stores. In 1973, however, the regime made it legal for East German citizens to possess Western currency and even encouraged them to spend it in the *Intershops*. The first group of *Exquisit* stores were established in mid-1961 before the construction of the Berlin Wall. By January 1962 there were 31 *Exquisit* stores throughout the GDR. Many more were created in the 1970s. The *Delikat* stores were started in 1966. My thanks to Judd Stitziel for this information.

30. Berdahl, *Where the World Ended,* p. 124.

31. Stefan Pahlke, "Warten auf ein Telefon, mit Permanenz und Penetranz," in *Wunderwirtschaft*, p. 168.

32. See for example Philipp Heldmann, "Negotiating Consumption in a Dictatorship: Consumption Politics in the GDR in the 1950s and 1960s," in Martin Daunton and Matthew Hilton, eds., *The Politics of Consumption: Material Culture and Citizenship in Europe and America* (Oxford and New York: Berg, 2001), p. 186.

33. Erica Carter, *How German Is She? Postwar West German Reconstruction and the Consuming Woman* (Ann Arbor: University of Michigan Press,1997), p. 5.

34. Ibid., p. 21.

35. Ibid., p. 23.
36. Ibid., p. 43.
37. Ibid., p. 25.
38. Ibid., p. 31.
39. Wildt, "Changes in Consumption as Social Practice in West Germany," p. 315.
40. Ibid., p.315.
41. See Jonathan Zatlin, "The Currency of Socialism: Money in the GDR and German Unification, 1971–1989," PhD dissertation, University of California, Berkeley, 2000, Chapter Four.
42. Robert Moeller, *Protecting Motherhood: Women and the Family in the Politics of Postwar West Germany* (Berkeley: University of California Press, 1993).
43. Carter, *How German Is She?,* p. 7.
44. Ibid., pp. 62–5.
45. Ibid., p. 71.
46. Ibid., p. 7.
47. Ibid., p.71.
48. Ina Merkel, "Working People and Consumption Under Really-Existing Socialism: Perspectives from the German Democratic Republic," in *International Labor and Working Class History*, No. 55, Spring 1999, p. 106.
49. Merkel, *Utopie*, pp. 278–86.
50. The time women had to devote to shopping frequently took them away from their jobs and reduced productivity.
51. See for example: Konrad H. Jarausch, ed., *Dictatorship as Experience: Towards a Socio-Cultural History of the* GDR (New York and Oxford, Berghahn, 1999); Lindenberger, *Herrschaft und Eigen-Sinn in der Diktatur*; Kopstein, *Politics of Economic Decline;* Corey Ross, *Constructing Socialism at the Grass-Roots: The Transformation of East Germany,1945–65* (London: Macmillan, 2000) and also Corey Ross, *The East German Dictatorship: Problems and Perspectives in the Interpretation of the GDR* (New York: Oxford University Press, 2002).
52. For a sampling of recent research on the 1950s and 1960s see Hanna Schissler (ed.), *The Miracle Years: A Cultural History of West Germany, 1949–1968* (Princeton: Princeton University Press, 2001).
53. Axel Schildt, *Moderne Zeiten: Freizeit, Massenmedien und "Zeitgeist" in der Bundesrepublik der 50er Jahre* (Hamburg: Hans Christians Verlag, 1995). See also his *Ankunft im Westen: Ein Essay zur Erfolgsgeschichte der Bundesrepublik* (Frankfurt: S. Fischer, 1999).
54. See A.J. Nicholls, *Freedom with Responsibility. The Social Market Economy in Germany, 1918–1963* (Oxford: Clarendon, 1994).
55. Ludwig Erhard, *Wohlstand für alle* (Düsseldorf and Vienna: Econ, 1957).
56. See for example Alf Lüdtke, Inge Marssolek, Adelheid von Saldern, eds., *Amerikanisierung: Traum und Alptraum im Deutschland des 20. Jahrhunderts* (Stuttgart: Franz Steiner Verlag, 1996).
57. See Ralph Willett, *The Americanization of Germany, 1945–1949* (London and New York: Routledge, 1989) and Reiner Pommerin, ed., *The American Impact on Postwar Germany* (Providence and Oxford: Berghahn, 1995).

58. Uta Poiger, *Jazz, Rock and Rebels: Cold War Politics and American Culture in a Divided Germany* (Berkeley,Los Angeles and London: University of California Press, 2000).

59. Arnd Bauerkämper, Martin Sabrow, and Bernd Stöver emphasize the importance of such a "double" and combined narrative of postwar German history in the introduction to the volume they have edited on *Doppelte Zeitgeschichte: Deutsch-deutsche Beziehungen 1945–1990* (Bonn: Verlag J.H.W. Dietz Nachfolger, 1998).

60. See Eric Weitz, "The Ever-Present Other: Communism in the Making of West Germany," in Schissler, ed., *Miracle Years*. pp. 219–232; Dieter Vorsteher, ed., *Deutschland im Kalten Krieg, 1945–1963* (Berlin: Argon Verlag, 1992); and also the online version of the exhibition by the German Historical Museum, Berlin (Deutsches Historisches Museum) of "Deutschland im Kalten Krieg. Deutsch-deutsche Feindbilder in der politischen Propaganda 1945 bis 1963," at http://www.dhm.de/ausstellungen/kalter_krieg/imp.htm

61. This does not of course mean that we can ignore the GDR's relationship with the Soviet Union and the ways in which the "Sovietization" of the DDR transformed East German society, especially in the 1950s. See for example Michael Lemke, "Foreign Influences on the Dictatorial Development of the GDR, 1949–1955," in Jarausch, ed., Dictatorship, pp. 91–107.

62. Burghard Ciesla and Patrice G. Poutrus, "Food Supply in a Planned Economy: SED Nutrition Policy Between Crisis Response and Popular Needs," in Jarausch, ed., *Dictatorship,* pp.145–6.

63. Since 1989, some East Germans have developed a certain nostalgia for GDR-era products. However, this so-called *Ostalgie* does not mean that East Germans now share a higher opinion of these commodities. It has much more to do with cultural conflicts between Easterners and Westerners in post-Wall Germany. By declaring their attachment to products that were part of growing up in the GDR, East Germans can assert their own identities in the face of West German economic and cultural domination of the new united Germany. See for example Paul Betts, "The Twilight of the Idols: East German Memory and Material Culture," *Journal of Modern History*, 72 (2000), pp. 731–65.

2

"A World in Miniature": The Leipzig Trade Fairs in the 1950s and East German Consumer Citizenship

Katherine Pence

> Glass and ceramics; textiles and clothing at the international Trade Fair fashion show; published, printed, and paper goods; toys and musical instruments; household technology, clocks, jewelry, leather goods and also crafts are the focal points of the Model Fair. Here the national and international assortment is concentrated. Here reigns the typical turbulence of the first Fair days in Leipzig. Here contracts will be signed that often commit a whole year's capacity for the exhibiting firms . . . Here is Leipzig "a whole world in miniature."[1]

In these celebratory terms, a guide to the 1957 Leipzig Trade Fair described the array of goods on offer at this semi-annual exhibition. Yearly Spring and Fall Fairs featured a "technical fair," displaying industrial machinery, and a "model fair," exhibiting consumer goods. Producers and traders would meet at the fair to settle contracts for export and domestic distribution of goods, but consumers also visited the exhibition to view the spectacle of economic abundance. Dubbed a "world in miniature," the Leipzig Fair aimed to offer universality in the display of commodities and in the international participants at the event; the Fair also worked to be a primary site for the German Democratic Republic (GDR) to take its place on the world stage as an economic power and crossroad of trade. Visitors to the Fair were given the opportunity to marvel at socialist progress and production as exemplary within the international arena. However, as this chapter will consider, the experience of viewing the commodity exhibition mobilized alternative readings of the displays and opened the GDR to critique from women who were the nation's most vigilant, concerned consumers. The Fair not only gathered citizens to be convinced of the material and ideological benefits of socialism, but also provided bustling public spaces for meetings of men and women engaged in wary criticism of the regime or even illicit behavior that the regime could not stop.

Bridge between Past and Future

Reemerging immediately after the war in the period of rationing and chronic shortages, the Leipzig Trade Fair became an early symbol of projected normalization of the German economy and of promised prosperity in the years to come. Trade Fairs were important symbols of the reemergence of Germany as an economic force after the debilitating years of reconstruction. Since the original Leipzig Fair dated from the Middle Ages, it provided the GDR with a way to trace continuity between a long tradition as a center of trade and its desired role as an industrial nation on the world stage. The postwar fair organizers drew frequent references to the long legacy of trade activity to which they were now heir in the German Democratic Republic.[2] Just as the GDR emphasized Leipzig's ties to pillars of German culture like Goethe, Bach, and Luther,[3] the Fair became an institution that offered a route to legitimacy for the GDR as an economic and cultural leader.

However, the Third Reich, wartime destruction and the postwar emergence of separate German states disrupted the long historical continuity of this event. In the postwar era, the GDR struggled to recast the Fairs as both embedded in this history and as a sign of the new socialist age. In doing so, the reestablishment of the Leipzig Fairs mirrored the challenges the GDR faced in creation of a consumer economy as a whole. The early history of the Fairs' reconstruction is one of overcoming obstacles and shortages. Damage to over three-fourths of the display halls by Allied bombing raids became the first issue that beset Fair planners. Despite these rough conditions, the Fair Administration resumed activity already in August 1945 with a small fair displaying Leipzig products from 751 firms.[4] By the following year, 3000 exhibitors attracted around 170,000 visitors from East and West.[5] This beginning prompted the Fair organizers to initiate bigger fairs in 1947, which would become the basis for yearly Spring and Fall Fairs.[6] Despite the hard winter of 1946 –1947, which hampered the construction work on the Fair site, the first major Fair was still proudly able to meet its deadline of February 15, 1947.[7] With this kind of success, in 1947 the Leipzig newspaper described the Fair as 'exemplary for all German reconstruction.'[8] Still, as one account described, the displays at the 1947 Fair left much to be desired. Displays were somewhat makeshift, and "The assortment of goods also caused headaches. Mostly just display pieces made from wartime material or ersatz materials were available. This was especially the case for many household and kitchen appliances, which were often made from old steel helmets or gas mask canisters."[9]

In the first years of resumption of the Fairs, political constraints stemming from the Allied military occupation in Germany, the country's division, and the beginning Cold War also hampered easy rehabilitation of the event. The control of the Soviet Military Administration (SMAD) in East Germany was a mixed blessing for the Leipzig Fairs. The SMAD had to grant approval for the reopening of the exhibition. It willingly provided such support with a military Order,[10] but also made Fair organization difficult by issuing the Order for the 1947 Fair at such a late date that it was hard to solicit Fair participants.[11] While the Fair administrators were frantically trying to rebuild exhibition space, they also had to contend with the effects of SMAD agendas to exact reparations and expropriate capitalist and noble Junker elites.[12] For example, a November 1946 report revealed that the Soviets had ordered a demolition of four exhibition halls, presumably as an expropriation measure, even though wartime bombing had already destroyed many other halls. Immediate protests from Fair organizers ensued, leading the SMAD to send a delegation from its offices in the Berlin suburb of Karlshorst to Leipzig to reverse the demolition order for three of the four buildings. To prevent further problems the Fair administration saw it as urgent and compelling (*dringend und zwingend*) to transfer the halls from private ownership to the Sachsen Provincial Administration and the Soviet Administration in Dresden, "so that the occupational authority will be freed from the thought that these are Junker-owned halls."[13] Just as German industries struggled with Soviet programs for state appropriation, dismantling, and reparations, the Leipzig Fair also dealt with sometimes seemingly arbitrary constraints of such policies.

The division of Germany, beginning with separate occupation zones in 1945, was another hurdle for the rebirth of German and international trade that the Fairs hoped to epitomize. When dual currencies were formed in 1948 and the Berlin Blockade followed for a year thereafter, leading to the founding of two separate states in 1949, the ease of exchange hit a low point. As the Leipzig Fair was trying to get back on its feet, its organizers feared that these conditions would make currency exchanges for purchases at the Fair more difficult, especially since sales to Western buyers based on the West Mark were deemed "undesirable."[14] The global tensions caused by the Korean War from 1950 to 1953 also affected development of the Leipzig Fairs. Since the United Nations, under pressure from the United States, passed a resolution to set up a trade embargo against North Korea and China in 1951, trade between socialist and capitalist countries suffered.[15] The Spring Fairs were cancelled from 1952 to 1954[16] as the GDR economy went through this difficult transitional period during which provisions reached such a crisis point that it contributed to the major 17 June 1953 uprising.

After 1953 when the armistice in Korea, the death of Stalin and the aftermath of the June uprising eased tensions and prompted reform, the GDR began to focus more concertedly on developing its consumer economy. As the German economies began to recover and to strive not only to regain prewar standards of living, but also to surpass them, the Fair reflected these advancements as well as the struggles to achieve them. The state-sponsored program called the New Course, instituted in 1953, purported to place greater emphasis on raising the standard of living of the population through better consumer goods. The following year was dubbed "The Year of the Great Initiative" in which the population was entreated to band together to bring the New Course to fruition. Within the context of these programs and as part of the new Five-Year Plan, starting in 1956, a series of initiatives were put in place to modernize the consumer economy. New emphasis was placed on electric appliances, fashion and modern home furnishings. These efforts gained new impetus when, at the Fifth Party Congress of the SED in 1958, Party Chairman Walter Ulbricht declared that the principle economic task of the GDR would be to catch up with and overtake West Germany in per-capita consumption.[17] To fulfill this goal the economic ministers introduced initiatives in 1958 like the chemical program entitled "Chemistry brings bread, prosperity, beauty" to produce products like plastics.[18] A program called "The 1000 Little Things of Daily Life" also debuted to produce a multitude of small consumer goods.[19] In 1959, the second Five-Year Plan was interrupted with a new Seven-Year Plan designed to help the GDR reach the world standard of consumption by 1961.

The Leipzig Fairs were meant to display the benefits of each of these programs, though successes of the programs and their displays were sometimes equally difficult. Although the Fair was clearly growing, throughout the 1950s the Fair planners faced a continuing series of logistical problems mirroring the problems in the consumer programs themselves. These troubles were often associated with the cumbersome bureaucracy of the provisioning system or shortages of funding and material. Sometimes goods were plentiful and in other cases shortages plagued both the Fair's merchandise selection and the general provisions for the Fair guests. This condition reflected the overall condition of the socialist consumer economy, in which, as Ina Merkel has suggested, "This coexistence of shortage and surplus was characteristic for the supply problems in the GDR."[20] Both durables and foodstuffs presented problems. Individual Fairs could be seen as case studies for both the progress and the setbacks in the economy from season to season. For the 1955 Fall Fair, for example, planners noted that for industrially produced durables, "In contrast to the Spring Fair a good and sufficient merchandise selection was available."[21] In some cases improvement in supplies meant that surpluses resulted, as in the sale of butter where "the situation substantially changed compared to the Spring Fair and only weak demand occurred."[22] In other cases shortages led to complaints within the Leipzig population. At the Fall Fair in 1955, eggs were in short supply as was game and fowl. A report complained that although artichokes, capers, truffles, wild mushrooms, cooking wine, and goose liver pâté had been ordered, there was none to be found. The report concluded,

> The absence of these articles does not make it possible to offer a selection of dishes that the international character of the Fair demands. The demand for timely delivery of Fair commodities so the [local] population won't schedule their own shopping during the

> Fair, a demand that has justifiably been raised for years, was once again not fully satisfied. There is discussion now as before that everything is there [in the stores] for the Fair, but beforehand and afterward everything is gone again. It must be checked why, if the organizational preparations and orders were given in a timely manner, that such unpleasant situations have arisen for focus commodities in particular.[23]

The suggestion that delicacies like pâté and truffles should be an expected part of the menu at the fairs demonstrates how the GDR had clearly advanced beyond the subsistence level of the immediate postwar years by mid-decade, when both halves of Germany famously took part in an "eating wave".[24] However, the passage also reveals the difficulties in achieving the world standards toward which the Fair strove. Additionally, the statement reveals the falsity of the presumption that the Fair would represent the standard of living in the GDR as a whole to its guests. The suggestion that more goods were available during the Fair than at other times reflected a common critique that the Fair put on a privileged show of consumer goods that was exceptional rather than typical.

The ongoing struggle to achieve an international standard at the Fairs was seen not only in the varying supply of goods, but also in the difficulty in exhibiting cutting-edge design and fashion. Designers and marketers from the GDR would travel to trade fairs in other countries to learn from them and hoped that their trading partners would reciprocate. Elli Schmidt, head of the Institute of Clothing Culture,[25] worked to raise the level of fashion on display at the Fairs to international levels of couture. For the 1956 Fall Fair she proposed a Parisian haute couture show complete with 18 invited luminaries from the fashion world, 200 models on display, and a modest reception for the guests.[26] However, due to lack of funds, this plan could not be implemented.[27] So instead of bringing the fashions to Leipzig, which would have helped underscore its role as a trade and design center, she planned a trip for her designers to France and Italy to learn about the latest fashions there. This more inexpensive plan gained approval even from a Minister President of the USSR who suggested that the Soviet Union should also send a delegation with the GDR group to the haute couture shows.[28] While this instance shows how designers in the GDR were genuinely concerned with competing internationally and with using the Leipzig Fair as a showcase for their successes, the material constraints evident here demonstrate some of the frustrations in bringing these goals to fruition.

The attempts to display world-class commodities also faced the problem of suitable display spaces. The reconstructed Fair halls and the displays within them were increasingly designed to represent modern aesthetics corresponding to the ideal of progress the GDR hoped to embody. Proudly, the press continually reported on the expansion of the Fair into increasingly larger and more modern display halls throughout the decade. The Leipzig Fair Administration constructed more buildings to house its ever more international set of exhibitors. By 1959 the Fair boasted 22 display halls and 21 pavilions totalling 606,168 cubic meters.[29] Buildings in the inner city had been rebuilt to house most of the displays of consumer goods, and a separate area for the Technical Fair featured great halls for display of agricultural and industrial machinery and products.

Ideally displays of goods were to use modern, eye-catching techniques, such as dynamic forms created with new display equipment like flexible wire stands, artful lighting effects, and fantasy-rich arrangements.[30] Larger windows were introduced to showcase more wares with a "better decorative effect."[31] However, there was still a sense that the Fair was struggling to keep up with global standards. In 1959 a report suggested that the development conditions (*Bebauungszustand*) "in no way correspond to the demands of a modern global trade fair." Planners decided that a "fundamental modernization of our Fair in the inner city is necessary. Several Fair buildings that in part were built over 50 years ago are un-modern, technically imperfect, antiquated and unsuitable and must be replaced in the course of the next decade by new, modern Fair buildings."[32]

As a showcase of achievements in the GDR's socialist economy, the Leipzig Fair seemed to have mixed results. The exhibitors and visitors grew in numbers and showed the advancement in the economy beyond the reconstruction years of the late 1940s and early 1950s. But the development of the Fair in the 1950s often displayed not only the achievements of the East German "economic miracle,"[33] but also the continual shortcomings endemic to the transition to a planned economy. Even as it coped with these difficulties, planners hoped the Fair would exhibit the best side of the GDR economy, because it was still its most prominent commodity showcase for both an international and a domestic audience.

Crossroads of East and West

In the 1950s, the Leipzig Fair aimed to play the role of a "bridge" or a "mediator" between East and West,[34] since its position in central Europe made it a long-standing crossroad for trade. Traders and tourists from around the world were invited to visit the Leipzig Fairs.[35] The official poster for the fair adopted in 1956 emphasized the meeting of the orient and occident at the Fair in the stylized image of a Western salesman in a fedora walking in tandem with an Eastern counterpart in a turban and beard.[36] Directives from the fair celebrated the links between European traders and Asian businesses, especially those "people's republics" such as Mongolia, Korea, and Vietnam.[37] Other imagery from the Fair stressed how it promoted the international, universal connection of a community of nations. This spirit was embodied in the mascot of the Fair adopted in 1965, the "Little Trade-Fair Man" (*Messemännchen*) dressed as a businessman whose head was in the shape of the globe. This figure became one of the most popular Leipzig souvenirs.[38]

The Fair could give this role as bridge new political weight by bringing together traders from both halves of the newly ideologically bi-polar world. It was clear that underneath the spirit of universality and cooperation lay virulent competition between the socialist and capitalist camps. While planners noted that the fair would offer an opportunity for "international comparison of achievements, especially between East and West,"[39] they wanted this comparison to yield recognition that the socialist East was better off. Beyond objective comparison, the Fair planners hoped to use the event as an opportunity for "agitation" or propaganda about the economic achievements of the socialist bloc and the political agenda of the SED. A publicity brochure in English from 1959 intended for foreign audiences boasted of the high profile of socialist countries at the Fairs. For example, "The sensation of the Spring Fair 1951 was the first appearance of the young People's Republic of China at Leipzig. The victory of the people of China, the most significant event in world history since the Great October Socialist Revolution fascinated both friend and foe. China at the Leipzig Fair . . .! That was the dominating topic of all home and foreign visitors to the Fair.'[40] The GDR was also pleased that the Leipzig Fair could showcase its role in welcoming newly decolonized states into the trading fellowship of nations:

> Shaken up by the great Chinese people's revolution, a significant number of people who had been suppressed and exploited by colonialism freed themselves. That is reflected in the Leipzig Trade Fair through the presence of representatives from such independent nation states as Egypt, India, Indonesia, Lebanon, Syria, the Sudan and others. The official collective exhibition of the young Egyptian Republic at the 1954 Fair and of the Indian Union at the Spring Fair in 1956 already demonstrate high points in this process. The government delegations from Egypt and India underscore the meaning that the German Democratic Republic has earned in international political and economic events.[41]

The presence of these new socialist republics at the Fair functioned partly as propaganda for the strength of the socialist bloc globally and of the centrality of the GDR in that group. Exhibition halls and pavilions were organized by national origin to emphasize this concert of nations represented at the universal fair.

Visitors from capitalist countries were invited to witness these socialist achievements. Political messages underscored the link between the GDR's commodity culture and its political and economic system. Economic authorities, such as the Ministry for Light Industry, planned propaganda to be shown at the fair that combined display of goods with overt political messages. For example, a plan for a display to be shown at the 1958 Spring Fair juxtaposed images of the latest fashions with party slogans; ski clothes were to be described in terms of "Vacations for workers – Cooperation of socialist countries." A graphic depiction of the development of underwear in the last 100 years was to be accompanied by the text "The further development and care for fashion is a task of socialist production."[42] Particularly in moments of heightened political tension, such as the 1958 crisis when Khrushchev's ultimatum to the Western powers threatened GDR seizure of control in West Berlin, the Leipzig Fair administration proposed that the East German retailers and producers had the "duty, to promote an exchange of opinions among the Fair guests and to influence them actively themselves" since they would have the opportunity to "perform political enlightenment work to support the fight for peace."[43] In this context, the Fair's testament to the "ability for achievement and rapid tempo of development in the socialist countries"[44] would help the GDR's larger political goals.

The heavy use of political slogans led Western critics to suggest that the urban decorations in Leipzig celebrating the Fair made the event look more like a "day of a Party Conference" rather than the traditional trade exhibit.[45] A US Army report described the center of the city during the Fair as 'slightly reminiscent of [George Orwell's novel] '1984'" in the following account:

> Loudspeakers around the Karl Marx Square blared news, martial music and "folk-songs"of the "people's democracies" all day and evening. Red flags and the red-black-gold of the GDR were much in evidence (probably in honor of the Fair); outsize posters of Stalin, Pieck, Grotewohl and all the heads of the "people's democracies" faced the main station; ubiquitous slogans urging the "fight" for peace and support for the October elections were posted in every conceivable place where the eye might light . . . All these trappings were cheaply done, and the whole effect was one of inexpressible dreariness.[46]

Despite such criticism, the Leipzig Fair took the opportunity to underscore the link between its burgeoning prosperity, its prominence as an international trading center and its socialist system. Casting its commodity displays in juxtaposition with political slogans may have seemed imperative particularly since this once securely all-German trade fair now faced competition from new fairs established in West Germany.

New Competition: The Cold War Context

In the new context of heightening Cold War tensions, Fair planners remarked in 1947, "We know that the Leipzig Fair has many friends as well as many adversaries (*Gegner*), domestically as well as abroad."[47] The Cold War had injected this threatening tone into the world of German trade. Germany had long been the premier European center for trade fairs.[48] Besides the pioneer in Leipzig, the German marketplace has boasted Fairs in Cologne, Munich, Berlin, Frankfurt am Main, and other cities. Whereas before the war they had formed a community of trading sites, the Cold War added a new political dimension to the competition between these Fairs. West German fairs now competed ideologically and politically as well as economically with the Leipzig Fair, traditionally the most important fair in Germany.

After the war, even during the height of Germany's economic breakdown in the late 1940s, a number of fairs resurfaced as proof of Germany's ability for miraculous material recovery. Berlin had long boasted several specialized fairs such as the Automobile Exhibition that started in 1897,[49] or the Green Week (*Grüne Woche*) for agricultural products, which dated originally to 1926.[50] As a divided city in the 1940s, West Berlin revived a number of these exhibitions and started a new German Industrial Exhibition in 1950 all as signs of recovery in the context of Ludwig Erhard's new social market economy.[51] Other major West German cities also revived traditional fairs. Cologne, whose fairs dated from the 1920s, started exhibiting consumer goods again in 1947. Frankfurt am Main Fairs followed suit in 1948.[52] The trade fairs in all of these cities offered specialized exhibits dedicated to branches of consumer-goods industries such as textiles, household goods, and furniture. In this sense, they didn't compete as directly with the universal offerings of the Leipzig Fair. While none of these fairs dated as far back as Leipzig's, they all had some claim to tradition that they could combine with Cold War political goals in the postwar era.

The biggest threat to the Leipzig Fair was a new Fair launched in 1947, overtly as a Cold War competitor to Leipzig. This was the Hanover Export Trade Fair, an invention of the British and American military occupiers.[53] As one account suggested, the Hanover Fair "should, according to the explicit political will of the British, outshine Leipzig and leave it appearing pitiful."[54] The Hanover Fair's focus on Cold War competition was underscored by the fact that at the debut Fair its 1,298 exhibitors[55] came not from the Soviet Zone, but only from the Bi-zone, the administrative union of the British and American Zones that was a precursor for the Federal Republic (FRG).[56] As in the early struggles with material reconstruction that faced the Leipzig Fair, the Hanover Fair also had to cope with shortages and destroyed buildings that made it difficult to open its gates on schedule. However, in its first year, the Fair was successful in closing export deals totaling 31.58 Million US Dollars. [57] After overcoming a crisis caused by the 1948 general strike in West Germany that threatened to shut down the Fair,[58] it continued to grow. With the invaluable assistance of former members of the Leipzig Fair Administration who had fled to the West,[59] Hanover was well on its way to becoming the site of an internationally competitive Fair.[60] The Hanover Fair did not emphasize geographical origin of exhibitors, as did the Leipzig Fair, which organized the exhibitions by nationality; rather, it featured primarily West German products and incorporated individual foreign companies into exhibits of product groups.[61] In other ways it directly rivaled Leipzig by dividing its offerings in 1949 into a technical fair and a consumer-goods fair, by offering a universal array of goods, and by casting the Fair as a showcase not only for use by traders but also as an event to be experienced by the whole German population.

The Leipzig Fair planners asked themselves in 1948 whether the postwar Leipzig Fair would continue to represent all of Germany instead of becoming just a local exhibit of East German goods. The GDR planners' answer was a resounding "yes," because they claimed that just as "the strongest argument for German unity is the organic growth and the organic dependency and unity of the German economic arena," over the course of centuries the Leipzig Fair had become an integral part of that organic economic unit.[62] When West Germans offered competition to the Leipzig Fair with new establishments like the Hanover Fair, East Germany reasserted that only its traditional Fair remained the true all-German trading center.[63] In fact, the Hanover Fair would remain an "interesting experiment," because as SED functionary Fritz Selbmann suggested in an internal meeting,

> [The Hanover Fair] must give an old Trade Fair expert the impression that it is like the establishment of an economic center in Alaska, just because gold was found there by chance, or like an attempt to create a fair just as one would produce a film or some other propaganda event. This attempt is already a failure. Hanover will never be a Trade Fair center, just as in the past all attempts to make Frankfurt, Munich, Cologne and Königsberg into German trade fair centers were failures . . . The Hanover Trade Fair will be just such an ephemeral appearance.[64]

The Leipzig Fair thus aimed to become a beacon of German unity by emphasizing the GDR's hold on German tradition.

In fact, West Germans also acknowledged the Leipzig Fair's status as a traditionally central trade fair. In a statement echoing similar East German assertions, the West German advertising trade journal *Die Werbung* commented, "The [trade fairs] have proven themselves to be organically growing institutions of the German economy – one thinks here of the Leipzig Trade Fair – able to adapt to the structural changes resulting from the postwar period."[65] This journal also noted how problematic the position of the Hanover Fair was in 1950 since it "lives more or less off of the 'Iron Curtain.' – It says a lot that after the eventual reestablishment of true economic unity in Germany, the Leipzig Fair would win back its traditional role as show window of the Reich [*sic*] in its entirety and Hanover would thus become irrelevant."[66]

Despite mutual predictions of doom for their rival Fairs, both the Leipzig and Hanover Fairs continued to expand and thrive throughout the life of divided Germany, even if the Cold War competition did cause them some difficulties.[67] The division of Germany and of its trading centers did have severe effects on the Leipzig Fair. Holger Möller suggests one of the major effects of the postwar era was a parceling out to local fairs in West Germany the responsibility for exhibiting branches of consumer goods that used to fall to Leipzig or Berlin. As East German companies who used to exhibit in Leipzig relocated to the Federal Republic, West German fairs gained a new hold on what used to be the "Leipzig and Berlin heritage."[68] Since few locations could rival Leipzig's expansive space for housing exhibits, the shift to exhibiting goods in West Germany happened through the proliferation of smaller local fairs like the Düsseldorf fair for sports supplies or the Offenbach Leather Goods Fairs that complemented the universal fair in Hanover. Still, despite this pressure, Leipzig continued to thrive as a trading center. Möller attributes this success partly to the central location of Leipzig with its good transportation links,[69] a quality that the Leipzig Fair administrators emphasized in its role as a long-standing crossroads between East and West. Although many West German companies began to exhibit in West German fairs, many also continued to travel to Leipzig.[70]

Throughout the 1950s and until German reunification in 1989, then, trade fairs on both sides of the Iron Curtain became showplaces of the economic achievements and political ideologies of both the GDR and the FRG. Just as the Hanover Fair was touted as a "Showcase of the West," the Leipzig Fair was also called a "show window" for the best achievements of socialism. The meaning of this "show window" changed as the political situation in Germany shifted. In the late 1940s, the press emphasized the role that the Leipzig Fair played in promoting German unity, calling it a "show window for the whole German economy, since a quarter of all exhibitors come from the German West."[71] As the hopes for immediate reunification faded, the Fair highlighted the continuing interaction between the two halves of the divided nation and continually reasserted the image of supremacy in the East. As economic functionary Heinrich Rau suggested in a speech opening the 1961 Leipzig Spring Fair, as a site for East – West trade the Fair aimed to promote "peaceful coexistence." Rau thought this "peaceful stance side by side of the two societal systems that dominate the present day – socialism and capitalism" – would entail "simultaneously a competition between these two systems" that would ultimately prove "that the victor would be socialism."[72] This made the Fair a stage to enact the Cold War competition between East and West and made the visitors to the event actors within this drama. Although the Leipzig Fair was important to the GDR's foreign image, it also worked to appeal to average citizens who looked to the Fair for signs that the promised utopia of prosperity would be fulfilled in concrete material terms.

Scrutinizing the Spectacle

As seen above, the GDR officially promoted the Leipzig Fair as a critical institution for underscoring the state's legitimacy within Germany and its status globally as a competent rival to capitalism. This goal made it clear that visitors to the Fair were meant to witness the exhibitions as symbols of the GDR's supposed success story. The main practical purpose of the Fair was the promotion of trade exchanges, in part to add to the GDR's economic success. Trades people were therefore the primary audience for the exhibitions. However, other visitors to the Fair such as tourists and average consumers were also important as witnesses to the spectacle. Consumers could visit the Fair to get a foretaste of new products, which they might expect to see soon on the market. Sometimes economic achievements on display offered hope of a better standard of living. However, just as Fair planners complained of ongoing problems in execution of the events, the consumers could also use the Fair to become aware of the discrepancy between ideal and reality of consumption in the GDR. Even when Fair displays approximated an ideal vision of abundance in the socialist economy, it often became evident that such a phantasmagoria often remained a utopian fantasy to average East Germans.

The visitors who perhaps most heavily scrutinized the Fair's offerings for how well they represented the everyday standards of consumption in the GDR were those who continued to bear the primary responsibility for household shopping in East Germany: women. Individual housewives and organized women's groups visited the fair to view the upcoming possibilities for consumption in the GDR. Critiques of fair offerings by official women's groups were meant to help the GDR economy by offering expert opinions of what should be produced. But their assessments, whether positive or negative, revealed the variety of ways that average consumers negotiated the commodity world constructed by the regime. Not just passive audiences of propaganda, these consumers' responses to these displays offer insight into the construction of the relationship between GDR state and a citizenry that could cooperate with state visions of socialist consumer culture or deviate from these ideals.

Consumption in the GDR was often frustrating to the average consumer. Rationing continued until 1958. Frequent shortages meant that shoppers had to queue in front of stores. Housewives and working women who were usually responsible for the daily shopping often complained about these problems.[73] To some extent the Leipzig displays were designed to reassure the population that socialist production was improving commodity selection. The attempt to channel frequent criticism of retail selections into a positive outlook on the progress of the economy was evident in the periodical *Das Magazin*'s report from 1954 about popular reactions to the Fair. A couple called Mr. and Mrs. Schrei from Naumburg reportedly answered, "The best thing is to take your wife with you these days. That way she can at least learn the real Fair life . . . After doing so, this happens: [The wife would say] You see, it made a difference that we always complained about the bad shoe styles. The ones on display here are really quite pretty. Look at the pretty crepe shoes. And from the GDR! And don't you want to buy those for me?"[74] This example suggests that the displays at the Fair were supposed to offer scrutinizing women a glimpse of better material standards soon to be available across the nation. In this anecdote, the brighter future ostensibly resulted from the constructive critiques of this female shopper.

While women's comments in the press and official reports showed some optimism and excitement about progress in commodity production shown at the Fairs, they also critiqued the inadequacies of the market. Their comments showed an early recognition that the spectacular displays did not necessarily translate into an improvement in living standards in everyday life. The gap between the displays and actual conditions was especially acute in the immediate postwar years when the population was still suffering from shortages of housing and material goods. A writer for the *Leipziger Zeitung* in 1947 underscored the discrepancy between the fantasy of the displays and the realities of shortage. She both praised the 'fantasy-rich' fashions seen at the Fair, such as 'festive evening gowns, true poetry in silk, tulle or brocade,' and also noted that 'the wish remains for every woman that these bewitching models presented here don't stay dreams and fantasy children from the magical realm of Frau Fashion, but will very soon become fulfillment and reality so that we will also be able to rejoice over a new and up-to-date (*am neuen*) dress!'[75] The *Leipziger Zeitung* featured another article from a "housewife" named Alexandra who criticized the Fair later that month. For Alexandra, the Fair teased visitors with images of abundance, while in reality they still only had limited housing and little means for purchasing the goods on display:

> In the Fair pavilions it was like a bath for the eyes to find so many beautiful things brought together at one time. Glass, porcelain, ceramics, color and form equally complete and balanced; handbags that couldn't be dreamt up any more beautifully; in the Ring Fair Hall the richness of dresses, fabric, accessories, curtains . . . How did the new furniture look? But there the expectations were disappointed. Amazed, one asks oneself, don't the interior designers, carpenters, and furniture producers have any insightfulness, or do they still have the opinion that each family lives in a multiple-room apartment. Nowhere does one see a truly fitting solution to the one-room apartment, in which so many are living today . . . Maybe the next Fair will offer that which we are missing now and will match – also in the prices – the needs and possibilities of our current lives.[76]

This housewife's critique represented a central problem in the Leipzig Fair: the fact that the goods on display did not always fit the needs of the population, and when they did, they were not always available or affordable. As consumer "experts", housewives in the 1950s became emissaries to the Fairs to examine the offerings of East German production and possible imports. As the consumer economy recovered from wartime shortages, these women sought to evaluate commodities on display in order to help the GDR make more commodities available that would meet shoppers' needs and compete with Western merchandise.

To help the economy modernize mid-decade as part of the New Course, East German women became particularly active in a continuing GDR effort to investigate and often to copy internationally developing technological innovations.[77] Women in the Socialist Unity Party (SED), the women's branches of the Free German Trade Union (the FDGB), and the women's mass organization the Democratic Women's Union of Germany (DFD) all went on excursions to the Leipzig Trade Fair to evaluate the appliances on display. Through official forays into trade fairs at Leipzig and in the West, these women familiarized themselves with new technologies and took on the role of consumer representative to test the new products and suggest which ones should be produced further. Their reports displayed their development as sophisticated consumers, increasingly savvy about technological functions, brand names, and especially the increased production of appliances aimed at easing the household workload. This official function also demonstrated how women were enlisted to fulfill their duties of citizenship in the GDR in part through their consumer role by helping the planned economy determine demand and improve selection.

Modernization of appliances was a major agenda in 1956 as part of the second Five-Year Plan, so women's groups paid particular attention to appliances on display at the Fairs in this year to assess whether the selection lived up to the promises of the Plan. Better production of household appliances was also key to the GDR's program for liberating women, since machines were thought to make housework easier so that women would have more free time to take part in socialist production. In their examination of the 1956 Leipzig Spring Fair, DFD women concluded that the household appliances on display proved disappointing,[78] although at the Autumn Fair that year DFD and the SED women reported being excited about the new products. They anticipated great improvements in the Fall because it was the first fair after the Third SED Party Conference at which the Five-Year Plan's commitment to modernization was declared.[79] The Fall Fair did seem to present promising innovations. For example, the SED women's division evaluated the Fall Leipzig Fair by enumerating the latest inventions and brands displayed there:

> There are a series of appliances which have proven themselves as practical and fit the demands of women: for example, the Combi-Washing Machine, the Union-Pressure Cooker, the Omega-Vacuum Cleaner, two multi-purpose appliances like Imme and Purimix. The Saalfelder washing machine with a greater capacity than the Combi, the

> Regeler Iron with settings for wool, silk, and Perlon, many smaller hand-held machines, the Lipsia-clothesline, and a water-heater.[80]

This list shows how the GDR was producing goods that were akin to appliances increasingly available internationally on a mass scale such as vacuum cleaners and washing machines. Other appliances such as the Imme and Purimix were more unique socialist innovations in that they conserved materials through multi-functionality. This trend also carried on the tradition from the postwar rationing period of extreme shortages: "out of one, make two." The DFD women's magazine *Frau von Heute* introduced the Purimix, "a leader among the new developments,"[81] with the glowing report:

> It made our hearts do leaps of joy, because it made a long-nursed desire into reality. Purimix does almost everything: it vacuums dust, it waxes, and with the same motor, but naturally with another attachment, it stirs, beats, mixes, pulverizes, chops, purees, and grinds. The most pleasing thing about it, is that it will cost only about 350DM and should be deliverable already in the first quarter of 1957. If it were purchasable with credit, many housewives' happiness could be complete.[82]

The Purimix became a banner of modern living, not only because it helped the housewife with multiple basic cleaning and kitchen tasks, but also because it supposedly enabled its owners to participate in the carefree, leisure activities of the 1950s, epitomized by modern entertaining. The magazine *Kultur im Heim* suggested: "The built in cross-blade made from stainless steel pulverizes vegetables and fruit most quickly for you, and – I nearly forgot that New Year's is on the threshold – naturally you can mix a few tasty shakes or flips for your guests for the new year."[83] Reports also welcomed the appliance Imme, because it served as a "mixer, meat-grinder, fruit press, grater, coffee grinder, and dough kneader," although it was still too expensive and too heavy for individual use.[84] Housewives had to wait until 1959 for smaller mixers, the Mixette and Komet, to come on the market.[85]

Molding a specifically socialist consumer culture that could rival the capitalist market became especially difficult because of continuing production and distribution problems. Unfortunately, the model goods on display and the multitude of additional suggestions by women frequently failed to make their way into production or onto storeroom shelves. Often the goods seen at Leipzig were produced for the purpose of export. The press tried to reassure domestic consumers that exporting GDR goods would not diminish the selection of commodities at home since they would be balanced by imports.[86] This comment failed to comfort many women who had whetted their appetite for the machines displayed at the

Leipzig Fair only to find they were seldom if ever available in stores.[87] Sometimes retailers didn't contract to sell the goods the women had seen in Leipzig, or new commodities were introduced briefly only to quickly disappear from sight. DFD women lamented that the Komet-brand heater was taken off the market for failing to meet safety standards and that retailers didn't choose to sell the much-desired Lipsia-brand clothesline.[88] In the case of some commodities, like refrigerators, production didn't seem to progress very expediently.[89] While GDR stores totally lacked some goods, other goods were produced in an absurd number of models. A hundred different firms reportedly produced some items, like irons, in 1956. Winnowing down the selection was difficult for economic planners, because private firms outside of direct control of the central economic administration produced them.[90] Given these production and distribution difficulties, by 1958 the FDGB women's division complained that,

> The indiscriminate manufacture of mass commodities in the years 1956 and 1957 is one of the reasons that our women are still always heavily burdened by running the household. To this is added the extreme expense of acquiring an appliance such as a washing machine. The current development in mass commodity manufacturing still doesn't guarantee that the need will be completely fulfilled. Many appliances are very urgently desired by women – such as electrical household appliances, washing machines, vacuum cleaners, and electric and gas stoves. The current planning for production of household appliances cannot be seen as sufficient. Therefore attainment of greater free time for women still remains hampered.[91]

The problems plaguing East German consumer culture became more evident to shoppers when they looked toward the West. To compare GDR achievements to advancing technologies in the West, women visited trade fairs in West Germany such as the Cologne Fair in 1956. Both the SED and the Economic Ministries promoted women's evaluative missions to Western trade fairs. The SED Women's Division declared that "especially the products at the Cologne Trade Fair display [show] which possibilities are available to relieve the daily tasks in the household."[92] The Ministry for General Machine Construction commissioned DFD women to evaluate the products at the Cologne fair. These DFD women drew up detailed accounts of household machinery for that Ministry as well as appraisals of other goods for the Ministry of Light Industry and an assessment of a Western department store for the Ministry of Trade and Supply.[93] The observations at the Cologne Fair provided these women with concrete examples of how to improve GDR products such as refrigerators. One report stated:

> Refrigerators: Demand for lasting, dependably working refrigerators of various sizes. Interior of the door should, as with West German products, be devised for storage possibilities; the interior fixtures, like containers etc. [should be made] out of good-

> quality plastic, which can be easily cleaned. The refrigerators should be offered with and without automatic interior illumination.[94]

The DFD women also returned with numerous suggestions for products similar to brands available through Western production. They proposed to the Ministry for General Machine Construction that a variety of small, inexpensive machines, not yet available in the GDR, such as automatic egg-cookers, trouser-presses, grills, and speed choppers, might sell well and help women with housework.[95] In their suggestions to the Ministry for Light Industry, they enthused about West German plastic products in "subdued and rich colored tones and beautifully formed workmanship." These included buckets, funnels, sieves, cookie cutters, egg cups, and children's bathtubs.[96] To the Ministry for Trade and Supply the DFD observers raved about foam-rubber products including brushes, sponges, and bathing shoes in "the most beautiful colors".[97]

In the women's concrete comparison of such goods with Western commodities, the faults of some GDR products became apparent. For example, the SED Women's Division declared that, "The available machines [in the GDR] don't always meet international standards, such as the Combi household washing machine. For example, the French Concord-brand washing machine features a pump that leads the water automatically to the drain. With the Combi, the housewife must let the water run off into a bucket and then she must pour it into the drain."[98] Another example was the Sicco-brand spin-drier, which the women judged as too large, unwieldy, and unsatisfactory. After evaluating the Cologne Fair, they demanded a spin-drier like the Western brand they saw there, the Xanta.[99]

The women's groups reported meticulously on these ongoing failings in East German consumer culture and compared them to Western achievements out of commitment to improve the fledgling state in the 1950s and to raise it to international standards. This activity was promoted by these state institutions as part of an ongoing effort to collect critiques of trade from the population which, Ina Merkel suggests, were promoted "because it promised both to channel displeasure into directed paths as well as to exert permanent control and direct pressure on trade workers."[100] The organized women's reports were passed on to economic functionaries and published in the DFD press organ, *Frau von Heute*.

These critiques of goods at the Leipzig Fair became part of a general trend in which women would evaluate commodities as a bridge between producers and consumers. Their reports helped inform industries in the planned economy of consumer needs in place of the regulating function of supply and demand in a free economy. At other smaller fairs and exhibits throughout the GDR, women's groups met with consumers, to introduce new products seen in Leipzig and to collect suggestions and critiques. The FDGB women's division held such meetings in conjunction with local product exhibitions:

> In the summer of 1956 we used a district exhibition in Magdeburg to assess with about 100 women the displayed mass commodities and to evaluate this assessment with the factory managers and trade functionaries in a following discussion. Thus, many suggestions were given to producers and retailers about how to improve further the quality of the displayed goods or about which new products should be manufactured. This example was spread to other districts, which use district fairs in a similar form for conducting consultations with women.[101]

As this example of the district meeting to discuss new products suggests, women's organizations used the trade fairs for several purposes: to try to take a position as consumer experts to help influence production and retailing, to involve a broad range of women in this effort to contribute to the socialist economy, and to bring these women into committed relationship with the planned economy and state.

However, it's unclear how much their critiques truly affected the developments in the GDR's consumer industry. The possibility that the women's critiques fell on deaf ears might be evident in the fact that by the end of the decade problems recounted by these women continued to plague the production of commodities. A report on the 1960 Leipzig Spring Fair by the GDR Institute for Market Research lamented that, "It can be said in general that we have not yet reached the world standard."[102] The Institute evaluated products themselves, especially the attempts to integrate plastic into new commodity design, and found them insufficient: "Household appliances should be especially attractive in form and color, and plastic is excellent for this purpose. The new hand-held vacuum cleaner from Omega (Model 70003) is not a good example of this by any means."[103] The availability of products was also still problematic; "A great step toward our goal for 1965 [to overtake the West in per-capita consumption] would be if for once the appliances shown in the Fair halls would come into retail trade in sufficient numbers."[104] The increased push to make the transition to socialism at the end of the decade made it increasingly difficult to actualize plans for sufficient commodity production, even if the suggestions from organized women were taken into account.

It's also unclear how much popular displeasure with the commodity array was channeled into what the regime would consider appropriate forms, emerging from commitment to help the regime. Indeed, encouraging housewife consumers to witness offerings of the GDR economy in comparison to the bounty of the West could certainly unleash a deeper critique of the socialist system at large that would stray from the bounds of acceptable GDR citizenship. In fact, the Leipzig Fairs did become a site for female visitors to test the boundaries between appropriate consumer citizenship and deviant behavior that had the potential to destabilize the goals of the regime projected in the Fair's displays.

Deviance at the Leipzig Fair

As one of the most important annual events in the GDR, the Leipzig Fair became emblematic for both the successes and the failures of the socialist system. By purporting to display the best image of GDR consumer culture, it became the focus of critiques not meant to be constructive like those of the DFD women. Housewives' critiques demonstrated how the Fairs illuminated a discrepancy between the ideal of prosperity promised by the regime and the realities of inadequate consumer goods. Such a revelation would not necessarily be taken as a sign of the growing pains of the Republic on the path to utopia, but could be seen as a reason to abandon hope in the GDR and flee to the "Golden West" as many more East Germans did toward the end of the 1950s.[105] In addition, the pressure to live up to the promise of abundance at the Fair led economic planners to send the best of GDR production to Leipzig during the fairs. This privileged status for Leipzig led to shortages in surrounding areas. As noted above, some GDR citizens noticed the discrepancy between the meager provisions in their local stores and the privileged assortment of goods at the Leipzig Fairs. This became a question of national security monitored by officials. One report by a Department of Security Issues recorded how, during long butter shortages in 1959, there were food lines forming in front of stores in cities near Leipzig such as Zittau, Bautzen, Riesa, and Dresden. The observer noted that, "As in previous years, it is also now discussed that they brought everything to Leipzig to the Fair. There is also a discussion in reference to the living standards in West Germany."[106] Such a statement is one sign that the Fair's attempt to showcase abundance backfired in the face of continuing everyday shortages and might in fact have led the population to look to the West for a better standard of living. Thus the Leipzig Fair became a lightning rod for critiques of the standard of living in the GDR in general. The regime's inability to control how the population interpreted the spectacle of the Leipzig Fairs demonstrates one way that these events mobilized possibilities for deviant uses of the fair.

Another way that the Fairs were open to unplanned or unacceptable uses was through illicit trading activity or covert personal meetings. While officially promoted trade was the centerpiece of the event, illegal forms of trade and smuggling could also take place at this crossroads. One report indicated that illicit trade such as the black market had the opportunity to flourish at the Fair and that some aberrant customers disrupted legitimate trade:

> This time [in 1947] admittance to the furniture fair was not made difficult, and the assumption may be correct, that barter and the "black market" flourished not only at the furniture fair, but also in the other fair buildings. Undesired people who were "just-looking" suddenly became people who were "also-shopping" that we didn't want. Liquors, English and American cigarettes, stockings and other everyday goods that have

> become rare took over the role of money, in cases when someone wanted to take a brand back home because it would be hard to get in one's own locality. The "black" exchanges constructed a dark side [of the Fair] with unexpectedly large number of participants. To make a repetition of this impossible, it will be indispensable for the Fair Office and the Reichsbahn train to make certain agreements allowing for a strict control over trips to Leipzig. Of course, that requires that the press will be enlisted to provide timely information that only those Fair visitors will be allowed in who have been legitimated by the Industrial and Trade Commission and the Craft Commission.[107]

The Trade Commission's response to the dangers of illicit trading was an increase of controls over the customers. However, despite such policing, the meeting of Eastern and Western populations at the Fairs would certainly continue to present opportunities for black-market activity and smuggling, which was an ongoing problem for the GDR.[108]

The status of the Fair as a vast international meeting place also meant that the nature of guests' interactions was beyond the control of the regime. Whereas the Fair was meant to be a crossroads of trade, families divided by the Iron Curtain could use this arena to maintain contact with each other, while ignoring the economic or propaganda purposes of the event. Holger Möller suggested that,

> The apparent reduction in the number of West German exhibitors in the 1950s and the continuous addition of visitors from the Federal Republic and from Berlin (West) is often seen as an indication of the thesis that Leipzig lost its meaning as a place of trade for all of Germany and that the visit to the Leipzig Fairs was used to foster human contacts such as meetings with relatives, friends, and acquaintances from the GDR.[109]

Particularly after the Berlin Wall was built in 1961, the Fair provided one possible avenue to visit relatives across the border for divided families who had few options for contact.

Another uncontrollable use of the Fair by its visitors was a form of consumption that took place outside the Fair exhibit halls: prostitution. Women were not only present at the Fair as consumers but also as objects of consumption. Businessmen from around the world commonly expected to meet women in Leipzig. Indeed, the assumption that the Leipzig Fair was also a traditional site of sexual liaisons can be seen in the anonymous novel, *Julchen and Jettchen: The Attractive Sales Girls – or Julchen and Jettchen's Erotic Adventures at the Leipzig Fair*, a book that the 1971 edition claims is one of only three German works of erotica written during the nineteenth century.[110] Although the activities of the actual Fair are overshadowed in the text by the explicit tales of lovemaking, the setting is not coincidental but shows how much this crossroads of trade was taken for granted as a site of "erotic adventures." Accounts from the 1950s suggest that this tradition also continued after the war, even when the GDR officially outlawed prostitution. In her study of GDR prostitution, Uta Falck notes that, "The Leipzig Fair as a center of attraction for prostitutes – that was apparently known by everyone."[111] An article from GDR's *Das Magazin* in 1954 asked Fair visitors what they would report about Leipzig when they returned home. A woman working in one of the lavatories at the Fair responded:

> If I wanted to talk – I could speak volumes. The "reputations" of many ladies from around the world are destroyed right in front of me. Even now many easy girls from around the world come along with the tradesmen to Leipzig, even if there aren't as many as before. Totally by coincidence they all have their birthday during the fair and let themselves be entertained and given gifts by their "fiancé" or "husband." But there are also respectable girls, and I naturally stick with them. Only yesterday I let two girls go out through the rear exit, because they didn't want to pay back two openhanded Dutchmen with the customary tribute.[112]

Das Magazin investigated the presence of "easy girls" again in 1955 and reported, "Let's stick first of all with the Fair city of Leipzig. Although for many it isn't as widespread as before, there is still a whole array of such girls here, whose number is not to be overlooked, especially during the Fair, when it's increased through the influx [of women] from all the same countries that the men come from."[113] Throughout the life of the regime, the Leipzig Fair was a well-known site for prostitution to the extent that the city gained the nickname "VEB Brothel."[114]

In a more officially acceptable way, the symbol of Leipzig as a romantic meeting place representing freedom and fantasy was memorialized in a popular musical produced by the East German DEFA studios in 1968 called "Hot Summer." The cinematic romp about teenage flings starts when a group of young men and women meet hitchhiking in Leipzig while numerous posters for the September 1967 Leipzig Fair adorn the city as a backdrop for the flirtatious opening dance numbers.[115] Beyond being a locus for trade and commodity display, Leipzig could also be the city of "Hot Summer," where an acceptable sense of romantic freedom could be fostered to give socialism a "human face," or "VEB Brothel," a site for illicit liaisons counter to socialist morality. In either case, as Uta Falck concluded, "Leipzig was a city with two faces. During the Fair the somewhat provincial regional city was turned around and changed itself into a pulsing metropolis."[116]

Conclusion

The Leipzig Fairs, while aiming to present a glowing showcase of socialist achievement to a domestic and international audience, actually had many faces.

Visitors to the fair could use the event as it was intended, to promote international trade or to witness the growing prosperity brought by socialist production. Housewives who attended the event could fulfill their duties of GDR citizenship by participating in bringing about this greater prosperity by offering helpful critiques of commodities on display. However, scrutinizing the exhibition of GDR commodity culture could equally lead to recognition of the discrepancy between promised prosperity and the reality in which goods failed to live up to the international standards they aimed for. The imperative to reach global standards of living prompted Fair visitors to gaze Westward: this comparison with the West could either provide input for improving socialist production or it could leave the spectator wanting what the GDR found it difficult to provide. The discrepancy between ideal and reality can also be seen in the illicit side of the Fair, where the meeting of East and West could become a site of smuggling – seen officially as insidious sabotage – and prostitution, the continuing existence of which refuted socialism's claim to end what it saw as commodification of women.

Did these mixed messages from and uses of the Leipzig Fair lead the population to call the legitimacy of the regime into question? Western critics hoped so. Observers from the U.S. Army in 1950 levied severe criticism of the Fair as a reflection "for the most part [of] its sponsor's general lack of interest in consumers' goods," except when it came to exports. They remarked that "most of the exhibits and the goods examined were shoddy-looking, with the exception of china, glass and such like."[117] Such an evaluation suggests that the Fair represented the ultimate failings of the regime and would lead to general dissatisfaction of the population.

However, the overall conclusion made by the U.S. Army delegation to Leipzig and its Fair was more complicated. They suggested that the socialist system on display did indeed present a challenge to the West.

> Aside from an examination of the Fair itself, which was superficial, the visit to Leipzig was of interest and even of considerable value in that it refocused generally current ideas concerning the Soviet Zone and corrected some apparently distorted notions, which probably must inevitably result from conversations and a study of reports unchecked by first-hand observation. That is not to say that previous conclusions concerning the Communist system's throttle-hold on the East Zone population are exaggerated, but rather that the balance of pressures is somewhat different than is often believed. Romantic notions of an elaborate spy system ought probably to be trimmed as far as the mass of the population is concerned. Since the Western world's picture of the Soviet Zone is formed to a very large extent by the victims of the Soviet Zone spy and purge system, it is probably too often overlooked that Communist pressure upon the mass of the population works in a rather different way. It is not so much overt as insidious, utilizing mostly economic and psychological weapons. In short, conditions are better and at the same time worse than is often generally recognized. To the population's struggle for daily existence, which is not impossible but difficult, is added a constant sense of insecurity, a growing

> isolation from the free world, continuing elimination of Anti-Communist leaders and harassing Communist propaganda tactics. The strategy points to a conquest of the population by attrition rather than terror. The chief danger seems to be that if such conditions persist over an extended period of time and the Soviet one is increasingly cut off from the Western world, even the inward resistance to Communism, which is considerable at the moment, will gradually wither from within.[118]

This reconnaissance memorandum cast the Fair as a threat to the fight against Communism, because its persuasiveness lay not in direct propaganda or the coercion of spying or purges but through wearing down resistance to Communism in more subtle ways such as the display of material evidence of advancements in GDR consumer culture. Even in cases where these achievements appeared meager in comparison to those of the West, the Fair provided a focus for consumer citizens, especially female shopping "experts," to solidify their cooperation with the regime by working toward concrete improvements in consumption. The women of the DFD, SED, and FDGB were ostensibly to exemplify this role. Thus, the Fair could become a site for actively building socialist prosperity, even if it could also be seen as a focus for critiquing socialist failures. Uses of the Fairs reveal how it could take on these multiple meanings that might, but didn't necessarily lead to resistance to the regime.

The illicit uses of the Fair, such as prostitution, could also lead to a variety of conclusions. Certainly the uncontrollable presence of an underground world of prostitution could unmask the hypocrisy of official monolithic images of a socialist paradise presented in Fair displays. At the same time, the coexistence of DFD women taking part in accepted consumer activity and of "easy girls" taking advantage of the opportunity to earn some hard currency from traveling salesmen, showed how life in the GDR was more complex. Official displays of the proper socialist economy could live alongside behavior that was completely at variance with socialist ideals and that survived despite policing and restrictions. In this sense, the Leipzig Fair really did become a "world in miniature" – a crystallization point for a regime rife with contradictions and mixed messages that were endemic to the complex and problematic nature of life under German socialism.

Notes

1. Bundesarchiv (BA) Coswig, G4/I 1342 Pk1 Ministerium für Leichtindustrie, Leipziger Messeamt, *Leipziger Messe Technische Messe und Mustermesse, 3.–4. März 1957.* Brochure.

2. Ibid.

3. Heinz Kahlow, "Mein Leipzig lob' ich mir," *Das Magazin*, 3(7), March 1960, pp. 34–5.

4. *The Leipzig Fair: A Historical Survey. Published on the Occasion of the 10th Anniversary of the Founding of the German Democratic Republic* (Leipzig: VEB Messe- und Musikaliendruck, 1959), p. 16.

5. Holger Möller, *Das deutsche Messe- und Ausstellungswesen: Standortstruktur und räumliche Entwicklung seit dem 19. Jahrhundert* (Trier: Zentralausschuß für deutsche Landeskunde Selbstverlag, 1989), p. 149.

6. Ibid., p. 149.

7. BAP DL-1 2473 Ministerium für Handel und Versorgung, Leipziger Messe, Spring 1947, Vorbereitung, p. 4.

8. Walter Seidel, "Schaufenster der deutschen Wirtschaft," *Leipziger Zeitung*, March 4, 1947, p. 5.

9. Leipziger Messeamt, *Vom Jahrmarkt zur Weltmesse: Ein Streifzug durch die Geschichte der Leipziger Messe* (Leipzig: Urania-Verlag, 1958), p. 205.

10. The order stated that, "to develop industry and trade in the Soviet Zone of Occupation, and the exchange of goods between the Soviet and the other Zones of Germany as well as with foreign countries, the Leipzig Fair is to be held again every year. The first Leipzig Fair will be held from the 8th to the 12th of May 1946." *The Leipzig Fair*, p. 17.

11. BAP DL-1 2473 "Bericht über die Tätigkeit des Leipziger Messeamts Körperschaft des öffentlichen Rechts, 30. Geschäftsjahr, January 1 to December 31, 1946," Signed Leipziger Messeamt, Dr. Pröpper, p. 6.

12. Norman Naimark, *The Russians in Germany: A History of the Soviet Zone of Occupation, 1945–1949* (Cambridge, MA: Harvard University Press, 1995), p. 183ff.

13. BAP DL-1 2473 Ministerium für Handel und Versorgung, Vertraulich! Niederschrift über die Sitzung des Verwaltungsrates des Leipziger Messeamtes am 13. November 1946 im Sitzungszimmer des Leipziger Messeamtes, p. 3.

14. Stiftung Archiv der Parteien und Massenorganisationen im Bundesarchiv (SAPMO BA) FDGB Buvo 0367 Berlin, August 5, 1948. Bericht über die von der Hauptverwaltung Interzonen- und Außenhandel der DWK veranstaltete Tagung, August 3, in Leipzig. Comment by Wandel.

15. *The Leipzig Fair*, p. 23–4.

16. Möller, p. 149.

17. Walter Ulbricht, "Der Kampf um den Frieden, für den Sieg des Sozialismus, für die nationale Wiedergeburt Deutschlands als friedliebender, demokratischer Staat," in *Protokoll der Verhandlungen des V. Parteitages der Sozialistischen Einheitspartei Deutschlands. 10. bis 16. Juli 1958 in der Werner-Seelendbinder-Halle zu Berlin* (Berlin: Dietz Verlag, 1959), p. 68.

18. Raymond G. Stokes, "Plastics and the New Society: The German Democratic Republic in the 1950s and 1960s," in Susan E. Reid and David Crowley, eds., *Style and Socialism: Modernity and Material Culture in Post-War Eastern Europe* (Oxford: Berg, 2000), pp. 65–80.

19. SAPMO BA, FDGB Buvo 1548, Frauenabteilung, Stand der Gewerkschaftsarbeit mit den Frauen im Kreis Jena Brigadeeinsatz des Bundesvorstandes, November 1959–

July 1960, "Vorschläge des Kreisvorstandes des FDGB an den Rat der Stadt und den Rat des Kreises Jena zur Erarbeitung des Kreisprogrammes für Dienstleistungen und Reparaturleistungen und die 1000 kleinen Dinge des täglichen Bedarfs."

20. Ina Merkel, *Utopie und Bedürfnis: Die Geschichte der Konsumkultur in der DDR* (Cologne: Böhlau Verlag, 1999), p. 88.

21. BAP DL-1 2476 Ministerium für Handel und Versorgung, 1955.

22. Ibid.

23. Ibid.

24. Michael Wildt, *Am Beginn der "Konsumgesellschaft": Mangelerfahrung, Lebenshaltung, Wohlstandshoffnung in Westdeutschland in den fünfziger Jahren* (Hamburg: Ergebnisse Verlag, 1994), p. 76ff.

25. Elli Schmidt became head of the Institute of Clothing Culture after she was ousted from the SED Central Committee in 1953, where she had held a high-ranking status within the Party. For more on Elli Schmidt and her relationship to GDR consumer culture, see Katherine Pence, "'You as a woman will understand': Consumption, Gender, and the Relationship between State and Citizenry in the GDR's June 17, 1953 Crisis," *German History*, 19(2), 2001, pp. 218–52.

26. BA Coswig G4/I 1643 Institut für Bekleidungskultur, Berlin, To Stellvertretender Minister Merkel, Ministerium für Außenhandel und Innerdeutsches Handel. July 10, 1956, Betr.: Modenschau der Pariser Haute Couture in Leipzig zur Herbstmesse. From Elli Schmidt, Chair.

27. BA Coswig G4/I 1643 Institut für Bekleidungskultur, Berlin, To Stellvertreter für Leichtindustrie, Kirsche. August 2, 1956, Betr: Modenschau der Pariser Haute Couture in Leipzig zur Herbstmesse 1956. From Elli Schmidt, Chair.

28. BA Coswig G4/I 1643 Institut für Bekleidungskultur, Berlin, To Stellvertreter des Ministers Kirsche, Ministerium für Leichtindustrie. September 10, 1956. "Planung der Reisen des Instituts für Bekleidungskultur im Jahre 1957," From Elli Schmidt, Chair.

29. SAPMO BA IV 2/610/57 ZK der SED, Handel, Versorgung und Außenhandel, Kammer für Außenhandel der DDR, Vorlage für die Leitungssitzung beim Minister, August 21, 1959. Betr: Bebauungsperspektive für die Leipziger Messe.

30. See the descriptions of displays in "Ein Messebummel gibt Anregungen für kulturvolle Warengestaltungen," *Wir werben und gestalten,* December 1955.

31. BA Coswig G4/I 1643 Institut für Bekleidungskultur, Abt. Leder, Berlin, September 10, 1956. Messebericht über das Schuhangebot zur Herbstmesse 1956. Signed, Albert Entwerfer für Schühe.

32. SAPMO BA IV 2/610/57 ZK der SED, Handel, Versorgung und Außenhandel (FBS 355/14632), Kammer für Außenhandel der DDR. Vorlage für die Leitungssitzung beim Minister, August 21, 1959. Betr.: Bebauungsperspektive für die Leipziger Messe. Berlin, August 8, 1959, Signed, Koch.

33. The GDR employed this term that was coined to refer to West Germany. Hans Müller and Karl Reißig, *Wirtschaftwunder DDR: Ein Beitrag zur Geschichte der ökonomischen Politik der Sozialistischen Einheitspartei Deutschlands* (Berlin: Dietz Verlag, 1968).

34. BA Coswig, G4/I 1342 Pk2 Ministerium für Leichtindustrie. "Direktive zur Leipziger Frühjahrsmesse 1958."

35. Publicity brochures were published in various languages and distributed internationally to popularize the Fair abroad. See for example Leipziger Messeamt, *Leipziger Messe, Édition en langue française* (June 1959).

36. BA Coswig, G4/I 1342 Pk1 Ministerium für Leichtindustrie, Leipziger Messeamt, *Leipziger Messe Technische Messe und Mustermesse, 3.–4. März 1957*. Brochure. This poster was the winner submitted by Margarete and Walter Schultze from Wittenberg in a contest sponsored by the Leipziger Messeamt and the Verband Bildender Künstler der DDR in 1956. It was the primary poster used between 1956 and 1965 distributed in 35 countries. Simone Tippach-Schneider, *Das Grosse Lexicon der DDR-Werbung: Kampagnen und Werbesprüche, Macher und Produkte, Marken und Warenzeichen* (Berlin: Schwarzkopf & Schwarzkopf, 2002), pp. 203–4.

37. SAPMO BA IV 2/610/57 ZK der SED Handel, Versorgung und Außenhandel, Kammer für Außenhandel der DDR. Vorlage für die Leitungssitzung beim Minister, August 21, 1959. Betr: Bebauungsperspektive für die Leipziger Messe.

38. The Leipziger Messemännchen was one of a number of advertising symbols developed in the GDR for various products. Simone Tippach-Schneider, *Messemännchen und Minol-Pirol: Werbung in der DDR* (Berlin: Schwarzkopf & Schwarzkopf Verlag, 1999), p. 45; Tippach-Schneider, *Das Grosse Lexicon der DDR-Werbung*, p. 203.

39. BA Coswig, G4/I 1342 Pk.2, Ministerium für Leichtindustrie, Information für die Presse, Leipziger Messeamt, "Grosses internationales Technik-Angebot auf der Leipziger Frühjahrsmesse 1958."

40. *The Leipzig Fair*, p. 22.

41. Leipziger Messeamt, *Vom Jahrmarkt zur Weltmesse*, p. 220.

42. BA Coswig, G4/I 1342 Pk.2, Ministerium für Leichtindustrie, Leipziger Frühjahrsmesse 1958, Ringmessehaus, Drehbuch II für die polit. Sichtagitation.

43. BA Coswig, G4/I 1342 Pk2 Ministerium für Leichtindustrie. "Direktive zur Leipziger Frühjahrsmesse 1958."

44. Ibid.

45. "Leipziger Herbstmesse," *Die Werbung*, 9, 1950, p. 438.

46. US National Archives, 446 HICOG Berlin Element, HICOG Eastern Element, September 15, 1950, "Visit to the Leipzig Fair," Signed George A. Morgan, Director.

47. BAP DL-1 2473 Ministerium für Handel und Versorgung, Industrie- und Handelskammer Leipzig, March 28, 1947, "Die Leipziger Frühjahrsmesse 1947," p. 1.

48. J.M.H. Huynen, *Trends in Trade Fairs: History, Environment, Marketing, Motivation* (Valkenburg-L, Netherlands: Uitgeverij Het Land van Valkenburg, 1973), p. 51.

49. Rupert Stuhlemmer, *85 Jahre Berliner Automobil-Ausstellungen 1897–1982* (London: Dalton Watson, 1982).

50. Messe Berlin, "Die Grüne Woche – ein Rückblick auf Berlins traditionsreichste Ausstellung," Presse-Information [1995?].

51. For example, the 1948 'Grüne Woche' exhibition emphasized the promise of a return of commodities during the postwar period of shortages through their hyperbolic manifestation in the form of fantastic giant vegetables – notably at a 3.3-kilo cucumber (Kastengurke), a 4-kilo 'Goliath-kohlrabi,' a 7-kilo white cabbage and a 40-kilo pumpkin – and huge stacks of foodstuffs. Leonie Holz, *Messestadt Berlin* (Berlin: Nicolai, 1986), pp. 54ff.

52. Other specialized fairs took place in Nürnberg, Düsseldorf, Stuttgart, Hamburg and other West German cities. The decentralization and specialization of these fairs in the Federal Republic is partly due to the strengthening of the federal system there. Möller, p. 184ff.

53. The Joint Ex- and Import Agency (JEIA) of the Bi-zone was the main organizer of the Hanover Fair under the approval of British General Brian H. Robertson and American General Lucius D. Clay. Max Walter Clauss, *Treffpunkt Zukunft: Die wirtschaftliche Entwicklung im Spiegel der Hannover-Messe* (Düsseldorf: Econ Verlag, 1984), p. 18ff.

54. Dieter Tasch, *50 Jahre Zukunft: Messen in Hannover 1947–1997*, Deutsche Messe AG, ed. (Hannover: Verlagsgesellschaft Grütter, 1997), p. 13.

55. Möller, p. 169.

56. Tasch, p. 14.

57. Möller, p. 169.

58. Tasch, pp. 19–20.

59. Möller suggests that without the assistance of these seasoned professionals "the construction of an independent Trade Fair and Exhibition structure in locations without any pre-war tradition in this area would only be imaginable with much difficulty." Möller, p. 193.

60. The number of visitors to the fair rose from 4,000 in 1947 to 80,000 in 1953. Ibid., p. 170.

61. Ibid.

62. BAP DL-1/2473, Ministerium für Handel und Versorgung, "Niederschrift über die Sitzung des Verwaltungsrates des Leipziger Messeamtes am 22. Oktober 1948 im Sitzungszimmer des Leipziger Messeamtes," Comments by Fritz Selbmann, p. 4.

63. Bö, "Unpolitische Messe?" *Neues Deutschland,* 52, March 4, 1948), p. 2.

64. BAP DL-1/2473, Ministerium für Handel und Versorgung, "Niederschrift über die Sitzung des Verwaltungsrates des Leipziger Messeamtes am 22. Oktober 1948 im Sitzungszimmer des Leipziger Messeamtes," Comments by Fritz Selbmann, p. 4.

65. Pl, "Grundzüge der Messewerbung," *Die Werbung,* 3, 1950, p. 135.

66. Werbeleiter Karl Röhl, "Messen und Ausstellungen: Das messepolitische Dreieck," *Die Werbung,* 7, June/July 1949, p. 112.

67. The Hanover Fairgrounds demonstrated its international prominence when it became the site of the World Exposition – EXPO 2000. Tasch, p. 152ff.

68. Möller, p. 181ff.

69. Ibid., p. 191.

70. As with many of the institutions of the East German economy, the dislocation of reunification has also had an impact on the Leipzig Fair. According to its official website, the Fair had to give up its traditional universal fairs in 1990, and followed the tradition of specialization that had become prominent in West Germany with a new series of smaller fairs. "City Guide: Historisch," n.d. <http://www.leipziger-messe.de/LeMMon/LMGWeb_G.NSF/frames?OpenPage&Code=0x00x11x> (1 November 2002)

71. Seidel, "Schaufenster," p. 5.

72. Heinrich Rau, "Ost-West-Handel – wichtige Grundlage der friedlichen Koexistenz! Aus der Rede anläßlich der Eröffnung der Leipziger Frühjahrsmesse 1961," in *Für die*

Arbeiter-und-Bauern-Macht: Ausgewählte Reden und Aufsätze 1922–1961 (Berlin: Dietz Verlag, 1984), p. 455.

73. Consumers could complain directly to government officials in petitions or "Eingaben" and they usually received an answer to their concerns. See discussion in Felix Mühlberg, "Wenn die Faust auf den Tisch Schlägt . . . Eingaben als Strategie zur Bewältigung des Alltags," in Neue Gesellschaft für Bildende Kunst, eds., *Wunderwirtschaft: DDR-Konsumkultur in den 60er Jahren* (Köln: Böhlau Verlag, 1996), pp.175–84. For more on the culture of complaint in the GDR see Ina Merkel, ed., *Wir sind doch nicht die Meckerecke der Nation! Briefe an das Fernsehen der DDR* (Berlin: Schwarzkopf & Schwarzkopf, 2000).

74. "Unsere Leserumfrage: Was erzählen Sie zu Hause, wenn Sie von der Leipziger Messe kommen? Kleine Interviews am Rande der Leipziger Messe," *Das Magazin,* 1(10), October 1954, p. 50.

75. Käte Gaul, "Phantasievolles Modeschaffen: 'Silberspiegel' und 'Am Kamin', der Wünschtraum jeder Frau," *Leipziger Zeitung,* March 6, 1947, p. 3.

76. Alexandra, "Nach der Messe: Rückblick und kritische Betrachtungen einer Hausfrau," *Leipziger Zeitung,* March 16, 1947, p. 5.

77. Raymond Stokes, "In Search of the Socialist Artifact: Technology and Ideology in East Germany, 1945–1962," *German History,* 15(2), 1997, pp. 220–39.

78. R.F., "Allerlei aus Leipzig," *Frau von Heute,* 11(11), March 16, 1956, pp. 4–5.

79. SAPMO BA DFD Buvo 324, Büro des Sekretariats, Sitzungen des Sekretariats 85.92. Sitzung, September 4–November 9, 1956, Zu protokoll Nr. 90, Anlage 4, Sekretariatsvorlage, Betr: Information über den Besuch der Leipziger Herbstmesse 1956, Berlin, October 5, 1956, Abteilungsleiterin, Diehl, Bundessekretarin.

80. SAPMO BA SED ZK Abt. Frauen IV 2/17/33, Information der Arbeitsgruppe Frauen über die Probleme der allseitigen Erleichterung der Hausarbeit [1957?].

81. SAPMO BA DFD Buvo 324, Büro des Sekretariats, Sitzungen des Sekretariats 85.92. Sitzung, September 4 –November 9, 1956, Zu Protokoll Nr. 90, Anlage 4, Sekretariatsvorlage, Betr: Information über den Besuch der Leipziger Herbstmesse 1956, Berlin, October 5, 1956, Abteilungsleiterin, Diehl, Bundessekretärin. Anlage, [list of new products] Berlin, October 4, 1956, Diehl.

82. R.F. "Noch einmal Leipziger Allerlei für die Hausfrau," *Frau von Heute,* 11(38), September 1956, pp. 4-5.

83. M.P. "Technik im Haushalt," *Kultur im Heim,* 4, 1957, p. 34.

84. R.F. "Noch einmal Leipziger Allerlei," pp. 4–5.

85. M.P. "Technik im Haushalt: Schnell noch einen Eierlikör . . .," *Kultur im Heim,* 1, 1959: pp. 42–3.

86. "Messe und Lebensstandard," *Konsumgenossenschafter,* 37, September 13, 1958, p. 6.

87. SAPMO BA SED ZK Abt. Frauen IV 2/17/33, Information der Arbeitsgruppe Frauen über die Probleme der allseitigen Erleichterung der Hausarbeit [1957?].

88. SAPMO BA DFD Buvo 324, Büro des Sekretariats, Sitzungen des Sekretariats 85.92. Sitzung, September 4–November 9, 1956, Zu protokoll Nr. 90, Anlage 4, Sekretariatsvorlage, Betr: Information über den Besuch der Leipziger Herbstmesse 1956, Berlin,

October 5, 1956, Abteilungsleiterin, Diehl, Bundessekretärin. Anlage, [list of new products] Berlin, October 4, 1956, Diehl.

89. Ibid.

90. Ibid. While many industries and retailers had been nationalized as part of state-owned "people's" industries, a sizeable number of private stores and companies continued to exist in the 1950s. During the major campaigns to complete the stages of building socialism in the GDR, as in 1952 and 1958, pressure was increased for private firms to join state networks. Still, private ownership of smaller shops and companies continued throughout the existence of the regime.

91. SAPMO BA FDGB Buvo 1547 Part II, Industriegewerkschaft Metall Zentralvorstand, an das Frauensekretariat des Bundesvorstandes des FDGB, February 8, 1958, Grothe Sekretariatsmitglied . . ., Abt. Arbeiterversorgung/Feriendienst, Berlin, February 7, 1958, Gro/Ste., "Bericht über die Verwirklichung des Programms der Gewerkschaften zur weiteren Verbesserung und allseitigen Erleichterung des Lebens der werktätigen Frauen und Mädchen."

92. SAPMO BA SED ZK Abt. Frauen IV 2/17/33, Information der Arbeitsgruppe Frauen über die Probleme der allseitigen Erleichterung der Hausarbeit [1957?].

93. SAPMO BA DFD Buvo 324, Büro des Sekretariats, Sitzungen des Sekretariats 85.92. Sitzung, September 4–November 9, 1956, Zur Protokoll Nr. 90, Anlage 3, Sekretariatsvorlage, Betr: Information über den Besuch der Kölner Haushaltsmesse, September 7–9, 1956, (Auswertung des Besuches der Messe, der Teilnahme an der Eröffnung der Messe, Rede des Bundeswirtschaftsministers Erhard und des Besuches der Warenhäuser und Geschäfte der Stadt Köln), Berlin, October 5, 1956, Abteilungsleiterin, Bundessekretärin.

94. SAPMO BA DFD Buvo 324, Büro des Sekretariats, Sitzungen des Sekretariats 85.92. Sitzung, September 4–November 9, 1956, DFD Buvo, Abschrift, Ministerium für Allgemeinen Maschinenbau, Betr: Auswertung des Besuches der Kölner Haushaltsmesse, September 7–9, 1956, Berlin, September 24, 1956, Signed, Diehl, Signed, Brassard.

95. Ibid.

96. SAPMO BA DFD Buvo 324, Büro des Sekretariats, Sitzungen des Sekretariats 85.92. Sitzung, September 4–November 9, 1956, DFD Buvo Abschrift, Ministerium für Leichtindustrie, Betr: Auswertung des Besuches der Kölner Haushaltsmesse, September 7–9, 1956.

97. SAPMO BA DFD Buvo 324, Büro des Sekretariats, Sitzungen des Sekretariats 85.92. Sitzung, September 4–November 9, 1956, DFD Buvo, Ministerium für Handel und Versorgung, Betr: Auswertung des Besuches der Kölner Haushaltsmesse, September 7–9, 1956, Berlin, September 24, 1956, Signed: Diehl, Signed: Brassard.

98. SAPMO BA SED ZK Abt. Frauen IV 2/17/33, Information der Arbeitsgruppe Frauen über die Probleme der allseitigen Erleichterung der Hausarbeit [1957?].

99. SAPMO BA DFD Buvo 324, Büro des Sekretariats, Sitzungen des Sekretariats 85.92. Sitzung, September 4–November 9, 1956, Zu Protokoll Nr. 90 Anlage 4, Sekretariatsvorlage, Betr: Information über den Besuch der Leipziger Herbstmesse 1956, Berlin, October 5, 1956, Abteilungsleiterin, Diehl, Bundessekretärin. Anlage, [list of new products] Berlin, October 4, 1956, Diehl.

100. Merkel, *Utopie und Bedürfnis*, p. 175.

101. SAPMO BA FDGB Buvo 1547, Frauenabteilung, Verwirklichung des Programms zur weiteren Verbesserung der Lage der werktätigen Frauen und Mädchen, Berichte der Industriegewerkschaften. January 1958–February 1958, Industriegewerkschaft Örtliche Wirtschaft Zentralvorstand, an Kollegin Käte Bombach Bundesvorstand des FDGB, Berlin, Febuary 7, 1958, Ku/Gl., Einschätzung der Verwirklichung des Frauenprogramms.

102. SAPMO BA SED ZK IV 2/610/40 Handel, Versorgung und Außenhandel. Institut für Warenkunde, Weltniveau auf der Leipziger Frühjahrsmesse 1960.

103. Ibid.

104. Ibid.

105. Patrick Major, "Going West: The Open Border and the Problem of *Republikflucht*," in Patrick Major and Jonathan Osmond, eds., *The Workers' and Peasants' State: Communism and Society in East Germany under Ulbricht 1945–71* (Manchester: Manchester University Press, 2002), pp.190–208.

106. SAPMO BA SED ZK IV 2/610/39 Handel, Versorgung und Außenhandel. SED Hausmitteilung an Genossen E. Lange, From Abteilung Sicherheitsfragen. March 3, 1959. Betr: Versorgungslage im Bezirk Dresden. From Borning. With copies to Honecker, Neumann, Lange.

107. BAP DL-1/2473 Ministerium für Handel und Versorgung, Industrie und Handelskammer, Leipzig, "Die Leipziger Frühjahrsmesse 1947." Leipzig, March 28, 1947, p. 15.

108. For general discussions of smuggling and East–West exchange see Merkel, p. 286ff.; Peter Kaiser, Norbert Moc and Heinz-Peter Zierholz, *Heisse Ware: Spektakuläre Fälle der DDR-Zollfahndung* (Berlin: Verlag Das Neue Berlin, 1997); Christian Härtel and Petra Kabus, eds., *Das Westpaket: Geschenksendung, keine Handelsware* (Berlin: Ch. Links Verlag, 2000).

109. Möller, p. 156.

110. I have no information to corroborate the claim that this novel is one of only three nineteenth-century works of erotica. Nor can I verify the actual publication date of this novel. Anon., *Julchen und Jettchen: Die reizenden Verkäuferinnen – oder Julchens und Jettchens Liebesabenteuer auf der Leipziger Messe*. Erwin Müller, ed. (Hanau: Verlag Müller & Kiepenheuer, 1971).

111. Uta Falck, *VEB Bordell: Geschichte der Prostitution in der DDR* (Berlin: Links, 1998), p. 52.

112. "Unsere Leserumfrage," *Das Magazin*, p. 51.

113. Helmut Lienemann, "Sterben die 'leichten Mädchen' aus?" *Das Magazin*, 4, 1955, p. 64, cited in Falck, p. 52.

114. VEB stands for Volkseigene Betrieb, or a state-owned company. Falck, p. 151.

115. "Heisser Sommer," 1968. Directed by Joachim Hasler, Starring Frank Schöbel and Chris Dodek.

116. Falck, p. 150.

117. US National Archives, 446 HICOG Berlin Element, HICOG Eastern Element, September 15, 1950, "Visit to the Leipzig Fair," Signed George A. Morgan, Director.

118. Ibid.

3

On the Seam between Socialism and Capitalism: East German Fashion Shows

Judd Stitziel

In May 1956 *Der Augenzeuge*, the official weekly news film that ran before feature films in theaters throughout East Germany, reported on a fashion show conducted by the consumer cooperative of Potsdam. The narrator's exclamations "New models in front of old scenery!" and "In Potsdam air, Parisian charm!" drew attention to the paradoxical mixture of Parisian-inspired, socialist haute couture set amid the classical architecture of Sans Souci, the park of the Prussian kings, and accompanied by swing jazz music. By describing one unusual dress as "a charming skirt in installments" (*reizender Rock auf Raten*), the narrator humorously noted the incongruity of displaying such extravagant and expensive clothes at a time when East Germans' buying power was extremely limited and many food products were still rationed.[1] In a similar vein, another *Augenzeuge* report from March 1957 featured designs from the fashion show of the Leipzig Trade Fair, the most prominent biannual showcase for East German products. The clip, however, began with the announcer's declaration, "setting the tone once again for 1957 are the fashion creators from Paris," and proceeded to show women wearing East German haute couture dresses in and around several automobiles.[2]

Given the well-known shortages and the poor quality of goods that plagued the GDR's economy and frustrated East German consumers, it may seem absurd at first glance that the regime not only tolerated but actively promoted displays of extravagant and virtually unobtainable apparel explicitly influenced by capitalist designers. Yet East Germans saw such images on an everyday basis throughout the 1950s and 1960s, whether at one of hundreds of fashion shows each year or in countless reports in newspapers, magazines, and films and on television. In explaining this peculiar state of affairs, this chapter examines many of the contradictions and tensions that arose from the broader attempts of the GDR's ruling party, the Socialist Unity Party or SED, to create a viable socialist alternative to Western capitalist consumer culture. Fashion shows under socialism in the GDR illustrate how a problematic combination of ideological imperatives, cultural continuities, and economic realities complicated, distorted, and partially blocked the SED's goal of building a new society and cultivating a new "socialist personality."

Despite the claims of the SED to influence and control every aspect of life in the GDR, the ideals of East German consumer culture did not result from a coherent and consistent party line dictated by a monolithic and all-powerful party-state apparatus. They instead emerged slowly as the result of informal negotiations that involved moments of conflict and consensus both within official institutions and between the regime and its citizens. Fashion shows illustrate well these political and cultural battles. Whereas some functionaries advocated proletarian and rural styles as the ideal aesthetic in the self-proclaimed "first workers' and peasants' state on German soil," others used Paris as their lodestar and sought to emulate international haute couture. While some rejected fashion altogether as a manifestation of female folly, others argued that women's new and growing public roles in the sphere of production required them to dress fashionably as a sign of their own self-confidence and as a model of good taste for men and children.

The story of East German fashion shows also complicates narratives of Americanization, Westernization, and Sovietization, whose top-down perspective has often led to one-sided models of political, economic, and cultural borrowing and contrasted 'modernization' in the West with "Stalinization" in the East.[3] While the Soviet Union exercised a constitutive influence on the GDR's economic and political structures, East Germans filled them with their own distinct content and joined their comrades from the Soviet bloc in emulating certain aspects of West European consumer cultures. The contested propagation of the transnational phenomenon of haute couture in Eastern Europe suggests previously undeveloped narratives of identification with and emulation of West European culture in addition to the well-known story of anti-Americanism.

Refashioning Taste, Class, and Gender

"Today we have in Germany – as a result of Hitler's war of conquest – neither raw materials nor processing industries that could be the basis for a fashion. The fashion goddess is, like so many other false gods, dethroned. Her 'leadership principle [*Führerprinzip*]' is over. No, here there's no fashion in the previous sense and there won't be any for years to come. But what will take its place? . . . That is a new problem."[4] This declaration in the socialist women's magazine *Die Frau von heute* in February 1946 expressed common hopes for a fresh start and for new cultural forms that could serve as the basis of transformed attitudes toward consumption and social distinction. The *Trümmerfrau*, or woman of the rubble, with her work clothes and a scarf over her pulled-up hair, personified for many Germany's "zero hour" – also in the world of fashion – and later became an important mythological component of West and East German identities.[5] However, she could serve neither as a personification of both states' promises of prosperity nor as a symbol of the differences between East and West. By the mid-1950s, female figures who performed these functions emerged as the chaos of the immediate postwar years subsided, and as both Germanies increasingly fought their Cold War battles on the grounds of consumption. Both East and West Germany used displays of consumer goods and discourses on consumption to prove the superiority of their respective politico-economic systems, to make claims to represent the German nation, and to establish the legitimacy of the state and encourage allegiance to it.

The combination of strong prewar traditions of publicly displaying commodities and Germans' dreams of returning to normalcy after years of hardship contributed to the rebirth of fashion shows in the Soviet Occupation Zone as early as August 1946. Yet the first postwar shows were qualitatively different from their prewar predecessors. Rather than representing flights of fancy, these early displays visualized the motto "make new from old," which the Nazis had already popularized during the war.[6] Reflecting Germans' everyday practices, shows featured apparel made from scraps of used material that appeared primitive by prewar standards.[7] Consumer magazines supported these practices by publishing countless paper patterns to help women make their own apparel.[8] The seemingly superfluous fantasies expressed in the public display of improvised yet nevertheless attractive and fashionable apparel, even amid the existential crises of the immediate postwar years, suggest the operation of more complex consumerist cravings than simply the wish to merely subsist and to satisfy supposedly objective, biologically based "basic needs."[9] By the late 1940s, the desires and fantasies of a well-developed consumer culture were already reemerging in the GDR.

East German functionaries soon began to instrumentalize these desires in attempts to draw the GDR's citizens into the project of constructing socialism. Already, during the gradual elimination of clothing rationing between 1949 and 1953, officials were beginning to call displays of commodities "achievement shows" (*Leistungsschauen*) in the hope that the public display of the GDR's best products would serve as concrete, visible proof of the potential of socialist production and as incentives for East Germans to work hard to achieve a higher standard of living.[10] By connecting displays and images of exclusive apparel with propagandistic promises like "as we work today, so we will live tomorrow," GDR officials implied that East Germans' labors and commitment to socialism eventually would result in the satisfaction of more elaborate sartorial desires.[11]

The visualization of these official promises and the evolution of East German fashion shows beyond the level of "make new from old," however, engendered intense controversy. In addition to criticisms that many official displays and images encouraged premature consumer fantasies, vehement attacks by dogmatic party functionaries on "fashion" made even the word itself taboo in official circles in the highly charged ideological atmosphere of the Cold War and the party purges of the late 1940s and early 1950s.[12] Anti-fashion East German Marxists claimed that capitalists deliberately stimulated the "unreasonable fickle moods of fashion," as Marx had called them in *Das Kapital*, and used them to manipulate the masses, to create "false" needs for new clothes, and thus to increase their profits.[13] Leading capitalist designers such as Christian Dior "dictated fashion" and strove for "newness at any price" in order to render "the latest old and unmodern" and to awake "new needs."[14]

Those who objected to giving fashion a place in socialism elaborated a familiar narrative both inside and outside socialist and communist circles that cast women as passive, malleable objects of the capitalist market, as "slaves to fashion."[15] Until the late 1960s, most East Germans considered women the primary consumers of fashion, which itself became mystified and reified through its personification as an arbitrary, fickle, and impulsive woman.[16] In the words of one contemporary, "it can't be prevented that Mrs. Fashion [*Frau Mode*] is a downright moody lady."[17] Even those who argued that fashion, by allowing women to appear always new and different, was their great "ally" and "servant" admitted that women's weaknesses and enthusiasm for the seductive powers of fashion occasionally undermined work discipline and productivity.[18] Anti-fashion functionaries posited that a combination of the advancement of production and capitalists' competition for customers artificially accelerated an otherwise natural process of gradual stylistic change.[19]

Many of those who rejected "fashion" as a capitalist, bourgeois invention instead celebrated the proletariat as representatives of the "true" interests of the German nation. Encapsulated in the term "*Proletkult*," or "cult of proletarianism," this broad strand of nationalist claims glorified "timeless" proletarian and rural forms, such as "good, solid" overalls, aprons, and dirndls, worn by stocky women performing hard manual labor or confidently standing with their hands on their hips, a typically working-class posture.[20] (Figure 3.1) The embodiment of a vision of Germanness rooted in work, these women spent rare leisure time in self-made dirndls, which were based on folk costumes and could be made out of old scraps of material. (Figure 3.2) Such "fashionable" work clothes were meant to encourage joyfulness at work while fulfilling "practical" purposes. A combination of the SED's emphasis on "culture" (*Kultur*), the regime's claims to represent the German nation, and the politically privileged status of rural workers in the GDR during the highly controversial efforts to collectivize farms in the early 1950s led state clothing designers to place special emphasis on the use of "motives of folk art following cultural heritage for the development of so-called traditional costumes [*Trachtenkleider*]."[21] Symbolizing the "timeless" dirndl's opposition to volatile

Figure 3.1 Marianne Schlegel, "Praktisch und doch ansprechend. Das Arbeitskleid unserer Bäuerin. 40 Modelle des Instituts für Bekleidungskultur diskutiert und bejaht," Die Bekleidung, *2(1), 1955, p. 27.*

urban fashions, women wearing dirndls were portrayed either in a nondescript indoor setting or out in a country field, but not on city streets. This was a very selective interpretation of the style. East Germans simply ignored both the dirndl's striking continuity with officially propagated women's clothing under National Socialism and its adoption by haute couture designers during the late 1930s and the Second World War.[22] The denial of the dirndl's more recent history allowed its advocates to portray it, along with overalls and aprons, as the embodiment of a socialist "clothing culture" (*Bekleidungskultur*) in the "first workers' and peasants' state on German soil."

But the *Proletkult* had a limited appeal, even in most official circles. Proletarian and rural work clothes and folk costumes may have symbolized the regime's celebration of work in the present, but proved inappropriate for embodying modernity and visualizing socialism's promises of future affluence. The *Proletkult* gradually gave way to the fundamental social conservatism of bourgeois values by

Figure 3.2 "Das Dirndl," Die Bekleidung, *1(2), 1954, p. 13.*

the mid-1950s, as expressed in official, gendered discourses on "culture" and "good taste." In the terms of contemporaries, the new socialist woman was to subscribe to the rules of *Herr Geschmack*, Mr. Taste, in order to resist the arbitrary moods of *Frau Mode*, Mrs. Fashion, which allegedly were dictated by Western, capitalist designers.[23] The new woman thereby helped to cultivate "clothing culture," which stood in opposition to ephemeral "fashions" and drew on "the great heritage of good taste that has been accumulating for centuries" that included classic figures of German culture such as Dürer, Holbein, Menzel, Goethe, Schiller, and Beethoven.[24]

This privileging of high culture created continual tensions and contradictions in the explicitly anti-bourgeois socialist state. East German workers were to "storm the heights of culture," in the words of a ubiquitous SED slogan, but only in order to take the place of the former bourgeois occupants, not to make any changes in substance or form. The tension between proletarian and rural role models on the one hand and urban bourgeois norms on the other found expression in schizophrenic fashion shows that often started with "female farmers" (*Bäuerinnen*) in work clothes and dirndls and ended with "working women" (*berufstätige Frauen*) modeling chic suits and extravagant evening apparel.[25] Another source of tensions and contradictions was the fact that official East German notions of good taste were virtually identical to dominant norms found in West Germany at the time, as seen in the dozens of best-selling manuals on good manners (*Benimmbücher*) in both Germanies.[26]

In the context of East Germany's planned economy, one of the biggest problems surrounding the issue of mutable styles was the common assumption that "one cannot plan fashion."[27] Signifying unbridled, irrational, uncontrollable feminine desires that defied regulation and rationalization, *Frau Mode*'s whims directly undermined state socialism's drive toward planning the economy and steering societal development through well-ordered and predictable production and consumption. Paradoxically, East German fashion shows themselves were supposed to counteract the disruptive forces of fashion. By exhibiting role models for East Germans to emulate, shows theoretically would help to cultivate "good taste" and "socialist consumer habits," which in turn would guide, domesticate, and channel consumers' – and especially women's – desires and thus help to harmonize production and consumption, supply and demand. Removed from their function under capitalism as instruments for the excitement of "false needs," fashion shows under socialism supposedly served as democratic forums for the collection of feedback from educated consumers, allowing "women themselves [to] choose their fashion!"[28]

The attempt to cultivate good taste through fashion shows often involved the presentation of images of "false" or "tasteless" fashions – especially Western ones – as a foil for "correct" styles. Under titles such as "Like this or like that?" (*So oder so?*), these shows sometimes were enlisted in the battle against "American cultural barbarism."[29] For instance, an article in the newspaper for young people, *Junge Welt,* from 1958 juxtaposed two pictures of the same young couple taken during an educational fashion show. In the first photo they are dressed "according to their own taste;" the girl, with her hair pulled up and back, wears a blouse and pleated skirt and carries a handbag while the boy is dressed in a suit and tie. In the other photo, labeled "Texas-Billy Masquerade," the girl sassily plays with her long, frizzy hair and wears a tight-fitting white T-shirt and equally tight jeans, while the boy wears trousers that are rolled up well above his ankles. The article claimed that "small squads" dressed in similar attire stood every evening on the Petersstraße in Leipzig: "The boys in jeans with skull-and-crossbones medallions and blaring radios, the girls in skin-tight tops [*Angströhren*] with tousled hair, clumsily garishly made up." These young people allegedly inspired the local Free German Youth group to put on a fashion show featuring the "Texas-Billy" parody in order to "put a mirror in front of them [and] show [them] how dumb and silly they look." The show's "practical, comfortable, modern, and tasteful" clothing would "demonstrate to them how one can leave a better impression on one's environment" through "fashionable clothing."[30] The article typifies official attempts to use "educational fashion shows" to contrast a supposed minority of East Germans whose clothing, mentalities, and behavior were still corrupted by capitalism with the alleged majority of GDR citizens who espoused "healthy" tastes.[31]

Another important function of displays was to facilitate the harmonization of production, distribution, and consumption. One aspect of this project consisted of encouraging the production and distribution of apparel that complied with the official "Fashion Line of the GDR," which theoretically unified good taste, consumers' demands, and productive capabilities.[32] As the regime stepped up its campaign for the rationalization and standardization of production at the beginning of the 1960s, fashion shows were to prove visually "that the frequently expressed fears that standardization amounts to homogenization" were "unfounded."[33] By "inspiring" producers and counteracting wholesalers' and retailers' allegedly conservative tastes, exhibitions were supposed to help overcome the forces within the GDR's economy that blocked the cultivation of "clothing culture."

But the GDR's textile and garment industry and its wholesale and retail trade organizations did not produce, could not produce, and had little or no incentive to produce "tasteful" apparel in sufficient numbers. The organization and logic of the GDR's industry and trade ran counter to the party's goal of producing and selling goods worthy of socialism's consumer utopia. The appearance of apparel in stores resulted from industry and trade officials' economic concerns and tastes, not from centrally propagated images, displays, or guidelines. The often complete lack of coordination among planners, producers, wholesalers, retailers, advertisers, and the media resulted in countless advertisements for goods that were unavailable in stores.[34] At the same time, the problems with both qualitative and quantitative connections between supply and demand resulted in growing stockpiles of unsold goods that plagued the GDR's economy – items that remained on store shelves for years because they were either too old-fashioned, low-quality, expensive, or damaged.[35] Yet another official purpose of fashion shows was to excite demand for and sell these otherwise overlooked or unattractive items as well as to increase lagging sales in general.[36] Immediately after "sales fashion shows"

(*Verkaufsmodenschauen*) wholesalers and retailers tried to sell the displayed items directly to consumers, thus theoretically helping to overcome organizational and logistical deficits in the GDR's planned economy.[37] These same economic shortcomings, however, made such shows very difficult to organize and the result generally fell far short of expectations.[38] Much more common were entreaties that fashion shows feature only items that actually were available for purchase in stores.[39] (Figures 3.3 and 3.4)

Figure 3.3 *Fashion show in the "industry store" of the women's garment factory VEB Damenbekleidung Fortschritt at Grünberger Straße 54 in Berlin, 1956. Producers were supposed to use such stores to sell their products directly to consumers, thereby receiving direct feedback and bypassing allegedly conservative wholesalers and retailers. Note the apparently mixed reactions of members of the audience. LAB, C Rep. 470-01, Nr. 89. Courtesy Landesarchiv Berlin.*

Figure 3.4 Fashion show in the "industry store" of the women's garment factory VEB Damenbekleidung Fortschritt at Grünberger Straße 54 in Berlin, 1956. LAB, C Rep. 470-01, Nr. 89. Courtesy Landesarchiv Berlin.

Socialist Haute Couture

Continuing the shift toward favoring modern, urban ideals and symbols of affluence, in late 1956 the central institution responsible for the official "fashion line of the GDR," the Institute for Clothing Culture, began to shift its focus from work clothes and daily wear to apparel "in *haute couture* character." This move found institutional expression when the Institute changed its name to the German Fashion Institute in 1957.[40]Although it may seem antithetical to the egalitarian claims of Marxist-Leninist ideology, the propagation of certain haute couture designs fit perfectly into dominant ideas about cultivating the socialist personality and "good taste" through a process of trickle-down cultural dissemination. In the eyes of both socialists and capitalists, (Parisian) haute couture represented the peak of a fashion pyramid from which "inspirations" spread downward and outward, reaching ever broader geographical and socio-economic segments of the population as it trickled down and was replicated in simplified, mass-produced forms.[41] This scheme also was in tune with party leaders' elitist and paternalistic conceptions of "education" (*Erziehung*), their mistrust of mass culture and celebration of high culture, and their goal of planning mass-production well in advance. Just as in the West, the media ideally would publicize a few exclusive designs which were either hand-made or produced in small series by specialized factories. These "fashionable forerunners," "test models," and "custom ready-to-wear apparel" would be expensive but provide feedback on the models' resonance among consumers and simultaneously stimulate demand for them.[42] This would give the textile and garment industries enough time to mass-produce simpler, less expensive versions of the original models starting in the following year.[43] East German officials partly justified this hierarchical structure by correctly observing that the new postwar social and economic structures had forced Western haute couture to broaden its base of customers. Fashion was becoming increasingly democratized as a growing share of the profits of couture houses came from licensing agreements that put their names on thousands of mass-marketed products, from dresses to perfumes to purses, that were sold in department stores.[44] By guiding and channeling tastes and serving as the basis for mass-produced models the following year, the promotion of haute couture could contribute to the regime's project of creating a relatively homogenous, mass consumer market and facilitating the long-term planning of mass-production.

A crucial and problematic component of this project was the creation of a socialist working woman devoid of class differences with claims to universal appeal. Many functionaries theorized that the eventual dissolution of class and social distinctions under socialism would reinforce and increase the importance of constructions of gender and heterosexuality. As the new working woman learned to confidently represent herself and "hold her own like a man" (*ihren Mann stehen*) in the sphere of production, she threatened to destabilize gender boundaries. Most fashion functionaries therefore were quick to assure themselves and others that women's new roles and legal equality with men in society and in the sphere of production did not necessitate the loss of femininity, classical ideals of beauty, or the so-called natural order. Instead, the new working woman's apparel embodied the masculine attributes of being "practical and appropriate for daily work," but at the same time corresponded to "the woman's sense of beauty." This duality enabled the working woman to embody a universal ideal of feminine beauty: according to German Fashion Institute officials, everyone – and most especially the working woman – wished "to be young and beautiful, slender and elegant."[45]

The predominant official orientation toward haute couture came under heavy fire from some functionaries and consumers who claimed that the promotion and universalistic claims of exclusive, individualistic designs were totally out of touch with the more down-to-earth tastes of the majority of East German women. Not only did such dress stand in opposition to women's new roles and rights under socialism, so the argument went, it also contradicted socialism's central egalitarian principles. In a letter to the Central Committee in 1958, the Women's Commission

(*Frauenkommission*) of the SED's regional leadership in Frankfurt/Oder sharply criticized the German Fashion Institute for not being in tune with what it claimed were working women's true needs. It asserted that working women, young girls, and garment workers unanimously rejected the Institute's fashion line. The line was "for a few extravagant [*Überspannte*] and crazy [*Verrückte*] ones, but most women consider it beneath their dignity to dress like that . . . This fashion trend does not at all correspond to our societal conditions and does not take into account that 43 percent of all women work." The Frankfurt Women's Commission claimed to speak for "women workers, female collective farmers, white-collar workers, [and] intellectuals" whose "life differed fundamentally from that of the past." The GDR was full of women whose main concern was work, both outside and inside the home, and who had little patience for the frivolities of high fashion, the Commission claimed. "It is not our thing to sit for hours in the afternoon over a little cup of tea in order to gossip about the most eccentric models and novelties. We would detest such a life. We pitch in and get down to business in order to fulfill our societal duties, sharing equal rights with men." A fashion institute, the Commission continued, should advise women how to dress "simply yet elegantly corresponding to a woman's dignity" in her profession, as a woman, and as a mother. In sum, the Institute's staff had "no connection" to the women of the GDR.[46]

The press resounded with calls for the Institute and the other leading producers of fashionable apparel in the GDR to "finally show something that we can really put on, what suits us, our lifestyle and habits."[47] The Institute allegedly lacked "direct contact to the people" and was "bloodless," in part because it did not have "customers" (*Kundschaft*), that is, it did not produce models for paying customers but rather simply in order to abstractly "lead" and "inspire" industry and consumers' tastes.[48] Many insisted that the Institute for Clothing Culture's mission was not to show that the GDR could make "high fashion," but rather to benefit all women.[49] *Neues Deutschland*'s fashion correspondent Inge Kertzscher summed up these tensions by asking whether the Institute and the GDR's industry should produce "runway-fashion or pretty dresses for everyone."[50]

The media and popular culture encouraged the popular myth of a battle of representatives of the "people's taste" against the GDR's elites in industry, trade, party, and state. In *Messeschlager Gisela*, a controversial musical that the regime banned only a few weeks after its debut in 1960, Gisela, a young, idealistic woman fresh out of school, designs an eponymous model "for every woman" which instantly gains the nearly unanimous approval of her colleagues in the textile factory VEB Berliner Schick. Robert Kuckuck, the factory's director, rejects her design, however, in favor of the ridiculously exaggerated "Melon" model, the "inspiration" for which he received during a trip to Paris.[51] At the play's climax Kuckuck's "Melon," modeled by his Western-oriented, uncouth secretary, flops and "Gisela" triumphs at the Leipzig Trade Fair's international fashion show, a clear victory for moderate "good taste" that suits and is affordable for "every woman" over "tasteless," Western, elitist decadence.

Fashion for "Stronger Women" as "Socialist Fashion"?

The organizers of fashion shows and the East German media also constructed hierarchies of women's bodies. Starting in the early 1950s officials propagated models designed expressly for "stronger" (*stärker*), "full-figured" (*vollschlank*), or "chubby" (*mollig*) women. Pictures of the models populated special spreads in every consumer magazine that covered fashion; several magazines even published special issues devoted solely to the needs of this supposedly distinct group of consumers. Consistent with dominant conceptions of "good taste" that stressed dressing according to one's "body type," the media sought to teach all women how to accentuate their bodies' "positive" characteristics while hiding the "disadvantageous" ones.[52] Officials felt obligated to educate the "woman with a stronger figure" who unfortunately bought "a dress made of fabric with large flowers because she thought that the same dress was pretty on her well-shaped friend."[53] While "full-figured" women had to "learn to abstain from the enchanting wide skirts," they were reminded that "there is no reason for mourning," because "good taste, creativity, and some initiative of one's own let even a chubby figure appear flattering and elegant."[54]

As calls for a distinct "socialist fashion" became louder at the end of the 1950s, fashion functionaries began to argue that special models for "stronger women" distinguished the aesthetic content and underlying role models of clothing in socialism from those in capitalism. In contrast to capitalism's objectification of women and its worship of the young and slender female body, under socialism all women supposedly enjoyed a right to clothing appropriate to their bodies.[55] However, despite the official insistence that "to be round is no misfortune," and that "the ideal of beauty of the socialist person does not allow itself to be influenced by measurements in centimeters and body weight," functionaries stressed that "of course the special attention to clothing for the stronger woman will not create an attitude that propagates or justifies an unaesthetic bodily fullness."[56] Implicitly and often explicitly the "normal" or "ideal" body remained thin, even under socialism.[57] As suggested by mottoes like "full-figured, yet nevertheless chic," special designs for heavy-set women aimed to create optical illusions – for example by using vertical stripes – in order to emulate the still-reigning ideal of slenderness.[58] Teaching women "how one with a chubby figure can have a refined, fashionable appearance without great luxury" implied that "chubby figures" were inherently unrefined (*ungepflegt*) and needed to be disguised.[59] Institute officials and others even advocated using tight-fitting underwear to "make the figure appear firmer and skinnier."[60] Indeed, the "stronger women" that appeared in the media and advertisements often seemed to be only slightly heavier than the models with Twiggy-like figures.

Rather than contributing to the emancipation of women from the strictures of narrow ideals of beauty and desirability, the East German media and fashion shows reinforced the social stigma attached to being overweight. The women who modeled the special designs were almost all middle-aged, despite the fact that half of the East German women with allegedly "stronger figures" were under 40.[61] When designs for overweight women appeared in fashion shows and magazine spreads, the announcer or the text usually explicitly differentiated them from the "normal" ones worn by younger, thinner women. While women with slender figures "enjoyed" wearing their clothes and were the subject of desirous male gazes, "stronger women" at best were consoled that they, too, could be "fashionable" and "refined" (*gepflegt*) with a little extra effort. Such practices made the "stronger" female body the exception and underscored East Germans' subscription to the same modes of visual pleasure as in Western Europe. Nevertheless many larger women resisted official definitions and insisted that their body types be included in the propagated norms. "I, too, despite my somewhat stronger figure, would like to be modernly dressed (I am 19 years old, 1.65 meters tall, and weigh 73 kilograms)," wrote Renate M. to the editors of the television show *Prisma* in 1968. "One must also consider that not all girls are slender like those, for instance, that [East] German Television showed yesterday as models. Would it not also be advantageous and more correct if one occasionally took into account next to them the stronger women and girls? That would certainly find a great resonance among the population!"[62]

By the end of the 1960s most official propaganda no longer pretended that "fashion today is for all age groups and figures" and that "the only thing that matters is to choose with reflection and taste."[63] Consumer magazines increasingly reminded the "stronger woman" of the only socially acceptable solution to her dilemma: "Resolve starting tomorrow to try a little more intensively and deliberately to reduce your weight by a few pounds, which separate you from the general ideal of beauty."[64] Since "the fashionable ideal image remains slim," the only way to match it was to lose weight: "As long as one has a few too many pounds, one must wear what is advantageous for the figure."[65] While young, slender women were free to follow the latest changing fashions, overweight and older women had to conform to certain stigmatized and unchanging rules – such as wearing vertical rather than horizontal stripes and avoiding broad belts.

Many women resisted or rejected official efforts at education and entreaties to conform to the "rules"of dressing according to one's "body type." An Institute official bemoaned in 1959 that "private tailors confirm that precisely the stronger women choose models from the fashion magazines that are to be worn exclusively by slim figures." These heavy-set women "do not like to let themselves be persuaded and convinced that such a model is not suitable for them."[66] Many fashion-conscious women did not want to seem like middle-aged overweight women trying to look thin, but rather like the svelte young models publicized by the media. While dogmatic party officials insisted on the "educational" role of images of clothing, designers and organizers of fashion shows realized that such displays served more as expressions of dreams and desires than vehicles for teaching women rational consumption habits and "rules" for dressing according to one's "body type." Two cartoons in the satirical magazine *Eulenspiegel* conveyed the insincerity and ultimate failure of official efforts to make all body types acceptable and even desirable. In one drawing a heavy-set woman sits at the dinner table eating a piece of cake and gazes longingly at a fashionable dress hanging on the door that is obviously too small for her to wear.[67] In the other, a woman attending a fashion show looks at the pant-suit being modeled by a "full-figured" woman and comments, "A delightful model. Too bad that I'm not so fat!"[68] Envy of larger women was as rare in the GDR as it was in the West – the ideal body was virtually identical on both sides of the Cold War divide. Despite the SED's conflicted attempts to establish special models for "stronger women" as a unique aspect of "socialist" fashion, here too the SED failed to create a desirable alternative to capitalist norms.

Official efforts to promote and sell special models for "stronger women" also encountered considerable obstacles on the supply side. Despite extensive efforts to facilitate the industrial production of "special" sizes, the GDR's garment industry and retail trade had significant disincentives to produce and distribute special models.[69] As was the case with haute couture garments, the state propagated models for "stronger women" at significant expense while industry refused to produce the models because they were too costly. Despite the state's promises and the plethora of propaganda for haute couture and clothes for larger women, the actual articles were very hard to find, a situation all too typical of East Germany's consumer culture in general.

Confronting and Competing with Western Europe

The failure of the promotion of fashion for "stronger women" was just one part of the GDR's larger and equally ambiguous confrontation with Western fashion in general. East German functionaries stood before a difficult conundrum. They hoped to create "socialist fashion" as a distinct, independent alternative and yet admitted that the haute couture of West European capitalist garment industries exerted a dominant, transnational influence on "international fashion."[70] Just as in other Soviet-bloc countries, officials in the GDR responsible for the official "fashion line" used West European fashion as their lodestar and traveled several times a year to Paris, Milan, Düsseldorf, and other capitalist fashion centers to attend haute couture shows and industrial exhibitions, justifying their trips by claiming that they could not afford to wait for months until the latest fashions and their imitations appeared in Western magazines.[71] The corollary of these attitudes and practices was the both official and unofficial goal, established by the mid-1950s, of "matching the rhythm of," "keeping up with," and "reacting quickly to" international fashion.[72] The East German textile and garment industries failed to achieve these goals, however, and criticism that fashion in the GDR "lagged behind international fashion" by at least one to two years littered East German newspapers and official speeches throughout the 1950s and 1960s.[73] The GDR seemed destined, in the words of two fashion functionaries, to be forever "lagging behind capitalist fashion happenings."[74]

The general acceptance of western European high fashion as the standard of a modern aesthetics of affluence presented the SED with the puzzle of how "socialist" fashion could "keep up with" and even influence "international fashion" from the position of an understudy that constantly borrowed from it. East German officials attempted a tricky and often contradictory balancing act between criticizing certain "capitalist" designs and promoting others. "Socialist fashion" essentially consisted of accepting western Europe's fundamental leadership, producing variations of "moderate" and "tasteful" Western designs, and nominally rejecting "extremes" and "exaggerations" that allegedly resulted from capitalists' competition for profits.[75]

One of the prime venues for official East German confrontations with capitalist fashion was the annual International Clothing Contest, renamed the International Fashion Congress in 1957.[76] Initiated by the GDR and Czechoslovakia in 1950 and held in a different Soviet-bloc country each year starting in 1955, the contests featured a fashion show during which a technical and an aesthetic jury evaluated scores of models designed by the central fashion institute of each country.[77] Through prominent coverage of the contests in the East German media, officials hoped to use the contest as a counterweight to capitalist haute couture shows. In the eyes of many East German officials the shows provided an important forum for the visual and material competition between the two "world systems" of socialism and capitalism, especially after the shows became integrated into the formal structures of the Council for Mutual Economic Assistance (CMEA or COMECON) in 1960.[78] East German officials even brought socialist and capitalist models together on the same runway at the biannual trade fair in Leipzig starting at the end of the 1950s.[79] The direct juxtaposition of similar models from capitalist and socialist countries, however, only reinforced the common prejudice that socialist designs could perhaps "catch up to" and "match" but never surpass or inspire western European ones.

Rather than presenting a distinct alternative to western European haute couture, these gatherings served primarily as an opportunity for the socialist countries to collectively look to the West and "critically" adopt only "the best" elements to fit each of their "national" circumstances while looking for "confirmation" that their designs had a "connection" to "international" fashion.[80] In reality, designs from Soviet-bloc countries were virtually indistinguishable from those of Western capitalist ones. While some may have paid lip service to an alleged "Marxist-Leninist aesthetic," if it existed, it certainly did not possess any characteristics that unmistakably differentiated it from Western fashion. In fact East German fashion functionaries themselves sometimes boasted that their models "in no way deviated from the colors and designs of the fashionable offerings of other [Western] countries."[81] Although official propaganda attempted to differentiate the "open" and "cooperative" proceedings of socialist fashion congresses from the cutthroat competition and fashion spies lurking at capitalist haute couture shows, the socialist countries continued the traditional format of such displays, including runway etiquette, orchestral accompaniment, and a male announcer.[82]

East Germany's adoption and superficial modification of modern Western visual and cultural symbols found further expression in the fashion shows of Heinz Bormann. Originally the owner of a private garment factory in Magdeburg, Bormann accepted partial state ownership in October 1956 and quickly became a highly publicized role model for the new category of half-state-owned enterprises. By heavily promoting Bormann, the SED could flaunt, both at home and abroad, socialism's achievements and capabilities, claim that the GDR could match the West on the runways of haute couture shows, and benefit economically from the firm's exports.[83] Continuing a prewar tradition of celebrating the genius of individual designers that owned firms, the media gave East German high fashion a face by emphasizing Bormann's personality and personal leadership of his firm and by explicitly comparing him to top western European designers. As one radio program declared, "in the GDR Mr Bormann is what Dior is in Paris and Schubert in Italy."[84] But such claims did not sit well with many party leaders, who periodically objected that Bormann's fashion shows were far too expensive and "did not work to steer and orient demand" toward products that corresponded to "our macro-economic possibilities" and "our socialist attitude toward life" but rather gave a "false orientation toward Western fashion trends" and "awoke demand for so-called 'Haute Couture' (Paris)."[85] To make matters worse, the East German media, having been given a green light to promote Bormann, sometimes went beyond the boundaries implicitly intended by party leaders. For instance, Central Committee functionaries severely criticized an article in the magazine *Freie Welt* entitled "Men with Millions" that dubbed Bormann "The Red Dior" and compared his lifestyle – including possession of a large house, antique furniture, and old paintings – with that of the West German designer Günther Sachs.[86]

In July 1958 the emphasis on keeping up with international fashion seemed to find at least indirect support at the highest levels of the party and state with the SED's declaration of the ambitious goals of the "economic main task," which stated that the GDR would surpass the FRG in per-capita consumption of all important consumer goods and foodstuffs by 1961. This goal encouraged many East German officials and members of the press to advocate rapid changes in styles and to emphasize "new" designs and types of clothing, in direct contradiction with previously articulated ideals of socialist production.[87] This in turn led to a backlash among more conservative functionaries, who warned that many officials responsible for fashion in the GDR were making Parisian modes into a fetish and called for a more critical and systematic evaluation of Western fashion.[88]

By 1959 the celebration and blatant imitation of Western fashion had gone too far for the tastes of most top party leaders, who feared that the GDR was trapped in a fatal never-ending cycle of trying to catch up to Western fashion. "When pointed shoes are the fashion in Italy," SED General Secretary Walter Ulbricht declared, "we make propaganda for pointed shoes one year later. Meanwhile in Italy or France broad shoes are already the fashion. We just can't keep up with the running behind!"[89] The GDR had to figure out "how one gets away from the 'running after' of fashion."[90] As hundreds of thousands of East Germans continued to resettle in the West and the German Cold War conflict intensified in 1960–1961, many officials called for the GDR to take the offensive and actively create and shape new and distinct fashions rather than simply react to Western trends.[91] Institute officials admitted in 1961 that in the "evaluation of international fashion there exist no ground rules, no systematization, no concrete instructions where a party-line [*parteilich*] evaluation begins and where it ends."[92] In that same year Ulbricht sarcastically asked, "When in the West someone coughs, do all our fashion designers catch a cold? When they [the West] go for the color of asphalt, we also come out with asphalt a year later . . . We must not ogle the Kurfürstendamm [the famous shopping avenue in West Berlin] so much. That is decidedly unhealthy."[93]

The same sorts of aesthetic preferences and consumerist norms that had fallen under the cultivation of "clothing culture" now became phrased in calls for the creation of "socialist fashion."[94] However, despite officials' claims that the construction of the Wall offered better conditions for the establishment of the GDR's own fashion line, no new initiatives were undertaken and the situation remained essentially unchanged.[95] Officials often admitted that stores' offerings "did not reflect comprehensively enough a distinct conception and a distinct line" and that the GDR's designs at the Fashion Congress did not support claims that "sooner or later" a "divergence" between Western and East German designs would develop.[96] By the mid-1960s calls for "a critical evaluation" of capitalist fashion according to the will of the Party (*Parteilichkeit*) had become so rehearsed that they lost credibility.[97] Officials had to perform self-contradictory verbal gymnastics to explain the GDR's unwanted but unavoidable connection with and dependence on Western fashion.[98] The criticism of the "extremes" of Western fashions became more pro forma and the emulation and copying of capitalist designs more blatant.[99] "Ideological ambiguities" about "Marxist aesthetics" and Western fashions continued to saturate official institutions for at least the rest of the 1960s.[100]

The official practice of selectively adopting and adapting fashions from the West to fit circumstances in the GDR seemed to preclude the creation of an entirely independent alternative. Unable to create independent and unique aesthetics and symbolic measures of prosperity, East German officials were left only to react to Western fashions, criticizing them and proposing more "moderate" East German variations. "Socialist" and "capitalist" fashion shared the fundamentals of a symbolic language that the West undeniably controlled. Fashion shows visually dramatized this relationship.

Behind the Curtain

East German citizens ultimately judged the achievements of socialism not by what they saw on display or in the media but rather by what they could actually purchase in stores. While fashion shows may have served well aesthetically as a showcase for socialism, they formed a crass contrast with the reality of stores' offerings. The displayed models generally were either one-of-a-kind, handmade garments or supposedly would be produced six to twelve months later in series sizes of only 200 to 300, of which four-fifths or more would be exported. Due to the GDR's cumbersome and disconnected apparatuses of production, trade, and the media, "inspirations" from the official fashion line and models on display rarely materialized on store shelves. The effect of such displays was, to quote a local party leader, "that our working people are being led by the nose."[101] (Figure 3.5)

The Berlin Fashion Week illustrates many of the tensions between the regime's efforts to display idealized apparel and consumers' resentment of these illusions. Starting in August 1958, the biannual event was to serve the typical political, educational, and cultural purposes of fashion shows described above. The "achievement show" was intended to demonstrate the "state of development" of the GDR's state-owned garment industry, to underline the GDR's commitment to the "economic main task," and to contribute to the recently revitalized goal of turning Berlin into a "fashion center" that could create and control "German fashion."[102] In addition to serving as "a school of good taste," the exhibition was meant to "directly politically influence the consciousness of the visitors" by presenting them with "concrete examples" of the achievements of East German industries.[103] The event was also to "establish direct contact" between production and trade on the

Figure 3.5 Caption reads "Gestatten, Deutsches Modeinstitut!" – "Gestatten, Einzelhandel!" ("May I introduce, Germany Fashion Institute!" – "May I introduce, retail trade!") Peter Dittrich, Eulenspiegel, *6(30), 1959, p. 12. Courtesy Eulenspiegel/Peter Dittrich.*

one hand and consumers on the other, a task which included introducing all three of these groups to the Institute's official fashion line.[104]

In keeping with these tasks the first three Fashion Weeks in August 1958, February 1958, and September 1959 were full of educational lectures and fashion shows. Fashion designers from the state-owned women's garment factories in Berlin, from the fashion magazine *Sibylle*, and from the German Fashion Institute staffed booths at the exhibition, informed the public "how fashion comes into being from the drawing board to production output," gave individual fashion advice, and drew sketches.[105] Fashion shows with titles like "Well Dressed – Feeling Good," "Does Your Husband Dress in a Modern Fashion?" and "The International Fashion" mixed displays of models meant to visualize socialism's achievements with educational commentary and a "cultural" framework that included a "good salon-orchestra" and dancers from opera houses.[106] Supporting the event's educational goals were lectures on such topics as "Cosmetics is a Part of Fashion," "Natural Beauty Through Healthy Nutrition," "Even the Stronger Woman Can Dress Fashionably," "Small Fashionable Transformations with Great Effect," "Sport: A Requirement of Fashion," and "To Each Type the Suitable Haircut."[107] A "Youth Forum" treating the topic of "how do some of our youth dress and how could and should they dress" included a fashion show and was supplemented by a question-and-answer session with "experts" from the garment industry, the German Fashion Institute, "a well-known athlete, and a well-known actor."[108] In addition to the large central events, smaller fashion shows were to take place in various districts throughout East Berlin and in factories during lunch breaks.[109] A central "high-class fashion ball' with 800 guests and an entrance fee of 20 DM per person was intended to be the week's "high point" as well as a "social event."[110]

The entries in the guest book of the fashion exhibition of the second Berlin Fashion Week in February 1959 provide detailed insights into the public's mixed and often contradictory reception of the event.[111] Reflecting a wide spectrum of tastes and expectations, visitors' overall reactions to the exhibition ranged from ecstatically positive to sarcastically negative. Not surprisingly, many judgments directly contradicted each other. While Hanke B. declared "never have I visited such an exhibition that was constructed with so much love," Genta P. found the exhibition "loveless" in comparison to the previous year's event. A small number of visitors gave unqualified praise, such as W. Jausch, who commented, "I am really enthusiastic. Definitely an advantage and sign for the development in fashion." M. Leischke even wanted to "personally find" those who had written "negative criticisms" in order to "ask them what they accomplish in *their* profession. My opinion: 'One can no longer overlook that the GDR has a presence and can have a say in the area of fashion!'" At the other extreme several visitors wrote nothing but critical comments about the models and the exhibition itself. Genta P. wrote, "the exhibition absolutely disappointed me," and joined several other visitors who resented the admission fee of 0.50 DM. Several visitors criticized the exhibition's partially improvised decor, including "makeshift bicycle lamps as additional lights," which failed to provide sufficient illumination, according to some. Echoing the well-known political debate over "lively, cheerful" colors under socialism, some visitors criticized the "dismal" colors of both the exhibition's decorations and its models. However, none of the visitors criticized the models for being too exclusive or for not matching the tastes of the "general public."

The vast majority of visitors mixed praise of the exhibited models with often blunt criticism of the visual contrast between the idealized images and their everyday experiences of shopping. Referring to the exhibition's title, *Berlin shows what one wears*, one visitor commented, "What is the meaning and purpose of this exhibition? It says that Berlin dresses as such! Unfortunately not." Other visitors were more tactful and optimistic: "This exhibition shows us what is supposed to be worn for 1959. Hopefully these charming models will also make it into [our] homes!" wrote Helger M. from Stendel. Most visitors wanted concrete information on how to immediately obtain the exhibited articles. "Where can one buy these things? That's what is of greatest interest," wrote R. Sunfer. Another visitor lamented, "The exhibited models are very pretty, but what use is that when one doesn't get to buy them?" Renate J. expressed skepticism about their availability in more sarcastic tones: "It would be desirable if the models would make it into production: and that hopefully before 1965."[112] Undertones of resentment saturated many comments that stressed the frustration of seeing the models in the exhibition but not in stores: Ilse N. entreated, "Please take care for us that all the beautiful things that are to be seen here also are really to be had in the stores for us." Closely following concerns about the availability of the displayed items were questions about their prices. Behind such questions was the common assumption, generally quite correct, that apparel on display without a price tag was expensive.

Another cluster of complaints concerned the lack of variety and differentiation of the displayed models. Sarcastically referring to the exhibition's title, F. Gross joined others in criticizing the limited number of assortments on display and the small exhibition space. A few visitors complained that the exhibition seemed exclusively oriented toward young, thin women. A certain "Kleimann" asked simply, "Does fashion exist *only* for young people?" Those who described themselves as belonging to a certain demographic group, including "chubby," "elderly," and "smaller" women, expressed feelings of neglect. "Once again I'm very disappointed," wrote Gisela B. from Berlin, "where are the models for the stronger lady? I am still young and would like also to be nicely dressed. When will one think for once of us?" Another visitor lamented, "One can marvel at very beautiful things here. But where again are we chubby ones? How often, almost always we get to hear: unfortunately only up to size 42." M. Gubler added, "Unfortunately in this exhibition one did not at all consider that there are also older ladies who like to dress well in the theater, in the afternoon, and also on the job." Mixing criticism of the exclusion of women who did not match the ideal young, slender figure with her frustrating everyday experiences of shopping, E. Becher wrote, "Please think of the older stronger women who would like to look nice on every occasion; the sizes 42, 44 are always there but 46, 48 are missing." But the exhibition also did not satisfy all of the young visitors. "Why wasn't more thought given to male youths?" asked L. Neumann. "They wear not only suits."

Partially in response to the criticisms of the disparity between the exhibited models and stores' actual offerings, officials increasingly sought to ensure that displayed models were indeed available for purchase.[113] This new emphasis gradually shifted the event's focus from educational and cultural to economic purposes. Officials expanded the assortments that were for sale at the Berlin Fashion Week to include not only accessories, jewelry, and cosmetics, but also shoes, dresses, suits, and children's clothing.[114] Sales doubled from 1.2 million DM in the spring of 1960 to 2.5 million DM in the fall of the same year. By the fall of 1961 they totaled 3.0 million DM.[115] In order to ensure an impressive display of models for sale at the Fashion Week, central authorities even ordered trade officials in Berlin to hoard goods in storerooms during the preceding weeks in order to ensure an impressive display of items for sale at the exhibition itself.[116]

Increased sales, however, did not indicate success in the eyes of many officials. After the fall 1961 Fashion Week state garment-industry officials complained that these trends diluted the event's "socio-political statement," undermined the goal of propagating a distinct "fashion line," and led visitors to view the event, particularly during the first two days, as "solely a good shopping opportunity, especially for scarce assortments."[117] In October 1961 state officials planned to hold the spring 1962 Fashion Week "with a new trend" that would stress the popularization of the official fashion line and fashion colors and feature specific assortments of clothing, such as apparel for young people.[118] Increased publicity was to help reinstate some of the event's original orientation despite its increasingly commercial character.

The Berlin Fashion Week ended quietly and abruptly in 1962. Although explicit orders have not been found, I would suggest that the decision most likely stemmed from the regime's sensitivity to consumers' growing impatience with industry's inability to deliver the "inspirations" on display. Another probable factor was the establishment and expansion of *Exquisit* stores, which offered "extravagant" apparel at extremely high prices. *Exquisit* could serve simultaneously as showcase and as store, thereby overcoming the seemingly unbridgeable gap between the fashion-show runway and the store shelf. By charging astronomical prices, the special stores were also to serve as a source of accumulation and as a method of soaking up consumers' excess buying power.[119]

Consumers became increasingly disillusioned with official displays of apparel during the course of the 1960s. The regime's own propaganda exacerbated consumers' anger about the gap between promises and everyday reality. Consumers expected to be able to buy the models that they saw in the East German media and in fashion shows and were outraged over the false advertising when they could not obtain the objects of their desires. The "object of the misery" of Gertraude L.'s months-long search, she wrote in a complaint to state trade officials in 1968, was "not some exaggerated demands, but rather very simply *plain, dark gray bouclé* [fabric] that one repeatedly presents to us as exhibition pieces in convention centers, exhibition halls, and store windows."[120] After receiving a rejection letter from the manufacturer of the women's dress "Anchor and Steering Wheels" shown in *Für Dich* in 1965, Ilse G. asked *Prisma* "why doesn't one forbid the magazines to publish such fashionable dresses?"[121] Typical of such criticisms was an article in the satirical magazine *Eulenspiegel* by a woman who described the resentment and disillusionment that she felt while viewing an "Exclusive Pre-Premiere" at the

Friedrichstadt-Palast in Berlin in 1967. Judging from the items on display, she wrote,

> I had to conclude that the female portion of our population consists of 16- to at the most 20-year-old featherweight beings, whose primary occupation is being a wife and whose side-job is supervising a cleaning lady, a cook, a nanny, and a chauffeur for the Wartburg 1000 [the more expensive of the GDR's two brands of cars]. For only such lady-colleagues have the time and opportunity to wear turquoise satin suits or bright red pants complemented with wildly frilled lace blouses in the morning . . . only they have the necessary petty cash at their disposal . . . only they have connections to certain stores . . . Perhaps I've once again unnecessarily gotten all worked up. The items from "Exclusive Pre-Premieres" mostly aren't available in the stores, anyway.[122]

Consumers also complained to official institutions that fashion shows did not reflect socialism's claims to fulfill the needs of individuals of all different ages and bodies. Hans M. from Wilthen, for instance, lamented to the East German television station in 1971: "I still haven't seen a fashion show where one shows . . . something for those of us who are older. Fashion for young people dominates (which certainly is also correct), but we are also still there (for your information: I am 46). Could someone tell that to Bormann, Luci Kaiser [a well-known designer in Leipzig], and the rest of the fashion designers?"[123]

The continued heavy propagation of paper patterns for home-made apparel added to these tensions. Official propaganda portrayed cutout patterns and fashion shows of home-made clothing as sources of "inspiration" and asserted that home sewing was a beloved "hobby" as well as a less expensive alternative for those who preferred to give their clothing "a personal touch."[124] In line with a trope that had long been popular in Protestant Germany, officials also praised home sewing and knitting as a "meaningful free-time occupation" (*sinnvolle Freizeitbeschäftigung*). Such claims certainly contained some truth, and early fashion shows of self-made and self-displayed models evidenced much pride and enthusiasm.[125] But during the early years of the GDR both the SED and consumers understood the practices of "making new out of old" and of tailoring one's own clothes as making a virtue out of necessity in order to cope with a presumably temporary situation, one that gradually would be supplemented with the option of buying an increasing number and wider variety of new, industrially made garments in stores at lower prices. The continued prominence of self-made apparel in East German wardrobes throughout the next four decades constituted an implicit admission that consumers themselves had to produce what the GDR's industry could not.

By the end of the 1960s market researchers and other officials increasingly argued that home sewing was "not primarily a gladly practiced hobby but rather a not always avoidable solution [*Ausweg*] when one does not find the right item in the offerings of ready-to-wear."[126] A survey of the readers of the women's magazine *Für Dich* in 1968 revealed that although 64 percent of all women sewed "a large portion of their wardrobes" themselves, only 4 percent listed tailoring as a "hobby."[127] Market researchers confirmed the common knowledge that stores' extremely poor offerings of larger sizes practically forced many "stronger women" to either make their own clothes or have them made.[128] Adding insult to injury, the officially disseminated patterns often were useless because of errors in the patterns themselves or a lack of appropriate materials. At the beginning of the 1970s the regime seemed to be as far as ever from the fulfillment of its implicit and explicit promises to eliminate the need for home sewing by providing plentiful, inexpensive, and attractive industrially produced apparel.

Fashion shows became less common and progressively lost their original political, cultural, educational, and economic purposes during the course of the 1960s.[129] By the mid-1970s fashion shows took place "relatively infrequently" and "only in selected locales," according to the GDR's Institute for Market Research.[130] Before Bormann's firm was completely absorbed by the state along with virtually all private and half-state-owned enterprises in 1971/72, state auditors had concluded that while his fashion shows should continue outside the GDR to strengthen the "reputation of our Republic abroad," the displays' function of representing "ideal values" was simply too expensive to be justified at home.[131]

The concurrent decline of fashion shows and expansion of *Exquisit* stores both signaled the abandonment of the political and cultural project of creating a distinctly "socialist fashion" and reflected the increasingly dominant roles within the SED's consumer politics of economic concerns and sensitivity to consumers' disillusionment. During the course of the 1960s, official attempts to create a distinctive socialist consumer culture gradually faded as its inherent contradictions and weaknesses remained unresolved and as officials increasingly turned their attention to the standardization and rationalization of production and to growing economic crises. Despite the regime's attempts at economic and industrial reform during the New Economic System from 1963 to 1970, quality stagnated, clothing became more uniform, and apparel drifted further and further from consumers' diversifying and increasing needs and desires. Party leaders had backed themselves into a self-constructed ideological and political trap and proved either unwilling or unable to fundamentally reform an ideologically inconsistent and economically unsound system.

Just as importantly, the GDR had failed to create a desirable alternative to capitalist norms. Since at least the mid-1950s, East German fashion shows had reinforced a modern semiotics of affluence and positioned "socialist" fashion as derivative of Western styles. Ideals of beauty and symbols of modernity and prosperity remained virtually identical on both sides of the Iron Curtain.

Fashion shows and other displays of commodities visualized a Western reality that was unobtainable for East German consumers, despite their hard work and the regime's promises. The crass contrast between these promises and propagated images on the one hand and the bleak reality of East German consumers' everyday experiences on the other both contributed to disillusionment with the entire system of state socialism and encouraged enchantment with the West. Continuing a pattern already established in western Europe before the Second World War, the individual consumption of goods in the GDR proved to be a more visible and convincing measure of affluence than the social consumption of public resources and services such as housing, health care, child care, cultural programs, education, and public transportation. In part because socialism shared with capitalism the goal of a modern consumer's paradise and many of the symbols used to visualize it, the SED proved incapable of creating a desirable alternative consumer culture based on distinctly "socialist" values and aesthetics. Instead, the unique consumer culture that had become established in the GDR by the early 1970s was a contradictory and tension-filled amalgam of "capitalist" and "socialist" images, promises, values, and practices. The regime's competition with the West on capitalism's own terms and the inability of the GDR's industry to fulfill the SED's promises can help explain why East German citizens judged their standard of living using the "capitalist" criteria of individual consumption while taking for granted subsidized social consumption. Only after the fall of the Wall, when prices for items of social consumption skyrocketed, did East Germans develop powerful nostalgia and pride about their former consumer culture. Fashion shows in the GDR embodied the ambiguities and contradictions that arose on the seam between socialism and capitalism, between images of abundance and experiences of scarcity.

Acknowledgements

I would like to thank Dirk Bönker for his helpful comments and the Social Science Research Council's Berlin Program for Advanced German and European Studies at the Freie Universität in Berlin for a fellowship that supported research for this chapter.

Notes

1. Bundesarchiv-Filmarchiv (BA-FA), DEFA-Wochenschauen *Der Augenzeuge*, 19/56 [May 11, 1956].
2. BA-FA, DEFA-Wochenschauen *Der Augenzeuge*, B14/57 [March 19, 1957].

3. For recent discussions and critiques of the terms Americanization and Sovietization see Heide Fehrenbach and Uta G. Poiger, "Introduction: Americanization Reconsidered," in Heide Fehrenbach and Uta G. Poiger, eds., *Transactions, Transgressions, Transformations: American Culture in Western Europe and Japan* (New York/Oxford: Berghahn, 2000), pp. xiii–xl; Philipp Gassert, "Amerikanismus, Antiamerikanismus, Amerikanisierung: Neue Literatur zur Sozial-, Wirtschafts- und Kulturgeschichte des amerikanischen Einflusses in Deutschland und Europa," *Archiv für Sozialgeschichte,* 39, 1999, pp. 531–61; Konrad Jarausch and Hannes Siegrist, eds., *Amerikanisierung und Sowjetisierung in Deutschland 1945–1970* (Frankfurt a/M/New York: Campus, 1997); Michael Lemke, ed., *Sowjetisierung und Eigenständigkeit in der SBZ/DDR (1945–1953)* (Cologne/Weimar/Vienna: Böhlau, 1999).

4. Gertrud Berger, "Frau Mode – Entschleiert," *Frau von heute*, 1, February 1946, p. 23.

5. Elizabeth Heinemann, 'The Hour of the Woman: Memories of Germany's 'Crisis Years' and West German National Identity," *American Historical Review,* 101, 1996, pp. 354–95; Ina Merkel, . . . *und Du, Frau an der Werkbank: Die DDR in den 50er Jahren* (Berlin: Elefanten, 1990), 31–47.

6. The phrases in German are *Aus Alt mach neu* or *Neues aus Altem*. Gloria Sultano, *Wie geistiges Kokain . . .: Mode unterm Hakenkreuz* (Vienna: Verlag für Gesellschaftskritik, 1995), 653. The mottoes also were common in West German magazines until the mid-1950s. Ulla Grum, "'Sie leben froher – Sie leben besser mit Constanze': Eine Frauenzeitschrift im Wandel des Jahrzehnts," in Angela Delille and Andrea Grohn, eds., *Perlonzeit: Wie die Frauen ihr Wirtschaftswunder erlebten* (Berlin: Elefanten, 1985), p. 141.

7. For early fashion shows, see "Darauf haben wir gewartet. Das schönste, was es auf die Punktkarte gibt," *Frau von heute,* 4(4), 1949, pp. 24–5; E.T., "Frauen wählen ihre Mode selbst! Modellschau des Demokratischen Frauenbundes Berlin," *Frau von heute,* 4(15), 1949, p. 29; "Frauenwünsche die jetzt Erfüllung finden!" *Für Dich,* 4(1), p. 5; "Modenschau . . . Neue Wege unserer Werbung,' *Konsum-Verkaufsstelle* 2(2), 1950, p. 20. On women's practices of transforming everything from old clothes, rags, and tablecloths to parachutes, uniforms, and military bed sheets into "new" dresses, or shirts, see "Phönix" GmbH Chemnitz Berufliches Bildungs- und Förder Centrum, ed., *15 Milliarden Stunden im Jahr: Ein Blick auf Hausarbeit und Haushalttechnik in der DDR* (Chemnitz: PrintDesign 1997).

8. Drawings and photographs of women modeling paper pattern designs appeared in both general women's magazines such as *Frau von heute* or *Für Dich* and magazines devoted primarily to displaying paper pattern models, including *Praktische Mode* (later *PRAMO*), *flotte kleidung*, *Die neue Mode*, *Modische Modelle*, *Saison*, and *Modische Maschen*.

9. I am suggesting a more complicated narrative than most retrospective accounts which claim that extreme shortages reduced Germans' desires for clothes, food, or shelter to a bare minimum, devoid of all aesthetic considerations. For example, in a speech in 1960 Elli Schmidt claimed that "back then [during the Second World War and the immediate postwar period] our women did not ask how the clothing that they wore looked. We were all very happy if there was enough to wear, when we got shoes on our feet." Stiftung Stadtmuseum Berlin, Modeabteilung – Modearchiv (SSB-MA), Schriftensammlung (SM) 6–7, p. 2. See

also Rainer Gries, *Die Rationen Gesellschaft: Versorgungskampf und Vergleichsmentalität. Leipzig, München und Köln nach dem Kriege* (Münster: Westfälisches Dampfboot, 1991).

10. See, for instance, D. Meyer-Wolf, "Die Konfektion zeigt, was sie bereits leistet," *Der Handel* 1(1), 1951, p. 14; Walli Haupt, "Leistungsschauen – ein Wertmesser unserer Wirtschaft," *Konsum-Verkaufsstelle* 4(31), 1952. It is interesting to note that the term *Leistung* also figured prominently in National Socialist rhetoric.

11. Slogans such as "*wie wir heute arbeiten, so werden wir morgen leben*," "*erst besser arbeiten und dann besser leben*," and "*so wie wir arbeiten, so werden wir kaufen können*" peppered party propaganda until at least the late-1950s. See Stiftung Archiv der Parteien und Massenorganisationen der DDR im Bundesarchiv (SAPMO-BA), NY4215/63, Bl. 323; Bundesarchiv, Abteilungen Berlin, Berlin-Lichterfelde (BA-BL), DE1/25687, Berlin, May 5, 1958, pp. 10–11.

12. One example of an early unrealistic display of dress was the feature film *Modell Bianka*, released by the state-run film company DEFA in 1951, which climaxed in a fashion show of extravagant evening dresses at the Leipzig Trade Fair. BA-FA, *Modell Bianka*, dir. Richard Groschopp, sw. Erich Conradi, DEFA, 1951.

13. Compare Anna-Sabine Ernst, "Mode im Sozialismus: Zur Etablierung eines 'sozialistischen Stils' in der frühen DDR," in Krisztina Mänicke-Gyöngyösi and Ralf Rytlewski, eds., *Lebensstile und Kulturmuster in sozialistischen Gesellschaften*, (Cologne: Wissenschaft und Politik, 1990), p. 92.

14. Hellmut Schurig, *Die Entwicklung der Textilindustrie in Westdeutschland und in der Deutschen Demokratischen Republik* (Berlin: Die Wirtschaft, 1959), 64; SSB-MA, SM1–12, p. 4.

15. Erica Carter, *How German Is She? Postwar West German Reconstruction and the Consuming Woman* (Ann Arbor: University of Michigan Press, 1997), p. 16.

16. The personification of fashion as a woman is encouraged by the fact that the word itself, *die Mode*, is femininely gendered in the German language.

17. Elfriede Philipp, "Bekleidung – aber keine Kleider. Ein geheimnisvolles Gremium bestimmt, was die Berlinerin tragen soll," *Die Wirtschaft*, n.d. [1955/1956], unpag., found in Landesarchiv Berlin (LAB), C Rep. 106-01-01, Vorläufige Signatur Nr. T/176.

18. SSB-MA, SM3–15, p. 2.

19. SSB-MA, SM3–7, p. 14; Schurig, *Die Entwicklung der Textilindustrie*, p. 64.

20. See, for instance, BA-FA, DEFA-Wochenschauen *Der Augenzeuge*, 8/55 [February 25, 1955]; SSB-MA, Geschäftsbericht (G) 5, pp. 13–14. Anna-Sabine Ernst and Eric Weitz have outlined the uneasy coexistence of two broad "strands of nationalist claims" in the GDR, which can be categorized in simple terms as "proletarian" and "bourgeois." Anna-Sabine Ernst, "Vom 'Du' zum 'Sie.' Die Rezeption der bürgerlichen Anstandsregeln in der DDR der 1950er Jahre," *Mitteilungen aus der kulturwissenschaftlichen Forschung*, 33, 1993, pp. 190–209; Eric D. Weitz, *Creating German Communism: From Popular Protests to Socialist State, 1890–1990* (Princeton: Princeton University Press, 1997), 371–4.

21. SSB-MA, SM4–4, p. 3.

22. Gerda Buxbaum, "Asymmetrie symbolisiert einen kritischen Geist! – Zum Stellenwert von Mode, Uniform und Tracht im Nationalsozialismus," in Hochschule für angewandte Kunst in Wien, ed., *Zeitgeist wider den Zeitgeist: eine Sequenz aus Österreichs*

Verirrung, (Vienna: Hochschule . . . in Wien, 1987), pp. 181–8; Valerie Steele, *Paris Fashion: A Cultural History* (Oxford and New York: Berg, 1998), p. 266.

23. For example, R. Kn., "Anarchie im Reich der Mode," *Die Frau von heute*, 3, March 1946, p. 20.

24. SSB-MA, SM3–7, p. 19; Christoph Kleßmann, *Die doppelte Staatsgründung: Deutsche Geschichte 1945–1955* (Bonn: Vandenhoeck & Ruprecht, 1991), p. 333.

25. See, for instance, a film advertisement for clothing from "Konsum" cooperative stores in 1958 that begins with work clothes for workers on a collectivized farm and ends with a fashion show featuring extravagant evening dresses at the local "cultural house" (*Kulturhaus*). Holger Theuerkauf and Michael Reinicke, directors, *Flotter Osten*, Mit-Schnitt-Film, 1990.

26. See Ernst, "Vom 'Du' zum 'Sie'"; "Beiderseits der Elbe: Küß die Hand," *Die Zeit*, April 9, 1965, quoted in Christoph Kleßmann and Georg Wagner, eds., *Das gespaltene Land: Leben in Deutschland 1945–1990. Texte und Dokumente zur Sozialgeschichte* (Munich: C. H. Beck, 1993), pp. 37–9; and the numerous books on good manners (*Benimmbücher*), many of which went through several editions in the following decade, including Karl Smolka, *Gutes Benehmen von A bis Z* (Berlin: Neues Leben, 1957); Walter Karl Schweickert and Bert Hold, *Guten Tag Herr von Knigge: Ein heiteres Lesebuch für alle Jahrgänge über alles, was "anständig" ist* (Berlin: Henschelverlag, 1959); Gertrud Oheim, *Einmaleins des guten Tons* (Gütersloh: C. Bertelsmann, 1955).

27. LAB, C Rep. 106-01-01, Vorläufige Signatur Nr. T/176, Vorschlag für eine Veränderung der Arbeitsweise in der Berliner volkseigenen Bekleidungsindustrie, um eine bessere und modischere Bekleidung für unsere Bevölkerung zu gewährleisten, Willy Maaß, Modeatelier Berlin, Berlin, June 9, 1955.

28. E.T., "Frauen wählen ihre Mode selbst!," pp. 29.

29. "Such a fashion show often educates [*erzieht*] better than a whole lecture on taste," proclaimed an author in the central organ of the East German youth organization *Freie Deutsche Jugend*. Eva Grabe, "So oder so?" *Steckenpferd. Beilage der Jungen Welt*, 1./2.11.1958. On similarities between East and West German concerns about the degenerative impact of American cultural influences in Germany during the 1950s, see Uta Poiger, *Jazz, Rock, and Rebels: Cold War Politics and American Culture in a Divided Germany* (Berkeley/Los Angeles and London: University of California Press, 2000).

30. Grabe, "So oder so?," pp. 1.

31. SAPMO-BA, DY30/IV2/1/283, Bl. 11–12.

32. Archiv des Verbands der Konsumgenossenschaften, Nr. 504 Vorstandssitzungen, Beschlußvorlage Nr. 96/62, March 30, 1962, p. 2; Sächsisches Staatsarchiv Chemnitz (SäStAC), VVB Trikotagen und Strümpfe, Nr. 2190, Entwurf Aufgabenstellung der Fachkommission "Mode und Werbung" . . . beim DMI, Berlin, n.d. [March 19, 1960].

33. BA-BL, DE1/26233, Standardisierung, n.d. [1960], unpag.

34. For instance, a director of the state-owned television station seems to have picked out the designs to be featured in a broadcast of a "Grand Fashion Show" in 1956 without consulting central state industry officials. LAB, C Rep. 106-01-01, Vorläufige Signatur Nr. T/238.

35. Judd Stitziel, "Konsumpolitik zwischen 'Sortimentslücken' und 'Überplanbeständen' in der DDR der 1950er Jahre," in Dierk Hoffmann, Michael Schwartz, and Hermann

Wentker, eds., *Die DDR vor dem Mauerbau: Politik und Gesellschaft*, (Munich: Oldenbourg, forthcoming).

36. LAB, C Rep. 900, IV/4/06/297, Sekretariatsvorlage Betr.: Analyse über die durchgeführte Überprüfung der HO-Industriewaren, Prenzlauer Berg, Kreisleitung SED – Prenzl. Berg, Abt. Wirtschaft, Berlin, April 22, 1954, p. 8; "Im Kreuzfeuer der Blicke. Rostocker Kolleginnen im Konsum-Kaufhaus 'Format' und die Mode," *Konsum-Genossenschafter,* 13(44), 1961, p. 8.

37. Bundesarchiv, Abteilungen Berlin, Außenstelle Coswig/Anhalt (BA-CA), DL102/28, p. 243.

38. *Konsum-Genossenschafter,* 11(35), 1959, p. 2 and 12(27), p. 1.

39. See for instance LAB, C Rep. 900, IV/4/06/318, Bericht, Erna F., Berlin, 23.10.53.

40. The *Institut für Bekleidungskultur* became the *Deutsches Modeinstitut*. East German officials never mentioned that the latter had been the name of Germany's central fashion institute during the Third Reich. On the Third Reich's *Deutsches Modeinstitut*, see Kenneth D. McDonald, "Fascist Fashion: Dress, the State, and the Clothing Industry in the Third Reich," Ph.D. Dissertation, University of California, Riverside, 1998, pp. 112–21.

41. Explanations of fashion based on trickle-down models can be traced back to Thorstein Veblen's ideas about "conspicuous consumption" and Georg Simmel's socio-psychological explanation of fashion impulses. Thorstein Veblen, *The Theory of the Leisure Class* (New York: Macmillan, 1912 [orig. 1899]); Georg Simmel, "Fashion," *International Quarterly,* 10, 1904, pp. 130–55. For the popularity of trickle-down theories to explain the relationship between haute couture and mass-market fashion in the 1950s, see Angela Partington, "Popular Fashion and Working-Class Affluence," in Juliet Ash and Elizabeth Wilson, eds., *Chic Thrills: A Fashion Reader*, (Berkeley/Los Angeles: University of California Press, 1992), pp. 145–61.

42. SSB-MA, SM1–13, p. 3.

43. SSB-MA, SM3–7, p. 27 and SM4–2, p. 9.

44. Susannah Handley, *Nylon: The Story of a Fashion Revolution: A Celebration of Design from Art Silk to Nylon and Thinking Fibres* (Baltimore: Johns Hopkins University Press, 1999), pp. 77–115.

45. SSB-MA, ML 1958, Modelinie der Nachmittags-, Fest- und Abendkleider . . ., pp. 1, 3.

46. SAPMO-BA, DY30/IV2/17/62, Bl. 54–7. I am grateful to Timothy Dowling for bringing this file to my attention. For the Institute's response see "Frankfurter Frauenausschüsse im Deutschen Modeinstitut," *Sibylle,* 3, 1958, p. 77.

47. Inge Kertzscher, "Wir blättern in Modeheften," *Neues Deutschland*, 11.1.1958, Beilage.

48. "Das Modehaus ohne Kundschaft," *Neue Zeit,* 11.11.1956.

49. Inge Kertzscher, "Wir machen internationale Mode – für wen?" *Neues Deutschland*, 18.11.1956.

50. Inge Kertzscher, "Laufsteg-Mode oder schöne Kleider für alle?' *Neues Deutschland*, Beilage Kunst und Literatur, 7.4.1957.

51. Kuckuck's secretary explained to a friend on the phone that Kuckuck went to Paris to "get himself inspirations [*Anregungen*] . . . no, not what *you* think . . . only fashion." Jo

Schulz, *Messeschlager Gisela: Operette in einem Vorspiel und drei Akten (vier Bildern). Textbuch* (Berlin: VEB Lied der Zeit, Musikverlag, 1961), p. 15.

52. BA-BL, DE1/26292, "Die Bekleidung für junge stärkere Frau," Referat der DDR, XII. Modekongreß Berlin, p. 2; "Taille: 92 – Na und?" *Für Dich*, 35, 1963, pp. 43–7.

53. SSB-MA, SM3–7, p. 20.

54. "Wenn die Taille an Zentimetern zunimmt . . .," *Konsum-Genossenschafter*, 12(40), 1960, p. 8.

55. BA-BL, DE1/26292, "Die Bekleidung für junge stärkere Frau," p. 1.

56. SSB-MA, SM5–16, p. 5; BA-BL, DE1/26292, "Die Bekleidung für junge stärkere Frau," p. 2.

57. Regarding the first official "fashion line" in 1954 an Institute functionary wrote, "when designing apparel we want to assume the normal proportions of the body . . . The overall picture is a slender silhouette." SSB-MA, Modelinie 1954, Rundschreiben Nr. 1 . . ., p. 3.

58. See also SSB-MA, SM5–16, p. 3.

59. 'Taille: 92 – Na und?,' p. 43.

60. SSB-MA, SM5–16, p. 5.

61. Inge Kertzscher, "Konfektion mit neuen Maßen," *Neues Deutschland*, December 12, 1959; BA-BL, DE1/26292, "Die Bekleidung für junge stärkere Frau."

62. SäStAC, Zentrales Warenkontor Textil- und Kurzwaren (ZWK TuK), Nr. 157, Renate M. to Deutscher Fernsehfunk, *Prisma*, Anklam, August 16, 1968.

63. SSB-MA, SM5–16, p. 2; 'Taille: 92 – Na und?,' p. 43.

64. SSB-MA, SM5–16, p. 2.

65. [Mia Heim], "Modelinie berät Mollige," *Für Dich*, 50, 1969, p. 43; [Mia Heim], "Modelinie berät Sie. Rund um die Hüften," *Für Dich* 48, 1969, p. 44.

66. SSB-MA, SM5–16, p. 1.

67. *Eulenspiegel*, 9(21), 1962, p. 14.

68. Pál Pusztai, *Eulenspiegel*, 9(18), 1962, p. 5.

69. See Judd Stitziel, "Fashioning Socialism: Clothing, Politics, and Consumer Culture in East Germany, 1948–1971," Ph.D. Dissertation, Johns Hopkins University, 2001, pp. 219–20.

70. The paradoxical goal was to create "a peculiar fashion with international character." SSB-MA, 3–9, p. 4.

71. See for example the extensive collection of travel reports by officials of the GDR's central fashion institute in the Stiftung Stadtmuseum Berlin, Modeabteilung – Modearchiv.

72. This mission was expressed with phrases like "*Schritt halten*" and "*dem Rhythmus angleichen*." SSB-MA, SM1–13, p. 2 and SM4–14, p. 9.

73. See Ursula Paulini, "Hinken wir der Mode hinterher?" *Märkische Volksstimme*, 9.9.1956; BA-BL, DE1/5446, Bl. 6; SSB, SM3–9, p. 1.

74. Karl-Ernst Schubert and Georg Wittek, "Zur Aufgabenstellung des Modeschaffens in der Deutschen Demokratischen Republik," *Mitteilungen des Instituts für Bedarfsforschung*, 2(2), 1963, pp. 53–70, quote p. 55.

75. SAPMO-BA, DY30/IV2/6.09/75, Diskussionsbeitrag von Elli Schmidt, DMI, n.d. [January 1959]; SSB-MA, SM4–14, p. 8.

76. *Der Internationale Bekleidungswettbewerbe* was renamed *Der Internationale Modekongress* in 1957.

77. BA-BL, DE 1/26292, Kurzer Abriß der Geschichte der Internationalen Modekongresse und ihre Bedeutung, Arbeitsplan II 10./1960 – Modekongreß, 3.11.1960. The Institute for Clothing Culture was in fact the youngest such fashion institute among those in the socialist countries. The Union House in Moscow, the Clothing Institute in Budapest, and the House of Models in Sofia all were founded in 1948, while the Central Laboratory in Lodz was created in 1946, the Institut Textilni Tvorba in Prague in 1949, and the Design Center in Bucharest in 1951. "Sieben Länder – sieben Modeinstitute – ein Ziel," *Sibylle*, 3(3), 1958, pp. 4–5.

78. CMEA, or COMECON, was designed to facilitate trade and economic aid among its members, which included the Soviet Union, East Germany, Bulgaria, Czechoslovakia, Hungary, Poland, and Romania. The GDR's "Permanent Working Group for Questions of Clothing Culture" (*Ständige Arbeitsgruppe für Fragen der Bekleidungskultur*) under the Permanent Commission for Light Industry and Food Industry within CMEA helped to organize the Fashion Congresses. *25 Jahre Modeinstitut der DDR*, n.d., n.p., unpag. For the political importance of the Fashion Congresses see BA-BL, DE1/26292, Vorschlag über die Vorstellungen der DDR für die Arbeit der Ständigen Arbeitsgruppe für Fragen der Bekleidungskultur, from Elli Schmidt, DMI, to Nindl, Sekretär der DDR-Delegation der Ständigen Kommission für LLI, Berlin, January 3, 1961.

79. "Pariser Chic als Messegast," *Frau von heute*, 11(39), 1959, pp. 6–7.

80. SSB-MA, SM3–11, pp. 11–12.

81. SSB-MA, SM1–13, p. 3.

82. See, for instance, BA-FA, DEFA-Wochenschauen *Der Augenzeuge* 45/58 [June 3, 1958], 55/58 [July 8, 1958], 32/59 [April 17, 1959], 30/60 [1960], 46/60 [1960], and 9/62 [1962].

83. The state owned 69.2 percent of Bormann's firm. LAB, C Rep. 470-02, Nr. 36, Bl. 1.

84. BA-BL, DE1/24938, Thesen zur Parteileitungssitzung am 20. Februar 1959 über die Probleme der Planerfüllung 1958 und den Plananlauf 1959, p. 2.

85. SAPMO-BA, DY30/IVA2/6.09/112, Information über die Durchführung von Modell-Modenschauen durch das Modehaus Bormann, Magdeburg, Briksa, Abt. Leicht- und Lebensmittelindustrie, und Steidl, Abt. Gewerkschaften und Sozialpolitik, Berlin, 18.3.1963.

86. Fritz Jahn, 'Männer mit Millionen,' *Freie Welt* 22/1967: 10–15; SAPMO-BA, DY30/IVA2/2.021/706, Bl. 11–12.

87. SSB-MA, ML 1958, Protokoll über die Absprache der Modelinie Frühjahr/Sommer 1958 mit den Fachabteilungen, Abt. Modellentwurf, Berlin, 26.11.1957, p. 3.

88. See SSB-MA, SM5–19, p. 6.

89. Walter Ulbricht, "Über Standardisierung und Mode,' *Neues Deutschland*, August 13, 1959, p. 4.

90. SAPMO-BA, DY30/IV2/6.09/72, Entwurf: Konzeption. Aufgabenstellung für die Tätigkeit der Arbeitskreise zur Vorbereitung der Textil-Konferenz 1960, Abt. Leichtindustrie, Sekt. Textil-Bekleidung-Leder, Berlin, 10.11.1959, unpag.

91. A small number of officials had long advocated this approach in vain. For instance, an official at the Ministry for Trade and Provisioning insisted in 1950 that state trade officials should not wait to see "which newest fashion cry comes from Paris or London, but rather we should get to the point of determining and influencing fashion ourselves." SAPMO-BA, DY30/IV2/1.01/133, Bl. 79.

92. SSB-MA, SM7-25, p. 6.

93. SAPMO-BA, DY30/IV2/1/255, Bl. 161–2. See also SAPMO-BA, DY30/J IV2/2/753, Bl. 72–4. For the reaction in the German Fashion Institute to Ulbricht's remarks, see SSB-MA, SM7–17, pp. 1–2.

94. These initiatives form numerous interesting parallels with efforts to create a "German fashion" during the Third Reich. See McDonald, "Fascist Fashion," pp. 93–112; Irene V. Guenther, "Nazi 'Chic'? German Politics and Women's Fashions, 1915–1945," *Fashion Theory*, 1 (1997), pp. 29–58; Sultano, *Wie geistiges Kokain . . .*

95. SSB-MA, SM7-17, pp. 13–14.

96. Schubert and Wittek, 'Zur Aufgabenstellung des Modeschaffens', p. 55; BA-CA, DE4/19893, Die Konzeption für das Modeschaffen im Industriezweig Bekleidung in Auswertung des VI. Parteitages, VVB Konfektion, Berlin, 4.4.19[63], p. 2 of second section.

97. See for example BA-CA, DE4/19893, Jahresarbeitsbericht 1962 des DMI . . ., p. 2; SSB-MA, G14, p. 8 and SM18–8, Band 6, pp. 1–2. On the term *Parteilichkeit*, see Alan L. Nothnagle, *Building the East German Myth: Historical Mythology and Youth Propaganda in the German Democratic Republic, 1945–1989* (Ann Arbor: University of Michigan Press, 1999), p. 17ff.

98. See, for example, SSB-MA, SM12–26, p. 1.

99. SAPMO-BA, DY30/IV2/6.09/70, Zu Fragen Sortiment – Qualität – Mode, 10.4.1959, p. 4.

100. For examples of the term "ideological ambiguities" (*ideologische Unklarheiten*), see SSB-MA, SM7-25, p. 6 and SM9–6, p. 4; Schubert and Wittek, "Zur Aufgabenstellung des Modeschaffens," p. 54.

101. SAPMO-BA, DY30/IV2/1.01/245, Bl. 92–3.

102. The goal of turning East Berlin into a "fashion center" was declared in 1953 as part of the regime's "New Course." LAB, C Rep. 900, IV/7/128–8, "Diskussionsbeitrag zur Kreisparteiaktivtagung am 18.11.1953," 18.11.1953, p. 1; LAB, C Rep. 625, Nr. 113, Maßnahmen zur Realisierung des Beschlusses der Bezirksleitung der SED von Groß-Berlin "Berlin zum Modezentrum zu gestalten," VVB Konfektion, Berlin, 30.5.1958; BA-BL, DE1/25687, Letter from berliner modewoche [*sic*], Organisationsbüro to Güntzel, Plankommission, Berlin, 21.8.1958.

103. Inge Kertzscher, "Eine Schule des guten Geschmacks: Zur 2. Berliner Modewoche," *Neues Deutschland*, 14.2.1959, Beilage; "Berliner Chic Begriff geworden"; LAB, C Rep. 113, Nr. 412, Entwurf der 4. Konzeption für die Berliner Modewoche September 1959, Berlin-Werbung Berolina, Berlin, 5.8.1959, p. 6.

104. LAB, C Rep. 113, Nr. 412, Entwurf der 4. Konzeption . . ., p. 6; LAB, C Rep. 625, Nr. 2 (BEHALA), Vorlage für die "Berliner Modewoche" 1959, VVB Konfektion, Abt. Ökonomie, Henkel, Abteilungsleiter, Berlin, 27.7.1959, p. 1.

105. BA-BL, DE1/25687, Nähere Programmerläuterung, n.d. [1958], p. 1.

106. LAB, C Rep. 113, Nr. 412, Entwurf der 4. Konzeption . . ., pp. 8–10.

107. Ibid., pp. 14–15.

108. BA-BL, DE1/25687, Nähere Programmerläuterung . . ., p. 2.

109. LAB, C Rep. 625, Nr. 2 (BEHALA), Vorlage für die "Berliner Modewoche" 1959 . . ., p. 3.

110. LAB, C Rep. 113, Nr. 412, Protokoll über die Beiratssitzung "Berliner Modewoche" am 12.8.1959, VVB Konfektion, Berlin, 13.8.1959, p. 2.

111. The following quotes are taken from LAB, C Rep. 625, Nr. 110, ausstellung der 2. berliner mode-woche 18.–25.2.1959, unpag.

112. Several *Augenzeuge* reports on fashion shows expressed similar sentiments such as "[It] remains to wish that these simultaneously demanding [*anspruchsvoll*] and practical models are also to be seen and to be bought in the stores" or "Let's hope that the people's owned industry brings these models quickly and inexpensively into trade." BA-FA, DEFA-Wochenschauen *Augenzeuge* 45/58 [June 3, 1958], 52/58 [June 27, 1958], and 55/58 [July 8, 1958].

113. LAB, C Rep. 625, Nr. 2 (BEHALA), Vorlage für die "Berliner Modewoche" 1959 . . ., p. 1.

114. LAB, C Rep. 113, Nr. 412, Protokoll der 1. Beiratssitzung zur 3. Berliner Modewoche, VVB Konfektion, Zahl, Hauptdirektor, Berlin, 28.7.1959, p. 2 and Protokoll über die Beiratssitzung . . ., p. 4; BA-CA, DE4/679, Bl. 91, 94.

115. BA-CA, DE4/679, Bl. 93.

116. SAPMO-BA, DY30/IV2/6.10/72, Bl. 76–7.

117. BA-CA, DE4/679, Bl. 91–2.

118. Ibid., Bl. 95.

119. LAB, C Rep. 900, IV-2/6/861, Wie hat sich die Einrichtung von Exquisitläden für den Verkauf hochwertiger Industriewaren schon bewährt?, pp. 2–3, 7.

120. SäStAC, ZWK TuK, Nr. 156, Gertraude L., Karl-Marx-Stadt, to Ministerium für Handel und Versorgung, Karl-Marx-Stadt, 25.4.68.

121. SäStAC, ZWK TuK, Nr. 32, Ilse G. to Deutscher Fernsehfunk Berlin, Prisma, Berlin-Adlershof, Brandis, 11.6.1965.

122. Katherina Schulze, "Ich kann mir nicht helfen," *Eulenspiegel*, 14(38), 1967, p. 1.

123. SäStAC, ZWK TuK, Nr. 292, Heinz M., Wilthen, to Dr. Karl-Heinz Gerstner, Deutscher Fernsehfunk, Wilthen, 30.7.71.

124. "Sie näht am liebsten alles selbst," *Frau von heute,* 12(5), 1957, pp. 5–6; *Modische Modelle: Hand und mit Apparat gestrickt*, n.p., n.d. [1960], p. 2; BA-CA, DL102/193, p. 9; Ruth Weichsel, "Zur Ausstattung mit Kinderoberbekleidung," 5 *Mitteilungen des Instituts für Marktforschung,* 1, 1966, p. 31; Jörg Börjesson and Hans-Peter Seliger, "Zur Einzelfertigung von Oberbekleidung," *Mitteilungen des Instituts für Marktforschung,* 10(4), 1971, p. 25.

125. "Wir schneidern selbst," *Frau von heute* 11(20), 1956, p. 17; "Selbst Geschneidert Selbst Vorgeführt," *Frau von heute,* 12(48), 1957, pp. 16–17.

126. BA-CA, DL102/294, p. 46.

127. Susanne Kluge, "Wie modern muss die Mode sein?" *Für Dich,* 23(29), 1968, p. 13.

128. One-third of "very strong women" had all of their apparel professionally tailored. BA-CA, DL102/471, pp. 24–9.

129. LAB, C Rep. 900, IV/4/06/297, Referat. Der Kampf zur Verwirklichung der Forderung des IV. Parteitages der SED, auf neue Art Handel zu lernen, Abtl. Wirtschaft; BA-CA, DL102/28, p. 250.

130. BA-CA, DL102/973, p. 17.

131. LAB, C Rep. 470-02, Nr. 36, Bl. 44, 47.

4

The Order of Substitutes: Plastic Consumer Goods in the *Volkswirtschaft* and Everyday Domestic Life in the GDR

Eli Rubin

> "Now look at this trash – always aggravation with plastics!" Incensed, mother Gestrig showed the object to her surprised family. What was originally a neat, lemon yellow polyethylene bucket, had turned into an ugly, deformed image. Now it looked like a cylindrical hat. She had of course just put it on the stovetop, but the stovetop was still warm, causing it to shrivel and melt.
>
> "In the past such things wouldn't have happened" chimed father Gestrig. "there weren't all these *ersatz* things yet. The newspapers can write all they want about the advantages of turning to plastics and their legendary properties. All humbug! People just can't satisfy themselves with the good old, solid materials. Chemistry and every other possible industry are tripping over each other to introduce this magical stuff everywhere . . . and what do you get out of it? Mother's bucket is a wreck, because it couldn't take the slightest amount of heat . . . And in general! Doesn't our Käthe always curse her dederon[1] stockings, and on top of that, doesn't she need a new raincoat because last winter her old one, of plastic of course, ripped at the seams and is broken now?
>
> . . . But in the end plastics are always supposed to have this great special worth. But no one can convince me, Otto Gestrig, of that. I stick by my opinion: plastics are suitable for nothing and only bring aggravation!"[2]

The fictional family Gestrig, appearing in Günther Just's 1962 *Es Geht Nicht Ohne Plaste*[3] ("It Doesn't Work Without Plastics"), presented a comic caricature of a family resistant to the increasing use of plastics in the production of consumer goods. The Gestrigs here are mockingly overdrawn as a foil against which the author proceeds to argue for the superiority of plastics in the household vis-à-vis older materials: plastics were lighter, cheaper, more durable, longer-lasting, and looked better.

The book was not only making a pragmatic argument, however. Also implicit in the clownish portrayal of the Gestrigs' rejection of plastic consumer goods was a political and cultural argument about the role of the home and its consumer goods within a modern socialist planned economy. The socialist planned economy of the GDR had just embarked on a sweeping "Chemistry Program" (*Chemieprogramm*) which promised to bring "bread, affluence (*Wohlstand*) and beauty" to its people. The mass-production of modern apartments, to be equipped with mass-produced modern furniture and technical home appliances, had just been launched. The declared goal of overtaking West Germany in consumer goods per capita had rocketed consumption to center stage in the SED's seven-year plan. The Party propagated programs such as the "Plan of New Technology," the "Scientific-Technological Revolution," and the New Economic System, and ideas like "cybernetics" dominated the discourse of Party leaders and economic planners. In such an atmosphere, to be against the turn toward plastic consumer goods in the home was to be old-fashioned, technologically unsophisticated, and to cling to the misunderstandings about the new modern society that was being built in the GDR. To be against plastics was to be against the project of building a modern, scientifically planned socialist utopia.

Similar tracts proclaiming the superiority of plastics can be found in western capitalist societies during the 1940s, 1950s and 1960s, although the two contexts were quite different.[4] Many of the pronouncements of plastic's superiority in the United States stemmed from industrial and business associations' attempts to boost sales and was driven by the rise of a broad postwar middle class that created a market for quickly and cheaply produced imitation goods. How then do we explain the similar phenomenon in a non-market society? If decisions about what to produce were made at the top, independently of market considerations, what was the need to convince the population of plastic's qualities? If the consumer had no choice between a plastic and an aluminum bucket, why write a book ridiculing those who missed their aluminum buckets and expounding on the virtues of polyethylene, polyamide, polyester, and so on? What might at first glance appear to be a banality, plastics, as a material and consumer good, stood at the intersection of industry, consumption, and political and cultural legitimacy for socialism in the GDR, and was thus a charged indicator or marker, a jumping-off point for a historian's larger questions.

Among the larger questions that inform this chapter are: what is the connection between planned industry and everyday life? How did the aesthetic surroundings of everyday life, especially in the home, change? Who or what was behind the change? What was the effect of this change, in terms of people's support for the government and in the transformation of social and cultural values and norms? Can objects, especially consumer goods, be "imprinted" with meaning? If so, how does the "imprinting" process take place, and how do we "read" objects as historians? To what extent can we take one consumer good, or group of goods, and use it/them to open up larger questions of the history of East Germany?

Plastics provide an interesting material to explore these questions in East German history.[5] The very *raison d'être* of polymers, their malleability and inexpensiveness, enables them to be used for a wide range of industries, goods, and cultural uses, in endless iteration. Their variability and omnipresence make them a natural touchstone for the production of cultural meaning, especially within a socio-economic framework. This chapter tries to use their production, design, projection, and consumption to tug at the complicated knot that bound government, party, economy, and consumers in the GDR. Specifically, did the production of plastic consumer products help to boost support for the SED and its "Chemistry Program"? To what extent were consumer objects in domestic everyday life made from natural materials such as wood, metal, or cloth replaced through plastics in the GDR? Can we talk about a "modernization" of the home through plastics, and did this "modernization" contribute to the relative stability of GDR society in the 1960s and 1970s?

The answers to these questions are complex. This chapter argues that the use of plastics in the GDR changed the look of everyday domestic life, and that the changes took place as part of a broader transformation of values toward the goals of living in a socialist, as opposed to a capitalist, culture and society. The changes were not, however, the result of exclusively top-down planning, but were rather the result of the "Brownian motion" of numerous institutions, traditions, communities, and economic factors both inside *and* outside of the GDR, from industrial designers to architects to bureaucrats. As will be discussed here, if plastics in the GDR never gained the perception of "cheapness" or became a synecdoche for the "throw-away" society of the West, they also did not convince East Germans of the scientific and technological superiority or validity of the promised socialist utopia.

The plastics and chemical industry, the industrial design community, and those responsible for providing consumer goods coexisted uneasily, and where their interests dovetailed, and then intersected with attitudes toward quality, consumption and domestic aesthetics, a constellation of values developed. This constellation worked through and bound together the realities of the planned economy, the vision of socialist consumption, and everyday life, and for a time at least represented the formation of a mainstream socialist *Wohnkultur* (domestic or home living culture) that contributed to the stability of the GDR's society-state relationship in the 1960s and 1970s.

Eli Rubin

The Power to Synthesize: Struggling to Produce Plastics in East Germany

The chemical industry historically played a crucial role in the rise of German power, not in the least because the chemical industry did not require a great deal of natural resources. Through a mix of some basic elements, such as sodium, calcium, sulfur, water, and coal, all of which were easily available within Germany, and scientific and technical ingenuity, also a traditional German strength, chemical concerns such as I.G. Farben, Hoechst, and BASF were able not only to make Germany a leading industrial world power, but to make German industry relatively independent of the need for natural resources that were available to colonial powers. The ability to synthetically produce otherwise natural materials played a crucial role in Hitler's ability to rearm within an autarkic economic system. For example, the I.G. Farben's Buna plant in Schkopau was the first in the world to produce synthetic rubber, without which Hitler, who had little access to rubber-producing tropical regions, could not have successfully launched his heavily vehicle-based *Blitzkrieg*.[6]

East Germany's new rulers resumed this same tradition of synthesizing at home those materials which could not, for political reasons, be found or acquired abroad. Between the embargo placed on the Soviet Union and its satellites by the United States and its allies, the extensive dismantling of the GDR's industrial infrastructure at the hands of its Soviet occupiers, and the use of a currency that carried little value in West Germany and as good as none in non-Soviet markets, it was crucial for the survival of the GDR and for the Soviet system in general to be able to synthetically manufacture scarce goods such as cotton, wood and aluminum rather than having to pay for them on the open market. In addition, having had other traditional industries relocated to various COMECON countries, the chemical industry was, along with automobiles and coal, one of the few that remained as a strength of the GDR, which gave the GDR a critical position within the entire COMECON system.[7]

Not only could the chemical industry churn out *Ersatz* goods, chemical products – especially synthetics – could help enhance almost every other area of industry. The SED leadership hoped that chemical products from insulation in electronics to cheap construction material and from synthetic clothing fibers to chemical fertilizer would catalyze a chain reaction of efficiency and growth that would make the GDR a modern, cutting-edge industrial state. Beginning in November 1958, these hopes were invested in the Chemistry Program, a comprehensive attempt by the Party and economic planners to shift investments to the chemical industry and to build up a major bureaucratic structure around the industry to direct the fruits of chemical production to boost several other economic branches.

The Chemistry Program, from the beginning, not only was intended to enhance production, but also had political significance for a relatively new regime still vying for the support of its own population. One aspect of its political significance lay in the fact that it was the first major program by the SED that was not a response to a crisis of one sort or another. Its unveiling, during the grandiose "Chemistry Conference" (*Chemiekonferenz*) held at the Leunawerke chemical factory, framed the GDR in a proactive light, comprehensively planning for the future rather than stumbling from one ad hoc policy to the next in a never-ending struggle to resolve shortages. Slogans such as "Chemistry gives beauty, affluence and bread" adorned the podium of the workers' House of Culture at Leuna as every major political leader in the GDR, representatives from every branch of the state, and several important personages from other COMECON countries listened to Walter Ulbricht deliver the keynote address. It was clear what was happening: the GDR's leadership was staking the success of German state socialism on the traditional strengths and future promises of the chemical industry. The naming of the land's largest chemical factories after the most powerful leaders in East Germany, such as the Leunawerke (renamed the VEB Leunawerke "Walter Ulbricht"[8]) or the VEB Petrolchemisches Kombinat "Wilhelm Pieck" in Schwedt, was only one example of the importance, or self-importance, the SED's leadership attached to its Chemistry Program. Nor was the importance of the chemical industry of the GDR only a matter of traditional German pride. The Chemistry Conference in 1958 was followed in 1959 by the announcement of a similar Chemistry Program in the Soviet Union and soon other COMECON states such as Romania, Poland, and Czechoslovakia followed.

The timing of the Chemistry Program and the Chemistry Conference in November 1958 was not entirely coincidental, because it followed on the heels of the landmark 5th Party Conference in July 1958 at which Walter Ulbricht pronounced that the GDR would overtake West Germany in per capita consumer-goods production in three years. Of major concern to not only the GDR but the Soviet Union as well was the role that the West German chemical and plastics industry was playing in fuelling the blossoming consumer society of the "economic miracle." Although the Chemistry Program was not conceived primarily as an engine to produce consumer goods, it nonetheless was key to setting up a modern industrial framework capable of convincing the population that the socialist system could outperform the West not only in terms of heavy industry but also in terms of creating a modern, consumer-oriented society. Chemicals and synthetics would be crucial to this daunting task: almost every consumer-oriented sector needed synthetics to be able to match the efficiency and production of the Federal Republic.[9] And yet, if Ulbricht's stated goal of overtaking the Federal Republic's per capita consumption levels was hopelessly unfeasible, so were many of the aims of the Chemistry Program, which were marked by the same unreal expectations as the 5th Party platform, thus compounding the problems of the consumer-goods production that was going to rely so heavily on the future successes of the chemical and plastics industry.

Despite the building of the so-called "friendship pipeline" and the subsequent petroleum refining plant in Schwedt, the GDR was never able to acquire enough oil from the Soviet Union to support the mass-production of new-generation thermoplastics.[10] The East German planners had counted on eventually getting over 40 million tons of oil a year from the USSR, but they were never able to get more than 19 million, whereas West Germany was already importing more than 74 million tons a year by 1965, a time when East Germany was still getting only about 8 tons a year.[11] The fact was, without similar amounts of oil, the GDR would never realize its goal of raising per capita plastics production from 7 kilograms in 1960 to 16 kilograms in 1965.

This put plastics immediately at the crossroads of tensions between the GDR's economic and international realities and its hopes and promises for a technologically advanced, world-class consumer society. Despite the promise of being able to manufacture materials out of thin air, thus freeing themselves of dependence on the West, in order to produce enough plastics to realize the consumption goals of both the Chemistry Program and the 5th Party Congress, the GDR had to import both oil and the technology to process it. Both eventually required hard currency. Without Western currency the GDR was unable to get oil from Arab states, despite repeated negotiations, especially with the Iraqis. In order to build a modern refining plant in Schwedt and in Leuna, the GDR had to import most of the machinery wholesale from Imperial Chemicals International in the UK, at an enormous cost.[12] At the same time as plastics were becoming an emblem for cheapness in the West, they were becoming a highly precious substance in the GDR, not only because of their scarcity or because of the propaganda invested in them through the Chemistry Program, but because they represented huge outflows of precious hard currency. The amount of plastics being produced in the GDR simply was not growing enough, and in some years, such as 1962, the production numbers actually regressed, while growth in the West continued almost exponentially. Many plastics products still had to be imported to cover the plan shortfalls, which then cost even more hard currency, in the case of imports from the West, or exchanges of other goods in the case of imports from COMECON countries.[13]

Numerous other problems combined to bring down the Chemistry Program, not least of which was its own euphoric promise. The GDR wasted enormous sums of money on ill-advised projects involving the precious amounts of petroleum it had, such as drilling for oil within the GDR based on shoddy geological data or attempting to use diesel fuel as a basis for growing animal feed, another wasteful project based on faulty scientific advice.[14] Another problem that the GDR's economic planners such as the State Planning Commission faced was that although the central chemical producers were concentrated in three or four huge factory complexes, called *Kombinaten*, as of the mid-1960s there were over 150 plastics-processing plants, where consumer goods and technical parts were actually molded, pressed, and extruded and a total of 450 factories that engaged in some form of processing of plastics.[15] Most of these were small, and many were private or "half-state" factories, making it much harder for the government to coordinate which factory was supposed to produce what and where the precious plastics feedstocks would go. As a result, there was a great deal of overlap, as the government saw it, between various plastics factories making different models of the same good, for example plastic eating utensils, while other goods were not produced.

To fix the problem of lacking coordination, a problem that also plagued other industry sectors, the government sought to extend its control to all the remaining private and half-state factories through the VVB Plastics Processing[16], put into effect in 1963. As part of the NES reforms,[17] the VVBs in general were to take responsibility for coordination among their component factories and force through certain features of the economic reforms, including quality control and streamlining of products. Instead of having 16 different small and medium factories producing combs of various plastic materials and designs, now there would be only one, the VEB Glasbijouterie Zittau, and only a few basic types of combs would be made, thus saving plastics for other uses.[18] "Standardization," "typification," and "rationalization" were among the most important watchwords of the NES reforms and, as will be discussed below, were ideas whose impacts stretched beyond the economic-planning directives and the factory floors and into the very living spaces for where these products were destined.[19] "*Sortimentsbereinigung*" (simplification of selection) enabled, theoretically, the VVB to control exactly how much raw plastics was going to exactly how many goods, but it also meant that almost all polyethylene bowls were the same, for example. It also meant that polyethylene and polystyrol would only be used for those goods where it was deemed that replacement with plastics was absolutely necessary.[20] This had a direct impact on the cultural life of consumption in the GDR. Rather than certain plastic items replacing older materials in some stores geared toward certain customers but not in others, as in capitalist market societies, plastic substitution tended to have the appearance of an all-or-none phenomenon: if plastic was better than aluminum in terms of its functional qualities and its cost-effectiveness for a certain good, say children's training potties, then there was no reason to continue producing the aluminum potties, and within a few years only plastic potties were to be found. If a selected good, or "position" as it was referred to by economic planners, was not better-off made of plastic, then it would conversely become very difficult to find in plastic.[21]

One major problem of the economic reforms, then, was that devolving power over planning to the individual factories and VVB contrasted with other aims of the reforms such as rationalization and *Sortimentsbereinigung*. Without resorting to a full market mechanism, plants themselves had little incentive to pay attention to quality or to agree among themselves on who should get what quantity of a given plastic. Planners and party officials, such as the Minister of the Chemical Industry Günter Wyschofsky began talking about the "most purposeful use" of plastics (*Zweckmäßigste Plasteinsatz*),[22] revealing a turn from the unrealistic belief that plastics could solve just about any material shortage and solve just about any economic problem. The Plastics Steering Office was created by the Council of Ministers and placed within the Ministry for Material Economy in March 1967.[23] It was the goal of the Plastics Steering Office to enforce the dissemination of plastics throughout the economy, according to a much more clearly framed set of priorities. Basically, other industries, such as construction, maritime and fishing, electronics, and machine building got first priority, plastic products for export, especially to the West but also to the Soviet Union got second, and whatever was left over went to consumers. Slowly, the use of plastics in the *Volkswirtschaft* was becoming ordered, more purposefully directed, and was moving away from fantasy and utopianism. Plastics were becoming a crucial element, a means to an end, in a larger social project of rationalization.

So for example the production of resins such as phenol or fiberglass-reinforced polyester, which was a relatively easy process for the outdated plastics-processing plants, figured heavily in the consumer world of plastics as it shaped up in the 1960s. With trade names such as Sprelacart, Sprelafaser, Dekafol, or Dehafol, these resins came to almost completely dominate the production of tables, kitchen cabinets and surfaces, and the one-piece shelf-chest constructions called *Schrankwände* which came to be ubiquitous in apartments throughout the socialist bloc. Because one of the few thermoplastic feedstocks that Buna could manufacture with efficiency, caprolactam, was the basic element of polyamide, the plastic used to make synthetic fibers, and because wool and cotton were so scarce in the GDR, the Plastics Steering Office ensured that plastics would dominate in the textile sector as well. From fashion shows to clothing racks in stores and closets everywhere, synthetic fibers such as Dederon and Malimo also almost completely replaced natural fibers, especially for women's clothing. Polyvinyl chloride, also a plastic that for the GDR was relatively unsophisticated to produce, was used widely in rain coats, shower curtains, and upholstery for Trabants and streetcars. Consumer goods that were relatively uncomplicated to injection-mold or to press from polyethylene, such as buckets, plates, toilet seats, casings for appliances, cake covers, medicine cabinets, cutting boards, and others were produced in high quantities. But other plastics that were already being mass-produced in the West for consumer goods were simply too precious to mass-produce for consumers in East Germany. Polyacrylate (Plexiglas, known as Piacryl in the GDR) did not replace glass except in technical or military functions, because in the end glass was cheaper to mass-produce. At a time when polyurethane was becoming the standard for everything from furniture stuffing to skateboard wheels in the West, it was used almost

Figure 4.1 An advertisement for the synthetic fiber "Wolpryla." "The promises of living culture have risen." From Kultur im Heim, *(4/1969).*

exclusively for insulation in construction in the GDR, and while polypropylene, because of its extreme lightness, was becoming commonplace in children's toys in the West, it was used mostly for electronics components and machines in the GDR.

In the wake of the failure of the first Chemistry Program, a second Chemistry Program was launched in 1966, one that included the plans to build a major low-density polyethylene plant in the new Leuna II factory, the completion of the oil refinery on the Polish border in Schwedt, and eventually, beginning in the early 1970s, the ability in Leuna and Buna to begin producing the GDR's own polyurethane and polypropylene.[24] Eventually, it became clear to even the SED leadership that many of the predictions of plastics and other chemical products radically transforming the industry and everyday life of the East German society were far too optimistic, because they were predicated on getting petroleum that would never be forthcoming from the Soviet Union. By 1980, the GDR had almost entirely resorted back to a brown-coal-based plastics industry. Slowly, the situation improved in terms of total plastics produced as well as for plastics consumer goods, although there never seemed to be enough to go around, especially for consumers.

Polymer Propaganda: Designing, Selling, Displaying Plastics in the GDR

In October 1959, in celebration of the GDR's tenth year in existence, the *HO* (*Handelsorganisation* or "trade organization") opened the store *Chemie im Heim* (chemistry in the home) on the Stalinallee in East Berlin. *Chemie im Heim* was a showpiece for the regime, intended as a jewel in the crown of the *Chemieprogramm*, then only one year in existence. It was instantly one of the GDR's largest stores, and its import was underscored by its location on the Stalinallee, which had been recently completed as the showpiece of the bombastic new socialist architecture and which housed other showpiece stores. Its opening was announced in full-page ads in the nation's largest circulating newspapers, such as *Neues Deutschland* and *Die Berliner Zeitung*, as being opened for the public in honor of the 10th-year anniversary.[25] Every conceivable plastic product for the home filled its shelves; polyethylene buckets, bowls, baby bathtubs, plates, eating utensils, cutting boards, shower handles, medicine cabinets, laundry and diaper baskets, egg cups, cookware, cake bells, lamp stands, sandals, foils, children's cups, and Tupperware-like containers, as well as other cosmetic, cleaning supplies and wash detergents. The store was not only a showcase for the new bounty of the plastics and chemical industry, it was a model of the modern *HO* and *Konsum* stores which were to become the key juncture in realizing the 5th Party Congress's push for a modern consumer society. It was a "self-service" store, meaning customers could actually touch and select their own goods, rather than waiting in line to be handed whatever was available in a back room, and it was staffed with "salespeople" who functioned more as product consultants, explaining the wonders of modern plastics and how to use them correctly (for example not putting thermoplastics on hot stovetops). By 1964, *Neue Berliner Illustrierte* described *Chemie im Heim* as "beloved" and gave it among the highest marks in a survey of the nation's best stores.[26] The *Chemie im Heim* model was copied elsewhere, such as in the Rosinenhof HO in Karl-Marx-Stadt.[27]

Despite the problems that plagued the plastics industry behind the scenes, plastic consumer goods were presented to the population as proof of the socialist economy's ability to provide the basis of a modern consumer society. In shops, advertisements, popular-science books and magazines, home, women's and design journals, exhibitions and fairs, and on television, plastics appeared as the vanguard of the changes that were being wrought in everyday life. Rationalizing and streamlining housework for women to increase their amount of free time, mass-producing apartments and their furnishings according to only one or two models, educating citizens on the actual science and technology involved in polymers, introducing modern design concepts into people's lives, and instructing citizens how to become conscientious rather than conspicuous consumers were all initiatives of various state organizations that formed the context surrounding the "plastics propaganda"

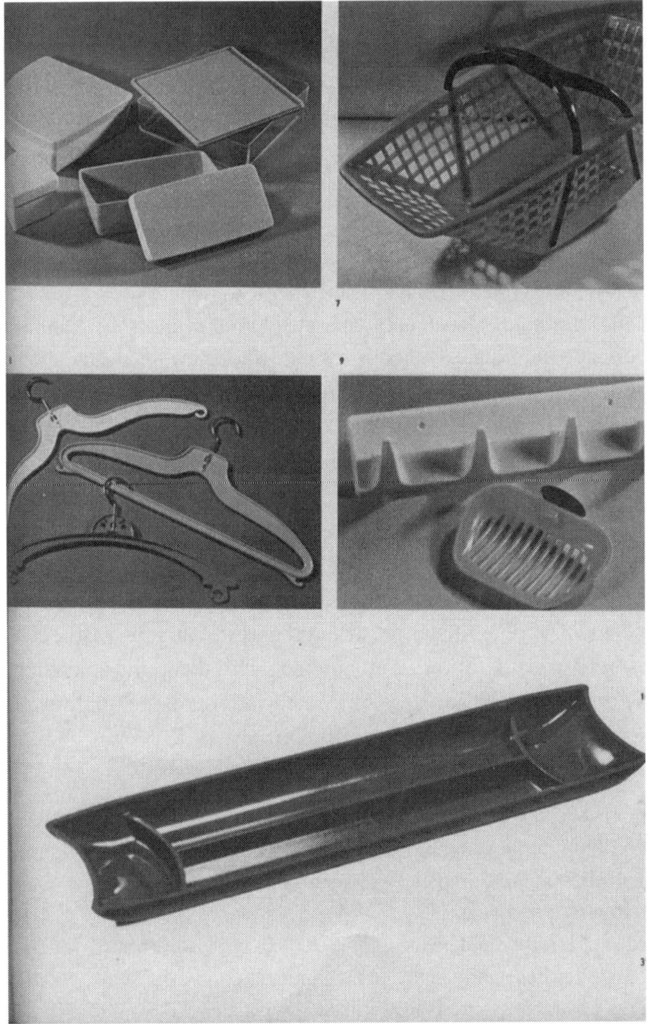

Figure 4.2 "Beautiful in form, purposeful, joyfully colored." The new range of polyethylene household products for the modern socialist household. From Kultur im Heim *(3/1966).*

inundating East Germans by the beginning of the 1960s. Through the image of plastics was formed a connection between socialism, modernity, technology, and functionality that would come to define the "mainstream" culture of consumption and the image of consumption of plastics in the GDR.

Numerous publications sought to educate consumers about how to correctly use and understand plastics. Paramount to many of these efforts was to convince the public that plastics were not substitutes of lesser value, *Ersatzstoffe*, but rather a new material in their own right. As such they could and should not be used to replace everything, but rather should be understood as something with a specific use and value. As the *Kleine Enzyklopädie die Frau* (Little Encyclopedia The Woman) expressed it in 1971:

> With modern technology, which is finding its way in increasing measure into the home, new materials are becoming widely known. They are labeled synthetics – or better, plastics – and are, in multiple ways, made to ease household work . . .
>
> Synthetics are not replacement materials (*Ersatzstoffe*). That cannot be stressed enough, because unfortunately there are many, who know this material only from afar, who are of the opinion that the prefix "*Kunst*" is a judgment of worth, meaning that the stuff is not an actual stuff. This is why "Synthetics" (*Kunststoff*) should be replaced with the term "Plastic" (*Plaste*) . . .
>
> A material always has "worth" if it has the right properties for the purposes toward which it is meant to be used.[28]

Kultur im Heim, a woman's and home-decorating magazine, pointed to the continual replacement of older materials through plastics, and the aesthetic desirability, but lest aesthetic consideration cloud anyone's judgment, the magazine also urged restraint by urging that, despite the new material's amazing qualities, it should be viewed functionally, as suited for specific purposes:

> If you think for a few minutes about how many things of today's daily use are out of plastic, you'll notice how comprehensively plastics have taken hold of our life. How can it be explained, that this completely new stuff has been introduced for so many different purposes in only a few years?
>
> The reason for this would be the multiple colors of plastic articles, which continuously please the eye . . . Especially in the kitchen more and more consumer goods (*Gebrauchsgegenstände*) from metal are being replaced by plastic.
>
> Of course this doesn't mean that plastics are appropriate for all purposes . . . It would be silly to put a container out of polyethylene on a hot stove plate. That's not good for it; then, it will melt.[29]

In order to help people understand the specific functions of plastics, many of these magazines explained the processes and technology behind them, such as the differences between different kinds of plastic. *Kultur im Heim* used its section "*Haushaltslexikon*" ("household lexicon") for this purpose, advising its (mostly) female readership that PVC flooring was much easier to clean, but that special care needed to be taken not to wash it with water above 100 degrees Celsius or to use certain chemicals such as turpentine because of its chemical properties.[30]

Popular-science magazines, like the widely read *Jugend und Technik* (Youth and Technology), included articles explaining how plastics were best used in almost every issue in the 1960s.[31] The book *Unsere Welt von Morgen* (Our World of Tomorrow), traditionally given to young adolescents as a *Jugendweihbuch* (a confirmation gift in the tradition of the workers' culture in Germany and carried over into the GDR), devoted an entire chapter to plastics. *Unsere Welt* also drove home the point that plastics were not *Ersatz* materials, as well as claiming that another big advantage they had was their ability to take on the colorful hues demanded of modern people.[32] Written in 1960, the book reflected the still somewhat unreal utopianism surrounding the *Chemieprogramm*, with fantastical illustrations of plastics being used for example as domes for underwater, polar, lunar, or Martian (socialist) cities. Yet the text of *Unsere Welt* displayed a distinct de-mystification of the material, devoting pages and pages to precisely detailing the science and technology of polymer production and clearly outlining each type of plastic's attributes as well as listing what products they were suited for and which uses were unsuitable. Hobby books such as *Wir basteln mit Plasten* (We're Doing Handicrafts With Plastics) explained exactly how to process and mold plastics at home, how to discern between different types of plastics (by knocking on them or singeing them for example), and gave several home-project ideas, such as making toy boats, planes, or laminate table tops, claiming:

> Plastics are a material [*Werkstoffe*] that do not exist in nature. They are the work of people, of chemists. This is proof that man is now able to re-pattern and to change nature according to his will. Our everyday life cannot be imagined without plastics any longer . . . as a material they are pushing out metals and other materials . . . their production, especially in the five-year plan of our *Volkswirtschaft*, will continually rise.[33]

The plastics propaganda extended beyond hobbies to other areas of free-time use. One of the most popular vacation and weekend activities for East Germans was camping, a practice actively encouraged by the government by arranging camping trips and securing camping places, often hard to come by, for workers of certain factories, special work brigades, the state workers' union (FDGB), the state youth association (FDJ), and by always maintaining a relatively high level of investment in the production of camping supplies and equipment.[34] Even more than in the home, plastics came to replace metal and natural fibers in the production of most camping supplies. The omnipresence of eating sets for camping made out of plastics, plastic table coverings, inflatable water toys, casing for portable beach radios, and so on was reflected in the widely read *Mosaik* comic book, which often took its main characters the Digedags, and thus its readers, on quasi-educational adventures through history and science. With a title that read "Summer Joy Through Plastics," the magazine depicted a scene of frolicking East

Figure 4.3 *"Summer Joy Through Plastics." The depiction of plastics in the context of leisure outside the home sought to broaden the material's appeal beyond readers of home and women's magazines. From* Mosaik *(40/1996).*

German campers (clearly identifiable by their Trabant parked nearby) using a palette of various plastic products, marking each one with a star, and on top the caption read:

> Winter has gone, and we are once again enjoying summer. Therefore we are showing you this scene, of this hilarious camping spot. But here there is something special: almost all the consumer objects are plastic. Each one is marked with a star, so you can see how big a role plastics play in our lives.[35]

Plastic consumer goods, and especially phenolic and polyester resins, fit perfectly into another of the GDR government's initiatives in the 1960s, namely, rationalizing housework in order to ease the burden of homemakers. Numerous articles and studies by government organs, especially the Institute for Market Research in Leipzig, attempted to apply methods of Taylorist analysis to household chores. Some studies talked of "mechanizing" and "technologizing" (*Technisieren*) the household, claiming the home was a "machine."[36] One 1964 study from the Institute classified housework into five major categories, listed by the amount of time each required: 1) food-related (shopping, preparing, cooking, serving, and cleaning); 2) cleaning the apartment; 3) cleaning clothes and linens; 4) heating the apartment;[37] and 5) other (childcare, gardening, etc.). Each of these activities was then broken down further (peeling, chopping, mixing, etc.) and the time spent on each carefully analyzed. The study then proposed scientifically informed solutions to lowering the amount of time spent in each area and, not surprisingly, plastics appeared in several of the suggestions. Plastic flooring was central to the goal of rationalizing "housework task group two (cleaning the apartment)" as it was called. Using plastic resins such as Dehafol and Sprelacart for kitchen surfaces, *Schrankwände* and tables would also contribute to a more smoothly functioning apartment.[38] Such strong recommendations from the Institute for Market Research helped propel plastic-laminate furniture and kitchens to the norm for the "rationalized" apartment blocks, such as the P2 model, that became ubiquitous in East Germany by the end of the 1960s.[39] Easy to clean plastic laminate furniture was featured in numerous popular media, often mentioned, as in one feature in 1965, in connection with the idea of the "apartment of the future."[40]

The benefits that plastics held for the consumer were not the only focus of the discourse on plastics in the media, however. Often plastics were extolled for the benefits that they would bring to the *Volkswirtschaft*. The television show *Prisma* for example aired a special feature entitled *Die Plaste Kommen* (Plastics are Coming) in 1970, showcasing the benefits that plastics had for the "material structure" of the *Volkswirtschaft*. As the program opened to scenes of shoppers browsing shelves stocked with plastic wares in *Chemie im Heim*, the narrator intoned that "Already today the material plastic has conquered a secure place in our lives." As the backdrop changed to a laboratory of the Institute for Light Chemistry (*Institut für Leichtchemie* IfL), the narration voiced "By producing with plastics instead of metal the amount of time spent by workers is lowered by 12 percent to 33 percent. This leads to the rationalization of the entire finishing process."[41] Focusing next on the Pentacon camera factory, the show detailed the replacement of metal parts with plastic in the new "plastic camera" model "Elektra." By mastering the "substitution process" of plastic for metal, numerous screws and joints could be eliminated, using instead only three injection-molded plastic casings, saving work time and saving the factory over 300,000 marks a year.

"The Elektra," *Prisma* went on, "is the most advanced plastic camera casing in the world." Even here, however, the *Prisma* narrator exhibited restraint, asking rhetorical questions such as "what are plastics really suited for? When is the substitution of metals through plastics really useful, and when is it an uneconomical decision? Designers (*Projektanten*) and engineers have a special responsibility here to always choose the right material."[42] By really understanding the properties of plastics, and only using them where their impact would be structure-determining (*Strukturbestimmend*), as opposed to treating plastics as a cheap replacement or wastefully squandering them on superfluous goods not essential to the success of the *Volkswirtschaft*, the GDR's economic planners, engineers, and designers were contributing to the collective good on behalf of the consumer, even if they were not always producing directly according to the wishes of the consumer.

The conception of plastics as a high-value material to be used only where they served the purposes of functionality was also a result of the particularities of the industrial-design community in East Germany. Many industrial designers in the GDR had little or no experience in designing with plastics; most had been trained as artisans in woodworking or porcelain, or as silver- or goldsmiths. The major design centers in Halle, the Burg-Giebichenstein school, and the Institute of Applied Art in Berlin initially produced, and continued through the GDR to some degree to produce, designs and dissertation projects based in older materials. However, many of the major figures associated with these two centers, such as Mart Stamm in Berlin and Selman Selamangic in Halle were direct disciples of the Bauhaus and, as *Bauhäusler*, trained the future industrial designers in the GDR to embrace mass-production and modern technology in order that the masses not receive tasteless, crudely designed kitsch. Although the Bauhaus itself was officially taboo following the "Formalism Debate" in the 1950s, many designers simply continued to work on "modern design," because they felt they had a better sense of the *Zeitgeist* of the times and of what people wanted. When Hubert Petras, one of the major pioneers in plastics design in the GDR, introduced cylindrical vases in 1962 at the Academy of Art exhibition in Leipzig, the design was slammed in the main Party organ *Neues Deutschland* for being "elitist" and "abstract,"[43] but the comments of visitors to the exhibition in the visitor's books reflected a wave of sympathy and excitement for the "look" Petras was expressing: modern and functional, but not overly abstract, bizarre, or hard to understand.[44] Defenders of this new aesthetic of moderated modernism appeared from throughout the design community, but also in the government and even the Party, causing *Neues Deutschland* to eventually accept a toned-down version of the very Bauhaus style that had only a few years earlier been described as "cosmopolitan" and "elitist."[45]

Some designers did serve the cause of the SED's Chemistry Program propaganda directly, such as Horst Redeker, director of the Institute for Applied Art, whose book *Chemie Gibt Schönheit* (Chemistry Gives Beauty) linked the power of the chemist with the image of Faust, and then portrayed Faust as a proto-socialist figure. Because chemistry radically altered the very nature of things, it provided man with complete control over the shaping of his environment, coinciding with the socialist faith in scientific planning, thus making it the perfect nodal point at which designers and communism could intersect.[46]

Most designers, however, did not overtly embrace the ideology of the regime at first. Many of the most prolific designers of plastics, such as Albert Krause in Halle, were not even Party members. Krause, who was originally trained as a silversmith, moved into industrial design and into plastics because there were simply no contracts available for silver in the *Volkswirtschaft*; boarding the Chemistry Program bandwagon was the only way to be able to continue working as a designer. Krause nonetheless carried over the same craftsmanlike attitude toward his work with polyethylene as he had with silver or porcelain; he viewed his work as a matter of creating goods that were of high quality, that fulfilled a useful need, and that were informed by a sense of "moderated modernism," and maintained that designing without the pressure of always thinking about what might sell he was able to design based on his and his colleagues' own sense of what people really needed, about what quality truly was.[47] It was a position staked out repeatedly by designers; plastics and consumer goods in the West were "Woolworth wares,"[48] cheap and kitschy, because the only factor taken into consideration by western designers, especially with plastics, was to please the whims of consumers at the lowest possible cost.

Although designers until the mid-1960s had trouble trying to gain influence over product decisions in industry,[49] their influence on popular taste was widespread in the media. From television shows to print media, designers and architects appeared frequently to "explain" what good taste was, and how, for example, to decorate apartments using the Sprelacart furniture available to consumers.[50] Only gradually did designers become more tied into the center of economic power; the young star of GDR design, Martin Kelm, used his personal influence with the Politburo leadership to transform the Central Institute for Design (*Zentralinstitut für Gestaltung* ZfG) from a lesser state organ into a powerful regulator of decision-making in product planning. The ZfG was placed directly under the DAMW, which was a representative of the Minister Council, and renamed the Office of Industrial Design (*Amt für industrielle Formgestaltung* AiF) in 1965; under a directive of the Minister Council, the DAMW had full authority to stop production of goods that did not meet its standards of quality.[51] What is most significant about this move, as well as two subsequent Minister Council directives in 1965 requiring VVBs to hire designers, is that designers entered industry under the aegis of quality testing, rather than under any pretense of providing aesthetic or creative counsel, reflecting the emphasis on notions of quality as opposed to aesthetic pleasure among East German designers.

Eli Rubin

Chemistry in the Home: Plastics and Politics in Everyday Life

What effect did the policies of economic planning, ideas of aesthetics in regard to product design, and representation in the media have on the significance of plastics in everyday life in the GDR? Did the propaganda surrounding the Chemistry Program invoke among the population support for the regime's goals? Did the "look" of modern design and high technology in the home, as in the case with plastics, shape people's attitudes toward socialism? Did people see plastics as a valuable material in its own right, or did they see it as yet another stop-gap measure by a *Volkswirtschaft* that could not function properly enough to provide them with a "real" consumer world? How does a historian approach the problem of reception, especially in regard to consumption in a country where there was no free choice for consumers in the marketplace? Furthermore, how should one explore attitudes toward a material, as opposed to a specific object or social "artifact" such as the Trabant or the "Goldbroiler" chicken roaster?[52]

One of the best sources of accessing popular opinion in the GDR that has emerged in recent research has been letters of complaint sent to various government bodies, as well as to media such as the television show *Prisma*. These letters, or *Eingaben*, have two drawbacks, however. First, until the Honecker regime began strictly enforcing Minister Council resolutions requiring ministries, VVBs, and other organs to vigorously respond to and archive *Eingaben* they were receiving in the early 1970s, many *Eingaben* were retained only with irregularity, meaning that searching for popular opinion from before approximately 1970 is often difficult. Second, *Eingaben* contained far more complaints than compliments or suggestions, for obvious reasons, so they have a tendency to overrepresent negative opinion.

The *Eingaben* to be found in the AiF, Ministry of Chemistry, State Planning Commission, *Prisma*, and other archival holdings related to plastic consumer products are overwhelmingly silent on the issue of plastics. The *Eingaben* held by the Ministry of Chemistry focus heavily on the problem of finding tires for Trabants, Ladas, and Wartburgs, and on problems with the quality of laundry detergent and with polyurethane-based paints. Occasionally the Ministry for Chemistry registered complaints about the "cheapness" and low quality of the plastics that were replacing metal and other materials in consumer goods, such as this letter from one Herbert Jellinek in Biederitz in 1978 to the Ministry of Chemistry, that questioned the positive effect that "substitution" really had on the *Volkswirtschaft*:

> I think that the positive economic effect of using plastics for the factory is counterproductive and is becoming a technological and political barrier, because the damages outweigh the advantages . . . [examples of] the substitution of metal parts through plastic

> parts include bicycle bells, air pumps, bicycle lamps, and rear lights. You bump into something once, and they're broken. *A bell with plastic gears* can usually be thrown out after a few uses, since it won't function anymore. The producer writes to me, "we don't have any record of returned products (*Reklamationen*)." That I believe, since almost everyone thinks that with such small things, that only cost a mark, there's no point in sending them back since you won't change anything that way![53]

Interesting here is how the author frames the problem in terms of what might or might not be good for the *Volkswirtschaft* and the producer themselves, as well as in terms of what might or might not change the situation for the better. This is a common feature in many *Eingaben*, because writers knew that presenting their problems as problems that were representative of the whole collective would get their complaints noticed further than by simply demanding or focusing on their own individual needs. Nonetheless, letters like Jellinek's are few and far between, and the absence of an overwhelming tide of complaints like the one above, as for example is seen in the case of Trabant tires, may suggest a general satisfaction among the population with plastic goods. From statistics kept on *Eingaben*, it appears that plastics did draw more ire than almost any other area covered by the chemical industry. Out of 19,697 *Eingaben* sent to the Ministry for Chemistry in 1975 for example, 3,062 went to the VVB Plastics Processing, over 15 percent of the total and almost three times as many as sent to the VVB Pharmaceuticals, for example, and only slightly fewer than those to the Buna and Leuna factories put together, which totaled 3,378.[54] Yet of these 3,062 *Eingaben*, only 429 were from consumers regarding the quality, availability, design, or price of plastic consumer goods. The remaining 2,597 were from workers or planners within the VVB, indicating once again that although the situation within the industry was chaotic, consumers were relatively satisfied with the products. Those *Eingaben* that offered suggestions rather than criticisms generally focused on the recycling of plastics. These *Eingaben* clearly display a concern that as a *material* plastic was not being conserved enough, and betray a deep level of discomfort with simply throwing away plastic bottles, as with this letter from Wolfgang Kott in Schmalkalden sent directly to Erich Honecker in early January 1978:

> It's hard for me to ignore that in our state a lot of goods out of plastic are produced that simply end up in the garbage after one use. As is well known, plastic is made from petroleum, for which we have to pay enormous sums. We are not after all so rich that we can toss around hard currency like this.
>
> I'm of the opinion that all the plastic garbage in households should be collected separately . . . a service organization (*Dienstleistungskombinat*) needs to collect the plastic garbage from households and return it to industry . . .[55]

Also helpful in determining the reception of plastics in the populace are references to and figures regarding sales from trade organizations, such as the Ministry for Trade and Provisioning or the Central Wares Office for Household Goods (*Zentrales Warenkontor Haushaltswaren* ZWK-HW), which frequently show an increasing interest among the public in plastic goods and an inversely proportional declining interest in the same goods out of older materials.[56]

Excerpts from interviews conducted by this author with former GDR citizens can provide a deeper and more qualitative view to complement the quantitative work done by the state and Party organs themselves. Those subjects who were more predisposed to have a positive opinion of the GDR, such as Party members or employees of the state bureaucracy, seemed to have a correspondingly positive judgment of plastic consumer goods, and to have had a large amount of plastics in their apartment. Margrete J., born in 1943, an employee of the VVB Light Chemistry in Berlin, and an SED member for 26 years, frequented *Chemie im Heim* for products for her abode. When asked about the store she replied

> Let's put it this way. Whenever you needed any kind of plastic product, didn't matter if it was an egg spoon or an egg cup, or anything that had to do with plastic or even rubber, this store was the best, it had the best selection.

Upon being asked how many plastic consumer goods were in her home, or everyday life, she replied: "Very many, very many. It went from plastic cups to plastic plates." Her kitchen, as with all the kitchens in the P-2 apartment blocks like the one in which she resided, in Berlin-Weissensee, featured Sprelacart-laminate cabinets, cutting boards and counter tops and polyvinyl chloride flooring, her bathroom featured polyethylene towel racks, medicine cabinets, soap dishes, shower rings, and polystyrol toilet seat all bought at *Chemie im Heim*, as well as polyester laminate *Schrankwände* that had been ordered from the Hellerau factory in the early 1970s. When asked about her judgment of the quality, or her overall opinion of these products, she reserved especially high praise for the Sprelacart, which had been installed when she moved in there in 1969.

> First, I'll say that Sprelacart was long-lasting (*Zeitbeständig*). It's now 30 years old. The surfaces where the Sprelacart is, they're not scratched or anything, they would stay that way for 100 years. And you could get it just like wood. Whatever you did with wood, you could do with Sprelacart. It was easy to take care of (*es war Pflegeleicht*), long-lasting, it was something like progress.

Describing how a Sprelacart cutting board compared to the older wooden one she grew up with, she replied:

> Let's put this way. In terms of their actual functions, they were almost the same. That was the one thing, but, when something new came along, something modern, then you said, I need to have that. Just like today. You said, yeah I am a modern person, I need to get modern stuff (*ich muss das Modernes zulegen*).

In terms of the Chemistry Program, she displayed a more skeptical and practical attitude:

> The Chemistry Program was so really overdone, and there were these slogans, with "Affluence, Beauty and Happiness" or something. Yeah, OK, you had to make as much as possible out of plastic because, look, we had the big brother Soviet Union give us the petroleum, and it was cheaper to make something out of that than wood, 'cause we're a country without lots of wood. A thing out of wood was simply too expensive and therefore we made so much out of plastic, like this plastic furniture or Sprelacart.

When asked whether she, either as a citizen/consumer or as a member of the Party and of the economic planning branch of the chemical industry, felt "proud" of the Chemistry Program or the industry's products, she answered:

> Proud, proud, I don't know, proud. It was definitely progress, but to be proud you need a little more. (*Laughing*). It was really nice when you got something new, but being proud, no.[57]

For those who felt themselves as outsiders in GDR society, interior design and fashion became one of the only avenues of expressing dissent, especially in the absence of free public speech, uncensored media, or unrestricted travel. Because plastics had become so associated with the officially sanctioned domestic environmental aesthetic, rejecting the use of plastics became by extension a means of "marking" oneself apart from the mainstream. The use of plastics had been officially encouraged as representative of rationalization in the household; their role had been to help subordinate taste and tradition to pure functionality. Plastics were not used when and where they appealed aesthetically per se, only where they served the end of further rationalizing the house *and* improving the aesthetic of the house, but only as measured by very simplistic categories of aesthetics, such as the possibility of choice between three primary colors. To reject plastics in favor of older materials, to choose materials like cotton or natural or antique wood, and thus materials that were against the people's economy, was to reject the order of values set out by numerous voices, from the Party to design institutes to magazines. As shown with another interviewee, Angela K. (born 1942), the decision to be intentionally non-plastic was not simply one taken in isolation from a broader cultural and political context. For Angela, who worked for two decades as a primary-school teacher north of Berlin and who finished her career working in Margot Honecker's flagship primary school in Berlin, surrounded by fervently pro-GDR colleagues, her desire to be more "cultured" or "educated" than the GDR mainstream of her colleagues manifested itself in the question of plastics in the home:

> When it came to discussions like these [about taste in interior decorating] a lot of my colleagues would say, . . . "well the things out of plastic, they have a nice form (*formschön*), they're modern, they're easy to care for (*pflegeleicht*) . . .
>
> . . . My friends loved *Chemie im Heim*. One of my girlfriends told me once "that's the best store in Berlin, there's only plastic to be bought there! *Chemie im Heim*. We always go there, shop there." I told them, yeah I can see plastics in the context with leisure time and camping and such, but they said "nah, it's nice, it's modern. It looks chic. There's really nice stuff there."
>
> . . . All this stuff they bought at *Chemie im Heim*. What else. Flower pots. Horribly ugly. That they had too, have it still. And my other girlfriend, she saw it that way too. She was so (*slightly mocking*) "yeah, [plastics] were nice; yeah they were replacements for what couldn't be gotten otherwise. And they weren't so bad."
>
> I found that always like that, like with this store *Chemie im Heim*, you know even this word "*Heim*" ["Home"] I even found awful! It's so, (*mockingly*) "little home, little home [*Heimchen, Heimchen*] stay in the apartment, just don't go out.
>
> . . . I couldn't believe it, that they couldn't see this background, this political background. That was politics, always supposed to come from behind . . . they wanted that you always looked away from it and just stayed in your little home [*Heimchen*]. They wanted to tape our eyes shut.

Perhaps as a result of not seeing the political background of the role of plastics in the home, Angela K. suggests, none of her colleagues or friends ever even spoke of the Chemistry Program nor did they ever give any "credit" to the regime for the chic, modern plastic things or other modern things they strove to decorate their apartments with in the 1960s and 1970s. Yet their attitudes toward *Chemie im Heim* bespoke a general constellation of tastes that Angela saw in endless iterations, especially in the homes of her town north of Berlin, whenever she made visits to parents. It was a taste she called alternately petite-bourgeois (*kleinbürgerlich*) and "*miefig-piefig*," a term translated roughly as "small" or "petty"-minded. What is interesting is the contestation over the term modern, because Angela believed herself to be a truly modern person, and in no way claimed her personal superiority over the GDR through moving into the "traditional." The GDR was not modern enough, or its plastics-functionality constellation was a false modernity for her. It was, in her words, "*Kitsch*," and her expression of political dissent was as much a personal journey of crafting a separate, more elevated taste based above all on a rejection of this "kitsch" and the plastics she associated with it:

> So narrow, so limited. But we were all that way . . . We only had the offer [of goods], the selection we had, that's all we had to decorate with. Horrible. Frightful. Whereas, I like to decorate modern. So, my tastes were a bit outside what was the GDR-norm. More modern, than what was supposedly "modern" in the GDR, the socialist modern.

As Angela became more aware of her sense of alienation within this "socialist modern," her search for an "authentic modern" led her to assemble a strange mix of abstract art and *Gründerzeit* furniture, various design ideas that may not have been found together in the West, but which found their way to her abode through her search for anything left out of the pages of *Kultur im Heim*. If she was trying to make a statement about the connection between an aesthetic and a political mainstream, she made it loud enough that she soon attracted the attention of the *Stasi*. Discovering after 1989 that there was a file kept on her by the secret police, she read how the Stasi had, after secretly breaking into her apartment, noted with disdain and suspicion that she was "unusually modern".[58]

For others in the GDR, rejecting plastics went further than expressing a sense of alienation from mainstream culture, it meant joining an entirely cohesive alternative culture. For Samantha C., a sculptor who had grown up outside Berlin in the 1950s and early 1960s as the daughter of a Stasi officer, subjected to rigorous indoctrination and enforcement of a cultural ban on any Western influence such as TV or radio, choosing the Bohemian life of an artist living in the hippie refuge of Friedrichshain in Berlin was as much driven by political and cultural motives as by an urge for personal rebellion. Yet the actual aesthetic of her run-down studio apartment reflected her intertwined personal and cultural rebellion against the GDR and its materials. When asked whether she ever wore the popular polyester/polyamide clothing line "Praesant 20," she replied emphatically,

> No, no, because I have good taste, always looking for nice things, textiles and clothes from cotton. I hate PVC, Praesant 20. I remember my mom had clothes from Praesant 20, but the smell from the polyester (*shaking her head*); and I think she was satisfied with this. In the 70s there was no choice, there was only Praesant 20.
> Q: How did you get cotton clothes?
> My grandmother, she produced for me clothes from cotton with the sewing machine and my skin was very sensitive to the polyester, and she had a good talent for making dresses.
> Q: When you walked around the streets of Berlin, and rode on the underground or streetcars wearing cotton clothes, did you feel different than all the people around you wearing polyester?
> Yes, back then, I felt different from the other people, because I liked being an artist, it was like my [girlhood] love of French castles, and no one knew what happened to this girl, and I wanted nice clothes, cotton clothes, and no one knew why, they thought it wasn't normal, but I had a very strong will . . .

For Samantha, much of her orientation of how to express her identity as an artist and resident of Friedrichshain came from the social connections among the other artists, dancers, and writers she met in Friedrichshain and Prenzlauer Berg. Friends directed her to the out-of-the-way antique furniture shops, which were not always easy to find in the GDR, a crucial step in rejecting plastic furniture such as Sprelacart or the Karat series of *Schrankwände* which she hated. "During this time I bought only old furniture. It was more expensive than *Karat*, but you could find really nice old things. It was wood, not plastic. Because I don't like plastic, especially for furniture, and so I bought old furniture, at specialty shops."

Being firmly within an alternative neighborhood meant that unlike Angela, whose circle of colleagues and friends constantly irritated her but from which she could never seem to fully distance herself, Samantha could completely disassociate herself from the cultural and material world of the GDR. Cutting herself off from the material world of the GDR's mainstream culture meant cutting herself off from the cultural activities with which this material world was by necessity connected. Whereas Angela still participated in some of the most basic GDR free-time activities, such as camping with her friends and colleagues, and at least accepted plastic plates and eating utensils as appropriate for camping culture, Samantha never needed to go camping, because none of her friends from the ballet or symphony orchestra ever went camping either:

> Oh no, I hated it. Only one time with a girlfriend, her parents were fans of camping, she said oh come it's on a lake outside of Berlin it's so nice. And when we went there it was 2,000 people camping there, 2,000! Only one night and I said oh my God, there was the ants, I said no, no, not for me, I would rather stay in a nice hotel. I think I was not a typical child of the GDR . . .

And so Samantha would never have had to experience the melamine camping food-service sets designed by prominent Burg-Giebichenstein plastics designer Hans Mertz in 1959 which were extolled by virtually every woman's or leisure-centered magazine and whose form influenced just about every other plastic camping service set in the GDR until the 1980s.

In the end, Samantha, who had already begun to disassociate herself from the GDR through her preference in materials and friends, completed the process by marrying a Dutchman and leaving the GDR in 1988, less than a year before it ceased to exist.[59]

Concluding Remarks: Substituting Legitimacy

In the euphoria of 1989 and 1990 it was easily forgotten that East Germans had not just been kept apart from their counterparts in the West physically, but that they had developed a separate cultural identity. This chapter has argued that by using the example of plastics, one can better understand how the structure of an industry and economy helps create cultural identity, that in the case of East Germany this separate and different identity had very much to do with the specific cultural, political, and economic values associated with materials like plastics, and that the way in which plastic consumer goods were talked about, designed, advertised, sold, and used and even thrown away all constituted part of a larger "order of things"[60] that defined, at least for a limited time, a mainstream of GDR culture.

For many Germans, whether from the former East or West, plastic consumer products have become a "node" of memory, meaning they are one of several focal points around which derision, fetishization, and nostalgia of GDR culture has crystallized. The sign on the Autobahn connecting Berlin with Dresden "advertising" plastics and elastics from Buna's Schkopau plant which read "*Plaste und Elaste aus Schkopau*" became a shared emblem for all West Germans who reflected together on their separate trips to the GDR.[61] The memory of that sign, one of several defining phrases or moments of GDR culture, still evokes a measure of contempt and amazement from Westerners: contempt, because the sign displayed pride in what was taken to be a fully unremarkable, banal, easy-to-make, cheap and disposable material;[62] amazement at the exotic nature of a culture that could elevate something so banal and functional to such exalted status. The slogan *Plaste und Elaste* was so fraught with cultural complexities of the differences and similarities between East and West Germany that it adorned the title of a "German-German Dictionary" written in the 1980s to help East and West Germans understand the many words like "*Plast*" that had evolved differently in the two countries.[63] The fetishization of GDR products in the post-*Wende* era, especially among Westerners, whether at flea markets or on individual websites, almost always displays plastic products prominently, such as the once-popular polyethylene chicken-shaped napkin holders and egg cups, worth probably less than 30 cents at one time, that now sell in markets for four Euros.

The tendency to either fetishize or to be condescending about, or both, products from the GDR including plastic products has characterized numerous academic or quasi-academic works in the last decade as well, both in Germany and in the U.K. and North America, a phenomenon which only serves to further veil plastics as a material that is particularly fetishized and derided, as a material node of memory, and thus block any attempts to use it as an opening through which larger issues of GDR history can be explored. In one of the first major works to go beyond precisely this blockage, Patrice Poutrus writes that the theme of consumption in the GDR has found itself somewhere between popular cultural history and daily feuilleton, accomplishing little more than to say "wow, what exotic stuff there was in the GDR."[64] Asking instead what the relationship between consumption and the legitimacy or hegemony of the government or Party was in East Germany, as

Poutrus has done, can move us past the fetishization of the memory of materials and products and even help explain why, for example, former East Germans often connect to their "*Ost-algie*" through their products, and why the memory of these products is so fascinating for Westerners.[65] That the *Vergangenheitsbewältigung*, or "mastering the past," for former East Germans often involves the memory of products and materials (rather than, say, dealing with guilt over genocide), that it is much more about *Kitsch* than about death, is an important clue about the importance of the meaning of these products and their materials in the *Bewältigung aus der Vergangenheit* or "the mastery from in the past."

This "mastery" or *Herrschaft* is a historical problem only beginning to take shape.[66] One of the major questions in the debate about *Herrschaft* is that of to what degree the GDR was able to legitimize its existence among its own population through the creation of a modern consumer society. A great deal of the propaganda surrounding the Chemistry Program and its plastics products certainly was meant to foster the belief among East Germans that the GDR, and by extension the SED and socialism, was going to meet their material needs through its unique combination of socialist willpower and planning on the one hand and a commitment to modern technology on the other. There is very little evidence that the Chemistry Program inspired any form of *direct* support or legitimacy for the regime, that anyone really believed in the slogans or saw the slowly growing selection of plastics for their homes as a direct triumph for the SED and for socialism. The failures of the Chemistry Program were not advertised, but everyone knew a small part of the story; the *direct* legitimacy of the regime's bombastic promises in terms of the production of plastics in the context of the Chemistry Program was undermined from a thousand small stories in a thousand small pubs, factory break rooms and dual-function P-2 model living-dining rooms.

Plastic consumer goods did, however, contribute to an *indirect* legitimation, perhaps best described as "stabilization" rather than legitimation, by helping to construct an image, an aesthetic of mainstream socialist culture, a culture based on certain values toward the meaning of materials and products that were shared by much of the population, as well as by the planners of industry, the government, and the designers. The above sketch of the production, propaganda, design, and consumption of plastics exemplifies this consensus: because plastics were a material in relatively short supply, it could not be wasted or used for disposable products by the consumer-goods industry. Instead of contributing to the "throw-away" consumer society of the West, plastic goods in the GDR were not meant to be temporary or disposable, but to be long-lasting.

Designers who worked with plastics were often those whose origins were as craftspersons, and so their approach to designing in polystyrol or polyethylene was much as it would be toward designing in wood or silver: their focus was on producing a quality product capable of fulfilling a specific function, rather than on pleasing the irrational wishes or whims of the consumer, and they were not interested in designing anything to be thrown away. As the Party and state struggled to find ways to streamline the malfunctioning *Volkswirtschaft*, rationalization and standardization became the watchwords that transformed the home. Standardization meant that there was very little difference between any apartment, kitchen, or furniture design. If a plastic was deemed by a VVB, the Ministry for Material Economy, or the State Planning Commission to be more cost effective than a natural material, such as Sprelacart kitchen cabinets, it would be present in almost every new apartment unit and be the subject of feature articles in almost every major home, women's, and design magazine. Rationalization meant that homes were to be transformed into modern factories for living, squeezing every available minute and mark out of the cost of living, and plastics were chosen by the state and by industry and designed by designers according to this principle. Thus, when plastics replaced natural materials in homes, it occurred not under the guise of cheapness, of *Ersatz*, but with the understanding that a particular plastic was valuable, and its value lay in its functional properties, which allowed it to serve the overriding purpose of streamlining the *Volkswirtschaft*.

This amounted to an "order of things," a functional constellation of modernity created out of the juncture of political and economic needs as well as design philosophies that, because there was little competition from any other order of things, at least in the 1960s and 1970s, simply became the mainstream by filling up homes and magazine pages. Furthermore, this order was explained per se throughout the media. Details on polymer technology and processing usually accompanied instructions in the popular media on how specific plastic products were supposed to be used, and exposés of specific designers and design institutes or schools in the media spelled out precisely their philosophy of designing according to the needs of the *Volkswirtschaft*, not the individual consumer. This contrasted mightily to the relationship of design and plastics in the West during this same time, in the 1960s, when for example designers such as Joe Colombo used plastic to realize fantastic, sinewy, playful forms seemingly inspired by the contents of lava lamps. To use such a valuable material for such a wasteful and obviously nonfunctional purpose in the GDR would have been unthinkable. Instead of appearing as detached from their production processes, in either fantastical forms or in piles of litter in parks, plastics in the GDR were distinctly not fetishized and not mystified. Only after the dissolution of the "order of things" that assigned plastics this functionality have they taken on a post-*Wende* aura of fetishization and exotica.

Because plastics became such a defining mark of the mainstream GDR culture, those who wanted to place themselves outside of this mainstream often chose synthetics as a point against which to define their alternative identity by seeking out natural materials even when, or specifically because, these were not as "rational" or "functional" as plastics. However, synthetics had in certain cases become the original material, the point against which what was once the primary, the natural material, was now measured. Even those who tried to go natural had to base their judgment of what was natural only in terms antithetical to what had become natural, namely, plastic: this choice was *dissent* but as dissent it was always in the secondary position, unable to fully reassemble its material memory and material continuity, because the natural order of materials had been interrupted, and an order of materials is as much an ordering of a memory of materials as it is any ordering-in-the-present. This interruption and reordering in the case of plastics is both a testament to the short-lived stabilization of socialist rule in East Germany and a metaphor for the GDR itself: an inauthenticity, a substitute that came close, for a few historical moments, to substituting itself for the original, a fundamental substitution between substitute and original, that did not last and perhaps never could.

Acknowledgements

A specific time frame has not been included in this chapter's title because the diffuse nature of the subject material has tended to resist such bracketing. Although the period of study here begins roughly in 1958 and ends with the end of the five-year plan in 1975, some of the work involves materials from the late 1970s and early 1980s, because one of the areas under investigation here is the gap between the acquisition of plastic goods and the memory or value-judgment regarding these acquisitions.

My thanks to all who have helped this project along, but special thanks go to Ray Stokes, Rainer Karlsch, Karin Goihl of the Berlin Program for Advanced German and European Studies at the Freie Universität Berlin, Konrad Jarausch, Silvia Rückert, and most of all my advisor, Rudy Koshar.

Notes

1. "Dederon" was the specifically East German term for Nylon. The term "Perlon" was used in West Germany.

2. Günther Just, *Es Geht Nicht Ohne Plaste: Ein Streifzug durch die Welt der Riesen-moleküle* (Leipzig: Verlag VEB Grundstoffindustrie, 1962), pp. 1–2.

3. "Plast" (plural, "Plaste") was a specifically East German term for plastic. The term used in West Germany was "Plastik".

4. See for example Jeffrey Meikle's *American Plastic: A Cultural History* (New Brunswick, NJ and London: Rutgers University Press, 1999).

5. The literature on plastics as an object of cultural or design history is, in relation to the German Democratic Republic, sparse at best. This chapter attempts to build off, in particular, Raymond G. Stokes' "Plastics and the New Society: the German Democratic Republic in the 1950s and 1960s," in Susan E. Reid and David Crowley, eds., *Style and Socialism: Modernity and Material Culture in Post-War Eastern Europe* (Oxford, New York: Berg, 2000), and Silvia Rückert's "Spürbare Moderne – gehemmter Fortschritt: Plaste in der Waren- und Lebenswelt der DDR," in Andreas Ludwig, ed., *Fortschritt, Norm und Eigensinn. Erkundungen im Alltag der DDR* (Berlin: Ch. Links Verlag, 1999), which are the only serious academic pieces to seriously consider the role of plastics from the vantage point of design, material, industrial, political, social, and economic history. Miekle's *American Plastic* is a pioneering and excellent work on precisely this topic, only it concerns American history; and Jorg Petruschat's "Take me Plastics," in Hochschule für Kunst und Design Burg-Giebichenstein, ed., *75 Jahre Burg Giebichenstein 1915–1990; Beiträge zur Geschichte* (Halle: 1990) is a well known and interesting chapter situating plastics as a cultural object within the context of design and the Chemistry Program in the GDR, although it is often too vague and too overdrawn. Two excellent chapters specifically on synthetic fibers and their cultural meaning in the framework of the GDR's Chemistry Program are Stefan Wolle's "'Chemie gibt Brot, Wohlstand und Schönheit.' Das Chemieprogramm der DDR – ein mißglückter Laborversuch" and Stefan Paul's "Die Dederon Kampagne 1959," both from Haus der Geschichte der Bundesrepublik Deutschland, ed., *Künstliche Versuchung. Nylon – Perlon – Dederon* (Cologne: Wienand, 1999); and for design and plastics in both Germanies in the 1960s and 1970s see Josef Straßer's "Utopien in Plastik: Die Kunststoff-Euphorie der sechziger und frühen siebziger Jahre," in the somewhat over-stylized *Plastics + Design* (Stuttgart: Arnoldsche, 1997) authored by Straßer and Renate Ulmer as an accompaniment to an exhibition of the same name at the Neue Sammlung, Staatliches Museum für angewandte Kunst, Munich.

6. For the most definitive treatment of the relationship between the German chemical industry and German politics, as well as other sources on this relationship, and I.G. Farben in particular, see Peter Hayes' *Industry and Ideology: I.G. Farben in the Nazi era* (New York: Cambridge University Press, 1987).

7. By the time the *Chemieprogramm* was launched in 1958, the GDR already accounted for 4.5 percent of the world's total chemical production, making it 7th in the world, and chemicals accounted for 14.5 percent of the country's total GNP, a percentage higher than that of any of the other leading chemicals producers. Per capita production of synthetic fibers, rubbers, and phenolic and melamine resins also put the GDR near the top in international comparison. See Rainer Karlsch, *Das Chemieprogramm der DDR von 1958 – Hintergründe, Ziele, Resultate* (unpublished manuscript, Zentrale Informationsverarbeitung Chemie GmbH, Berlin, 1990), pp. 1–3.

8. "VEB" refers to *Volkseigenerbetrieb* or "Peoples' own factory," a reference to factories or businesses owned by the state.

9. Cf. for example *Chemie gibt Brot, Wohlstand und Schönheit* (herausgegeben vom Zentralkommittee der SED, Abt. Agitation und Propaganda, Abt.s Bergbau, Kohle, Energie und Chemie, Berlin, 1959).

10. Petroleum yields a far higher amount of plastics, up to 15 times as much, especially thermoplastics such as polyethylene, because it is more easily "cracked" or split into ethylene, the basic building block of polymer chains. The processing of lignite, or brown coal, although far more available in East Germany, also produced far heavier amounts of pollution than did the refining of oil.

11. Raymond Stokes and Rainer Karlsch, *The Chemistry Must Be Right: The Privatization of Buna Sow Leuna Olefinverbund GmbH.* (Leipzig: Edition Leipzig und Buna Sow Leuna Olefinverbund GmbH, 2001), p. 31. Also cf. Stokes, *Opting for Oil: The Political Economy of Technological Change in the West German Chemical Industry, 1945–1964* (Cambridge: Cambridge University Press, 1994).

12. Stokes and Karlsch, p. 32.

13. In 1962, for example, the GDR was able to cover a domestic need of 79,470 tons of plastics with only 73,070 tons from its own industry, leaving 6,400 tons to be covered through import. BArchBL DE 1 VA 47643 "Hinweise zum gegenwärtigen Stand und der für 1965 vorgesehenen Versorgung der Bevölkerung mit Plasterzeugnissen," p. 4.

14. BArchBL DE 1 VA 48612 "Bericht über die Untersuchung des volkwirtschaflich zweckmäßigstes Einsatz von Plasten," May 11 1966, p. 9.

15. BArchBL, DE 1 VA 47643, "Bericht über Forschungsarbeiten zur Gewinnung von Futterprotein aus nichtklassischen Rohstoffen". Also see Bundesarchiv Aussenstelle Dahlwitz-Hoppegarten (hereafter BArchDH) Volkswirtschaftrat DE 4 VA 16140, "Ein neuer Weg von der pflanzlichen Zellwand zu Rohstoffen der Kunststoff-Industrie," in W. Voss, *Manuskript eines Vortrages vor der Sektion Chemie der Deutschen Akademie der Wissenschaften zu Berlin*" March 1961.

16. "VVB" refers to *Vereinigung Volkseigenerbetriebe*" or "union of people's own factories," and was a state-run umbrella organization grouping together VEB and half-state factories from within a given industrial area, in order to better coordinate planning and sharing of resources between them.

17. "NES" refers to the "New Economic System," a system of flawed economic reforms established under Ulbricht's leadership in an attempt to introduce some aspects of market economy into the GDR, such as making individual VVB and VEB more responsible for their own sales and quality control, especially when export markets were concerned.

18. BArchBL DE 1 VA 48612, p. 13.

19. For more on the NES and other economic reforms of the 1960s, the best work to date is André Steiner's tome *Die DDR-Wirtschaftsreform der sechziger Jahre: Konflikt zwischen Effizienz- und Machtkalkül* (Berlin: Akademie Verlag, 1999). See also Jörg Roessler and Dagmar Semmelmann's volume *Zwischen Plan und Markt: Die Wirtschaftsreform 1963–1970* (Berlin, 1990) and Janos Kornai's *The Socialist System: The Political Economy of Communism* (Princeton: Princeton University Press, 1992).

20. BArchBL DE 1 VA 42498 "Planvorschlag VVB El-plast/Qualität neue Produkte DAMW" from the Deutsches Amt für Messewesen und Warenprüfung, 1964.

21. This is not to imply that even the GDR had total control over its own economy. One could always, with hard currency, political connections, Western relatives, or the chutzpah

to participate in smuggling and the black market, get hold of goods not deemed "*volkwirtschaftlich,*" i.e. not produced by the state industries. Even when a good went entirely "plastic" there were always pockets of resistance who used these channels to continue to find these goods made out of natural materials.

22. BArchDH, Ministerium für Materialwirtschaft DE 3 CO 83, "Mündlicher Bericht über die ersten Ergebnisse der Untersuchung des volkswirtschaftlich zweckmäßigsten Einsatzes von Plasten," 1966.

23. BArchDH, DE 3 CO 85, 86, 90, 91, 129.

24. BArchDH, Ministerium für Chemie, DG 11 1143, "Polyester und Polyurethanprogramm 1966–1973," or BArch Hoppegarten DE 3 CO 146, 157, 159 or 161.

25. *Neues Deutschland,* October 7, 1959 and *Die Berliner Zeitung,* October 7, 1959.

26. *Neue Berliner Illustrierte,* 45, 1964, pp. 8–9.

27. "Mit dem Plast auf du und du," *Guter Rat,* 2, 1966, p. 18.

28. *Kleine Enzyklopädie Die Frau.* Irene Uhlmann, ed. (Leipzig: VEB Bibliographisches Institut, 1971), p. 291.

29. "Formschön, zweckmäßig, farbenfroh," in *Kultur im Heim,* 3, 1966, p. 27.

30. *Kultur im Heim,* 3, 1969, p. 21.

31. See for example *Jugend und Technik,* 2, 1960, p. 44, "Plaste überall."

32. Karl Böhm and Rolf Dörge, *Unsere Welt von Morgen* (Berlin: Verlag Neues Leben, 1960), p. 184.

33. Werner Schenke, *Wir basteln mit Plasten* (Berlin: Der Kinderbuchverlag, 1966), p. 7.

34. Cf. Anja Dähmlow and Viola Härtel, "Verreisen kann jeder, Zelten ist Charaktersache," in Neue Gesellschaft für Bildende Kunst, ed., *Wunderwirtschaft: DDR Konsumkultur in der 60er Jahren* (Cologne: Böhlau Verlag, 1996), pp. 152–5.

35. *Mosaik,* 40, 1960, back cover.

36. BArchDH DL 102/42. "Charakter, Umfang und Struktur der Hausarbeit in den Privaten Haushalten der DDR und Möglichkeiten der Erleichterung und Verringerung der Hausarbeit durch das Warenangebot und den Verbrauch von Konsumgütern," Werner Bischoff, Dissertation for Doctorate of Economics (Dr. rer. oec.) at the Hochschule für Ökonomie Berlin, Leipzig, November 1966, p. 15.

37. With the exception of the more modern apartment blocks built after the end of the 1970s, most apartments in the GDR were heated using an oven, requiring its inhabitants to acquire their own brown coal to burn for heat.

38. BArchDH DL 102/93, H. Koch, W. Nieke, E. Wieland, "Konzeption: Erleichterung der Hausarbeit," Dipl.rec.oec., June 2, 1964, pp. 3, 5, 8.

39. A report from the Ministry for Trade and Provisioning declared a 100 percent use of Sprelacart for kitchen cabinets and surfaces in 1968. BArchDH Ministerium für Handel und Versorgung DL 1 VA/19365, "Rechenschaftsbericht über die Erfüllung der Aufgaben in Planjahr 1968," March 3, 1969.

40. "Blick in die Zukunft," *Kultur im Heim,* 3, 1965, p. 40.

41. BArchDH DE 3 CO/132, Drehbuch, "Die Plaste Kommen," p. 139.

42. Ibid., p. 140.

43. *Neues Deutschland,* October 23, 1962.

44. BArchBL Ministerium für Kultur DR 1/8067, p. 81, "Bemerkungen zu den Gästebüchern." The modern style of design on display at the exhibition was roundly accepted by

the visitors: out of 55 comments 44 were positive and only one negative. Georg Demming and his wife for example wrote: "We came in admittedly because of the article in *ND*. We were however pleasantly surprised. Precisely those pieces that were criticized, we liked the most." Margarete Kühn of Berlin-Wildau: "I saw the exhibit of industrial design and liked it. The article from Mr. Hagen in *ND* is a one-sided and not well considered opinion and too subjectively colored. He does not take into consideration enough the discipline (*Gesetzmäßigkeit*) of industrial form under socialist conditions (*Bedingungen*)."

45. BArchBL DR 1/7961, letter to Minister of Culture from the Chairman of the Council on Industrial Form, Professor F. Engemann, Halle, October 23, 1962.

46. Horst Redeker, *Chemie Gibt Schönheit*, Berlin: Institut für angewandte Kunst 1959, p. 6.

47. Interview with Albert Krause, September 19, 2002, Halle.

48. Redeker, p. 31.

49. Especially the chemical industry, which because of its prominent position in the economic planning structure was resistant to economic reforms calling for more attention to quality and to producing consumer goods in line with customers' wishes, was particularly reticent when it came to hiring designers, or ateliers, to help consult on how products should be made.

50. *Prisma* brought the role of industrial designers into viewers' living rooms, for example, in a feature from 1977 entitled "Formgestaltung. Form – nur Formsache?" Deutsches Rundfunk Archiv, Babelsberg Bestand Prisma.

51. The power that designers, at least those who worked for Kelm at the AiF, had over production of consumer goods was unprecedented in the Eastern Bloc, and a source of pride for East German designers, as AiF designer Günther Reißmann expressed in a 1967 speech to his Polish counterparts. See BArchDH, Amt für industrielle Formgestaltung, DF 7 inst/47, Eröffnungsansprache von Günther Reißmann für die Form-Funktion-Qualität Ausstellung in Warschau, December 1967.

52. The Goldbroiler was, like the Trabant, a symbol of the GDR's consumer society. See Patrice Poutrus, *Die Erfindung des Goldbroilers: Über den Zusammenhang zwischen Herrschaftssicherung und Konsumentwicklung in der DDR* (Cologne: Böhlau, 2002).

53. BArchDH DG 11/2945, Eingaben 1978. Letter originally sent to the Ministerium für Handel und Versorgung, October 17, 1978.

54. BArchDH DG 11/3363, Eingaben 1970–1977.

55. BArchDH DG 11/2943, Eingaben 1977.

56. BArchDH DL 1 VA/19365, "Rechenschaftsbericht über die Erfüllung der Aufgaben in Planjahr 1968," March 3, 1969, p. 23. The report claims that for many articles, those made from plastic are increasingly asked for while the interest in those out of wood is "stagnating."

57. Interviews with Margrete J., August 27, 2002 and September 3, 2002, Berlin.

58. Interviews with Angela K., August 30, 2002 and September 6, 2002, Berlin.

59. Interviews with Samantha C., August 28, 2002 and September 7, 2002, Berlin. Please note that these interviews were conducted in English, at the subject's preference, and are transcribed word for word.

60. With all due respect to Michel Foucault, the phrase "order of things" as I use it here must be distinguished from its use in Foucault's *The Order of Things: An Archeology of the*

Human Sciences (New York: Vintage, 1973). The "order" I refer to is a set of commonly held value judgements about the economical worth of materials; the "things" specifically refer to the materials and the products that formed the consumer world of East Germany.

61. Cf. Simone Tippach-Schneider, *Das Grosse Lexikon der DDR-Werbung: Kampagnen und Werbesprüche, Macher und Produkte, Marken und Warenzeichen* (Berlin: Schwarzkopf & Schwarzkopf, 2002), where the slogan *Plaste und Elaste aus Schkopau* merited its own entry. See p. 272.

62. In particular, George C. Bertsch, Ernst Hedler and Matthias Dietz, *SED: Schönes Einheits Design/Stunning Eastern Design/Savoir Eviter Le Design* (Cologne: Taschen Verlag, 1994) described itself as an "archeology" of the design of GDR consumer goods still lingering in Eastern stores and derided the aesthetic and material choice of many products, calling the GDR the "Galapagos Islands" of the design world which preserved "fossils" from the West (p. 7), offering contrasts with the "Western sense of touch" that recoiled at the "brittleness of the 'Stromfix Junior II' cable reel that recalls old articles of Bakelite" (p. 9). Such condescension continues to evoke aggravation among former product designers in the GDR.

63. Cf. Theodor Constantin, *Plaste und Elaste: Ein Deutsch-Deutsches Wörterbuch.* (Berlin: Haude & Spener, 1982): see p. 63 for entry on "Plast."

64. Poutrus, p. 16.

65. There are in fact a number of brand names that have continued to sell in a reunified Germany that were popular in the GDR, many of which are products of the GDR chemical industry, such as "Florena" skin cream and "Spee" laundry detergent; their market is mainly former East German citizens who have turned back to what they consider to be higher-quality eastern products.

66. Perhaps the best work to date on the problem of *Herrschaft* is Thomas Lindenberger, ed., *Herrschaft und Eigen-Sinn in der Diktatur. Studien zur Gesellschaftsgeschichte der DDR* (Cologne: Böhlau, 1999).

5

Born Again in the Gospel of Refreshment? Coca-Colonization and the Re-Making of Postwar German Identity

Jeff R. Schutts

The *Haus der Geschichte,* Germany's state museum for contemporary history in Bonn, hosted a special exhibition during the summer of 2002, "Fascination Coca-Cola: Insight into a Legend." This blend of official public history and corporate public relations offered visitors a "journey through historical events and milestones in the history of Coke," from the soft drink's modest creation in Atlanta in 1886 to the ubiquitous trademark's status today as "the world's most recognized word after 'okay'." Moreover, seven interactive *Erlebnisinseln* ("adventure islands") promised to "transform familiar experiences into new and fascinating Coca-Cola experiences, telling the story of the omnipresence of Coca-Cola, which accompanies us on our journey through life."[1]

Although the exhibit, and its popularity, may have demonstrated, as maintained by Coke spokesman Klaus Hillebrand, "how deeply Coca-Cola is anchored in society,"[2] the insight it provided into Coke's role in shaping Germany's past was ultimately "*Geschichte-Lite*." In one of the more egregious examples of watered-down historical consciousness, the exhibit text noted, "In 1916 the world famous hobble-skirt bottle was created in the United States, meanwhile the First World War raged in Europe."[3] Likewise, filtered out of the *Haus der Geschichte* exhibit was any mention of the heated controversy in the 1950s over the rising tide of European Coca-Cola consumption and so-called "Coca-Colonization." Instead, as in the museum's standing exhibit, where a Coke bottle is encased next to Levi's jeans and Mickey Mouse,[4] the soft drink's high profile after the Second World War was celebrated simply as representative of the American-style consumer wonderland made possible by West Germany's *Wirtschaftswunder.*

However, Coca-Cola did more than add a bit of American flavor to the "economic miracle" that marked West Germany's postwar recovery. Coke helped make

German history. Like the Marshall Plan, Berlin Airlift and *Deutschmark*, Konrad Adenauer and Ludwig Erhard, Coca-Cola played an active role in the reconstruction of West German society and identity. In fact, a "world-historical force" can be identified in "refreshment," one of the most effervescent "ingredients" in Coca-Cola's commercial success. (The company formally lists as the soft drink's marketing formula: "joy of life, authenticity, refreshment, fun and relaxation."[5]) Although there is little validity to the local Cokelore about the soft drink's ability to derust snow chains, dissolve a piece of veal overnight, or free a sticky clutch in a Trabant 601,[6] the famous carbonated sugar-water was helpful to Germans in their efforts to wash away the Nazi legacy. As illustrated in this study, by consuming *köstlich und erfrischend Coca-Cola eiskalt* (delicious and refreshing ice-cold Coca-Cola), postwar Germans were Born Again in the Gospel of Refreshment.

Coca-Colonization

By the end of the 1920s, the Coca-Cola Company had granted bottling concessions in more than two dozen countries (including Germany), but it was the Second World War that launched the American soft drink as an unprecedented global phenomenon. Shortly after the bombing of Pearl Harbor, Robert Woodruff, the legendary "boss" of the Coca-Cola Company, promised to "see that every man in uniform gets a bottle of Coca-Cola for five cents, wherever he is and whatever it costs our company."[7] It was a shrewd promise. Coca-Cola employees were uniformed as official US Army "Technical Observers," or TOs, and sent to produce the soft drink wherever the American armed forces deployed. When the Second World War ended in 1945, not only had Coca-Cola been transformed into the "Universal symbol of the American way of life,"[8] Woodruff's Atlanta-based company was left with sixty-four taxpayer-subsidized Coca-Cola bottling operations scattered around the world. Exploiting this global beachhead, the company quickly recruited new franchised bottlers in more than two dozen countries and used aggressive marketing to increase per capita consumption in its already established markets.

By 1948, with forty-six international subsidiaries and over six thousand foreign employees, the company could claim, "Coca-Cola already has the distinction of dealing in more countries at one time and on a larger scale than any other trader in world history."[9] Within two years, a third of the fifty million Cokes consumed daily were sold outside the United States. In May 1950 *Time* magazine ran a cover story that acknowledged a new actor on the global stage, "Coke's peaceful near conquest of the world is one of the remarkable phenomena of the age." Nonetheless, even as it venerated the company's success at internationalizing its image and market, *Time* expressed misgivings about the cultural ramifications of

Coca-Cola's global success. "To find something as thoroughly native American hawked in half a hundred languages on all the world's crossroads from Arequipa to Zwolle is still strangely anomalous, somewhat like reading Dick Tracy in French or seeing a Japanese actor made up to look like Abraham Lincoln."[10]

What seemed odd to American journalists could appear outright ominous to Europeans. That spring a Viennese newspaper advised, "Tremble, Coca-Cola is on the march!" Other Austrian newspapers reported that atomic bombs were being manufactured at Coca-Cola bottling plants, and it was even suggested that soon the soft-drink company would be marketing cuckoo clocks whose birds would announce the hour by chirping, "Coca-Cola! Coca-Cola!"[11] In Rome a headline in *L'Unità* declared, "DRINKS COCA-COLA AND DIES," while another Italian newspaper warned that the soft drink would "turn a child's hair white overnight."[12] In Switzerland, where Coca-Cola lobbyists then sought to overturn health legislation that prohibited Coke because of its phosphoric acid, a political cartoon depicted a burly Coca-Cola vender harassing a Swiss peasant, "Dump out your apple-cider, drink Coca-Cola, and otherwise keep your mouth shut."[13] Across the continent, it seemed that flavored sugar-water had become the latest specter to haunt Europe.

In actuality, the high visibility of Coca-Cola's advertising and its all-American image made it an easy symbol for whatever one did not like about the postwar European society then under construction via the Marshall Plan. Traditional conservatives, long concerned about the dangers of so-called "Americanization," saw Coca-Cola as the elixir of the dawning god-less feminized materialist consumer mass society. In France, *Le Monde* reported, "We have accepted chewing gum and Cecil B. De Mille, *Reader's Digest,* and be-bop. It's over soft drinks that the conflict has erupted. Coca-Cola seems to be the Danzig of European culture. After Coca-Cola, *hola*."[14] Communists, on the other hand, saw Coca-Cola as an assault weapon in the establishment of an oppressive capitalist *Pax Americana*. An East Berlin newspaper explained, "Wherever the masters of Wall Street are able to take over and plant their artillery, invading batteries of Coca-Cola bottles will always follow."[15] Across Europe unexpected alliances were formed, often sponsored by the established national beverage industries, to orchestrate campaigns against Coca-Cola.

In Paris, communist delegates to the National Assembly, supported by wine growers and members of the moderate ruling party, introduced a bill to "prohibit the import, manufacture and sale of Coca-Cola in France, Algeria and the French colonial empire."[16] With the subsequent parliamentary debate making international headlines and local mobs overturning Coca-Cola trucks, the French campaign against the American soft drink became the most serious. "We must call a spade a spade and label Coca-Cola for what it is – the avant garde of an offensive aimed at economic colonization against which we feel it's our duty to struggle," insisted

Figure 5.1 Cartoon from Time *magazine, March 13, 1950.*

a neutralist Catholic newspaper.[17] *Le Monde* concurred, "What the French criticize is less Coca-Cola than its orchestration, less the drink itself, than the civilization – or, as they like to say, the style of life – of which it is the symbol."[18] (see Figure 5.1) In November 1949 the flagship French newspaper ran a front-page headline that helped popularize a communist-coined label for the controversial phenomenon, "Coca-Colonization." Again the issue was framed as a question of national identity and cultural survival: "Conquerors who have tried to assimilate other peoples have generally attacked their languages, their schools, and their religion. They were mistaken. The most vulnerable point is the national beverage. Wine is the most ancient feature of France. It precedes religion and language; it has survived all kinds of regimes. It has unified the nation."[19]

Although Germans could identify as strongly with beer and schnapps as the French did with wine,[20] the anti-Coca-Cola movement fizzled out as it crossed the Rhine. When the National Assembly in Paris passed a law in August 1950 meant to ban the soft drink,[21] members of the newly established West German *Bundestag* in Bonn were downing some fifteen thousand bottles of Coca-Cola a month.[22] "Thirst knows no season, nor political affiliation," declared a German Coca-Cola publicist. "Although inside parliament the debates may become heated and opinions widely divergent, here [at the soft-drink kiosk] everyone gathers peacefully."[23] In fact, whereas in France a "strange alliance" had been formed against Coca-Cola, in the *Bundestag* conservatives teased the socialist deputies for opposing a consumer tax that would harm Coca-Cola sales. "I am extraordinarily astonished to hear from you as a representative of the SPD such protective sentiments for one of the greatest capitalist corporations," quipped one member of the Bavarian Party to a colleague from across the aisle. "Even more so, [that you are] standing up for this big company that makes so much profit."[24]

In postwar Germany, as in the rest of Europe, Coca-Cola now symbolized the United States and its consumer-capitalist way of life. Hans Walter Hütter, director of the *Haus der Geschichte*, recently emphasized that to Germans during the 1950s Coke was "THE visual symbol of Americanization."[25] Historian Mary Nolan's extensive research on the American influence on Germany has supported this assertion. She noted, "No one person looms large in the post-1945 German imagination of America as Henry Ford did during Weimar. It was not personalities, such as Elvis or Kennedy, who commanded center stage, but rather commodities. The Coke bottle occupied pride of place."[26]

Nonetheless, Coca-Cola was also a product "made in Germany" since 1929. During the 1930s the soft drink had been able to establish itself as a successful German consumer product. Coca-Cola GmbH, the German Coke subsidiary headquartered in Essen, overcame the hardships of the Depression, and then the increasingly chauvinistic tastes of the Nazi Third Reich, to double its sales almost every year of its first decade. By 1939, Germans were enjoying almost 110 million ice-cold Cokes a year, and handing over 25 million *Reichmarks* in pocket change to do so. Capturing over 15 percent of the mineral-water-dominated market in non-alcoholic beverages, Coca-Cola was Nazi Germany's largest-selling brand-name soft drink. As the Atlanta headquarters noted in 1938, "The growth in volume of our business in Germany has been one of the most spectacularly successful chapters in the Company's history."[27]

This success was won despite occasional rumblings from local competitors that the soft drink was a "Jewish-American product."[28] The German Coca-Cola company neutralized such rumors by emphasizing the soft drink's decentralized production and its integral place in the German beverage industry. Celebrating its tenth anniversary in April 1939, Coca-Cola GmbH announced that through the company's more than five hundred local *Konzessionäre* (franchised bottlers and wholesale-distributors) the soft drink provided livelihoods for more than five thousand Germans. Moreover, countless others in the Third Reich saw their fortunes buoyed by the ripple effects of Coca-Cola's success. These included the more than two hundred sugar-beet farmers employed annually to meet the company's sugar requirements and the more than fifty thousand *Gaststätten*, grocery store, gas station, and kiosk proprietors who collected 25-pfennig for each Coke they sold retail.[29] As an Atlanta Coca-Cola executive would explain in the 1950s, "The growth of the Coca-Cola business overseas follows the same pattern of decentralization that helped make the business successful in the United States. It is the pattern of locally owned and locally operated enterprises. In Germany, it is a German business. In France, it is a French business. It Italy, it is an Italian business."[30] Because of this franchise structure Coca-Cola in Germany could be considered "as German as the milk that is milked by German farmers in German stalls from German cows of a Danish breed."[31] Although during the 1930s most of the "Coca-Cola Girls," hardworking men, jolly Santas, and chubby snowmen depicted in Coca-Cola GmbH advertising were "born in the USA," the soft drink's image and message resonated in Hitler's new Germany. Whether one was driving the Autobahn, training for the Olympics, or marching with the Brownshirts, Coke's German advertising promised that world-renowned ("*Coca-Cola hat Weltruf!*"), pure and wholesome ("*Rein und Gesund*"), ice-cold Coca-Cola ("*Trink Coca-Cola immer Eiskalt*") was the delicious and refreshing indulgence ("*Ein köstlicher Genuss,*" "*Die erfrischende Pause*") that at all times ("*zu jeder Zeit*") kept up your spirits ("*Erhalte Dir die Munterkeit*").[32]

As war loomed over Europe in September 1939, Max Keith, the Düsseldorf businessman who ran Coca-Cola GmbH from the mid-1930s until 1968, addressed those affiliated with the German company, "I am sure that each member of the great Coca-Cola Family is aware of his responsibility to *Volk und Vaterland.*" Noting that the situation demanded increased "awareness of duty and preparedness," Keith called upon his colleagues to answer the greater need for "good soft drinks, not only among the population but also in military circles." "However things may develop," he concluded, "we can all proudly look back on what we have accomplished, fully aware that our hard work over the recent years has not been in vain because the name and drink 'Coca-Cola' is now and forever firmly anchored within the hearts of millions of people throughout the *Reich*."[33]

Although the Second World War lowered production and cut off the supply of 7X, the concentrated "secret formula" that gave the soft drink its distinctive flavor, the German Coca-Cola subsidiary was able to stay in business throughout the conflict. With remarkable continuity, Keith and his chief counsel, Walter Oppenhoff, served as Coca-Cola GmbH's official administrators for the Third Reich's Commissioner of Enemy-owned Property.[34] Foreseeing already in 1940 that the German company would run out of its namesake product, Keith developed and started phasing in a new fruit-flavored soft drink, Fanta (short for *Fantasiegetränk*), made from un-rationed leftovers such as whey and apple-pressings. This ersatz "fantasy drink" was marketed consistently as "a product of Coca-Cola GmbH" long after Keith had patriotically directed the last cases of German Coke to wounded *Wehrmacht* soldiers in 1942.[35] "And funny enough," he remarked years later, "during the war the popularity of the trademark was not decreased but increased." Consequently, he noted, "The name Coca-Cola was a key to many possibilities to continue business which we otherwise would not have had. It was the key to almost everything – the good name we had already developed before the war broke out."[36]

Despite the increasing devastation caused by Allied bombing, for most of the war the German Coke company maintained profitable annual sales figures of about two and a half million cases, or sixty million bottles. Even as late as the summer of 1944 the production of Fanta was down little more than 10 percent from that of Coke in 1940.[37] Nonetheless, in May 1945 Coca-Cola GmbH experienced an apparent *Stunde Null* (Zero Hour) with the rest of Germany. Amid the socio-economic collapse and bombed-out rubble that had been Hitler's Third Reich, the German Coca-Cola company saw its production fall to less than a quarter of what it had been the year before; only some twelve million bottles of Fanta were sold in 1945.[38] After having "succeeded in making our organization survive a war," Keith found that an "even worse breakdown . . . followed it."[39]

The US Army brought "The Real Thing" back to the *Vaterland* in 1945 but the victorious GIs were resolved to keep their 5-cent Cokes to themselves.[40] The defeated and atrocity-tainted Germans had to, in the words of Franklin Roosevelt, "earn their way back into the fellowship of peace-loving and law-abiding nations."[41] With a vague policy of de-Nazification, democratization, and demilitarization, the occupying armies intended to fulfill the vow made by Allied leaders at the Teheran and subsequent wartime conferences: "Germany will never again be able to disturb the peace of the world."[42] The occupation's "basic objective," as stated in the American military order JCS 1067, was to show "the Germans that Germany's ruthless warfare and the fanatical Nazi resistance have destroyed the German economy and made chaos and suffering inevitable and that the Germans cannot escape responsibility for what they brought upon themselves."[43] Until the Germans were deemed sufficiently rehabilitated, there would be no "German" Coca-Cola.

Denied Coca-Cola concentrate, Coca-Cola GmbH was forced to continue Fanta production as best it could while Keith coordinated German support of the US Army's Coca-Cola operations. "As life around the plant took shape," reported one Coke TO in Stuttgart, "native Coca-Cola men became again part of a great business. From the fields and prison camps old employees returned to the business. Good machinists and diligent effort made what appeared to be a hopeless mess a shining success."[44] Sometimes in the same plant, Coca-Cola GmbH bottled Fanta for the hobbled German market while the TOs supervised Coca-Cola production for "the GIs and their Veronikas."[45] "It is prohibited at this time to sell Coca-Cola to Germans," observed a TO in April 1949, "but many of them as guests of the occupation forces get to enjoy the drink of hospitality, the symbol of friendship around the world."[46] Growing up in similarly occupied Austria, historian Reinhold Wagnleitner remembered "a rather special incentive for participating in [US Army-sponsored Austrian Youth Activities] . . . was the free distribution of Coca-Cola rations." He reasoned that the American military's expenditures on the soft drink "served two purposes: on the one hand, they improved the reputation of the U.S. Army with Austrian youths, an important group for long-term political goals; on the other hand, they also simultaneously laid the groundwork for a new market."[47]

Such US Army "sampling" activities and the GIs' own high-profile Coca-Cola consumption complemented Coca-Cola GmbH's marketing efforts to keep the trademark alive in German consciousness. In 1947, during the infamous "hunger years" when undernourished Germans were lost in the consumer no-man's-land between the *Stunde Null* of defeat and the coming currency reform, an advertising agency conducted a market survey to identify the brand names best remembered by the German public. More than five years after ice-cold Cokes had disappeared from German *Gaststätten*, Coca-Cola ranked 28th among the more than twelve hundred trademarks recalled, significantly above other familiar German beverages.[48] "Many families still had empty Coca-Cola bottles from the pre-war period," noted one recent German history of Coca-Cola. "During these 'bad times' they symbolized the time when 'everything was available.'"[49]

By this time the inability of the occupying powers to reach an understanding on how to address Germany's economic problems had prompted the British and Americans to lay the administrative foundations for West Germany's economic and political recovery. In January 1947 the two Western Allies fused their occupation zones into "Bizonia." The new entity's participation in the Marshall Plan later that year augured the West Germans' incorporation into western European political and economic life. When, in June 1948, the Western Allies introduced the *Deutschmark* to kick-start German economic recovery, the Soviets reacted by blockading Berlin. The subsequent drama of the Berlin Airlift encouraged Americans to see the Germans not as untrustworthy defeated enemies, but as appreciated allies in the West's "anticommunist consensus."[50] As the historian Thomas Schwartz has asserted, "the intensification of the Cold War during this period, and the belief that Germany's allegiance had to be secured quickly, led to a deplorable series of compromises with the legacies of Nazism."[51] Spotlighted center-stage in the developing Cold War, occupied Germany was transformed into two ideologically opposed states. Whatever the remaining stains of Nazism, the new West German Federal Republic created in May 1949 was to be a partner in the developing network of alliances that constituted the "free world." Capitalizing on this metamorphosis of German-American relations, in June 1949 Coca-Cola GmbH requested authorization to purchase Coca-Cola syrup through the US Army.[52]

Figure 5.2 Photo from Willy van Heekern, Fotoarchiv Ruhrlandmuseum, Essen.

On October 3, 1949, fifteen months after the currency reform and three weeks after Konrad Adenauer had become the Federal Republic's first Chancellor, Lee Talley, the Atlanta Coca-Cola company's European director, joined Max Keith for a ceremony at the gate of the Coca-Cola GmbH bottling plant in Essen. A snip of the scissors removed the last barrier to Coca-Cola's reintroduction to the German market. Freshly painted yellow and red delivery trucks rolled onto the German streets with signs announcing "*Coca-Cola ist wieder da!*" (Figure 5.2) At the same time as the French were beginning to raise concern about Coca-Colonization, German consumers celebrated "Coca-Cola is back!"

This emphasis on a product's "return" was characteristic of marketing in the new Federal Republic: "'Tradition' is one of the most important phrases, appearing in many early advertisements," a scholar of postwar German advertising has observed: "It suggests an era-bridging existence that makes the Nazi period disappear."[53] Equally significant, such nostalgia allowed Germans to overlook, or at least temper, Coca-Cola's association with the United States. As noted by British historian Ralph Willett, "the acceptance of the American presence since 1945 has never been total, and the rejection of [its] ideology was a constant feature of West German intellectual life until the 1960s."[54] Postwar Germans, Michael Geyer concurred, "wanted to be left alone, in control of their own destiny and, perhaps even more so, of their own history. A deep and quite vicious xenophobia, a rejection of anything and everything that was not 'their own,' can be seen throughout the public opinion polls of the 1950s."[55]

Germans, no longer forced to rely on a friendly GI for an ice-cold Coke, overwhelmed Coca-Cola GmbH's initial limited supply and Keith was forced to ration dealers to one case of Coca-Cola for every three of Fanta. During the remaining three months of 1949, five and a half million bottles of Coca-Cola were sold on the German economy. The following July the German news-weekly *Der Spiegel* announced, "Without US dollars, but with German initiative and attractive Pin-up-Girls, West German Coca-Cola dealers have successfully marched off and conquered their lost market."[56] With sugar rationing lifted that summer, the company reported that it expected to sell four million cases, or ninety-six million bottles. However, at the end of 1950 Coca-Cola GmbH had exceeded its expectations and sold over one hundred and forty million bottles. Considering the still war-ravaged economy and muted echoes of anti-Coca-Cola hysteria inside Germany, these sales figures were an impressive accomplishment. Nonetheless, in hindsight, they were a mere trickle before the flood.

Within five years, by 1954, annual Coca-Cola sales in Germany had jumped to over twenty-four million cases, a "miraculous" 600 percent increase that outpaced twelve-fold the overall rate of economic recovery in the *Wirtschaftswunder*. The following year, in 1955, the increase in Coca-Cola sales alone exceeded the total amount of Coca-Cola consumed in Germany in 1939.[57] In 1956, West Germans consumed more than thirty-five million cases of Coca-Cola; over eight hundred and forty million bottles, or roughly seventeen Cokes per person. Less than a decade later, when a *Der Spiegel* cover story declared Coca-Cola a "world power" in 1965, West Germans were drinking almost four and a half million bottles of Coke a day, over eighty-two million cases a year; nine times as much as the French. Whereas the typical German worker spent only 58 pfennig on soft drinks in 1950, and 1.57 DM in 1955, by 1963 the average outlay totaled 5.73 DM.[58]

In 1965, with Coca-Cola bottling subsidiaries in one hundred and twenty countries, West Germany was the soft drink's largest market outside the United States, and it had the next-highest per capita consumption, thirty-six bottles a year. Coca-Cola GmbH and its *Konzessionäre* then controlled almost a third of the country's soft-drink business.[59] Still today, Germany remains one of Coca-Cola's most important markets. The average German consumed nearly 200 Cokes in 2001, almost twice as much as the French and Italians.[60] In the 1950s, perhaps more than anywhere else, the Federal Republic of Germany was "Coca-Colonized."

The Gospel of Refreshment

How can historians explain postwar Germany's headlong dive into Coca-Cola-culture? Today, with "globalization" having superseded "Coca-Colonization" and even "Americanization" as the specter that seems to haunt traditional cultures and life-styles, scholars still struggle to make sense of the cultural confusion that follows in the wake of the ever-expanding and intensifying global market in consumer commodities. Does such internationalized mass consumption result in an increasingly homogenized McWorld of insipid global culture, or a multicultural bazaar that celebrates the kaleidoscope of human diversity? Reviewing the scholarship addressing these issues, historian Richard Kuisel recently differentiated between two general understandings of such cultural transfer. The first, which he tagged "Coca-Colonization," sees so-called globalization as a manifestation of cultural imperialism, where the largely American-based transnational corporations use their marketing power to clear-cut local cultural life in order to impose bland and invasive commercialized culture. The other approach to understanding such globalization stresses the cross-currents and complexity of cultural transfer. This view emphasizes how native cultures actively assimilate foreign commodities and practices, adapting them to local needs and inscribing them with new parochial meanings. As Kuisel noted, "In this second interpretation the Europeans, among others, have appropriated American mass culture and made it their own. In this vein, some have employed the phrase 'creolization' as an alternative to 'Coca-Colonization'."[61]

Any history of Coca-Cola in Germany should collapse the two concepts upon one another. By taking Coca-Colonization literally – by examining an actual case study in the international success of Coca-Cola (company, beverage, icon) – it is possible to sound out expressions of creolization while also acknowledging the role such cultural accommodation plays in the conquest of market share. In this case, to make sense of Coca-Cola's dramatic German success during the establishment of the global "Cokempire" profiled by *Time* and *Der Spiegel*, it is useful to first decipher the corporate ideology that inspired the Coca-Colonizers. Then, by analyzing how postwar West Germans were able to "creolize" this dimension of Coca-Cola-culture to their own needs, it is possible to illuminate Coke's role in the shaping of German history. This analysis, a mere sip from a rich brew of potential Coca-Cola historiography, suggests that there was more to The Real Thing than that which passed the lips.

At the turn of the century the Coca-Cola Company pioneered a decentralized system of independent bottlers as it conquered the huge American market. This franchise structure, tapping into local entrepreneurial capital and enthusiasm, was also used to create the international Cokempire. And, as before in the States, Coca-Cola's standards of uniform production and aggressive marketing were developed and maintained via company publications and periodic bottlers' conventions. When in March 1948 the company hosted the first such convention after the war, as reported (and manifested) in the company's new "in-house" journal, *Coca-Cola Overseas*, "the gathering emphasized from first to last the growing international aspects of the business."[62] Cokemen from thirty-two countries, representing over three hundred and fifty independent foreign bottlers, joined colleagues from the more than one thousand American franchised bottlers in Atlantic City at what was then the world's largest convention center. All in all, the five thousand attendees were, as one company spokesperson later wrote of the Coca-Cola community, "a group representing many races, many countries, and many cities within those countries. These men have no formal ties, no official organization. They are linked together by a common faith in 'Coca-Cola,' their belief in the honesty of the product and its value to mankind."[63]

While the convention's standardized sales plans and technical innovations were important to Coca-Cola's international success, it was this corporate ideology-*cum*-common faith that united and motivated the missionaries when they effected literal Coca-Colonization. Propagated through years of marketing, this "Gospel of Refreshment" was – and is – as familiar as the Coca-Cola trademark is ubiquitous. It offered a cosmology that linked and transcended the individual's physiological need for fluids and human society's chronic disharmony. Evangelized in an endless stream of Coca-Cola advertising, the Coke Gospel asserted that the consumption of a certain trademarked "Pure and Wholesome" "Delicious and Refreshing" carbonated beverage "Adds Life," because "Things go better with Coca-Cola" since "Coke is it," and one "Can't Beat the Feeling" of "The Real Thing." If accepted worldwide, the Coke Gospel promises that since "Life tastes Good" humankind no longer need suffer futile efforts to form more perfect unions, or bloody revolutions to free humanity from its chains. Instead, "The Pause that Refreshes" will provide global harmony if everyone would just "Always" "Enjoy Coca-Cola" and "Have a Coke and a Smile."

The Gospel of Refreshment evoked by this ahistorical ad-copy collage may seem as elusive as Hegel's *Weltgeist* but it can be found readily in the pages of *Coca-Cola Overseas* and testimonials of Coca-Cola employees. Roberto Goizueta, Woodruff's successor in Atlanta, attested, "Working for The Coca-Cola Company is a calling. It's not a way to make a living. It's a religion."[64] Codified into a model, this Coke Gospel can be used to understand the culture and logic that animated Coca-Colonization. At its core, the Coke Gospel maintains that Coca-Cola facilitates transcendence from the mundane reality of "thirst" to a "refreshed" state of youthful energy. Whether this is understood at the physiological level of digested caffeine-laden sugar-water or in metaphysical abstractions conjured forth by Coca-Cola advertising, it follows that making Coca-Cola available to the masses is a worthy calling, a true service to humanity. Thus, the key tenets of the Gospel of

Refreshment are the *universality* of Coca-Cola's appeal, Coca-Cola's inherent *goodness*; and the implication that Coca-Cola's *availability* is the measure of a Manichaean order – Coke is salvation; no Coke is wicked.

Upon this worldview an empire was founded. As Coca-Cola's franchise structure spread The Real Thing around the globe, *Coca-Cola Overseas* followed, in bi-monthly installments, giving testimony to the Gospel of Refreshment and homogenizing international Coca-Cola culture.[65] Most fundamental to the effort to create a global market was Coca-Cola's conception of "universality." In countless variations, the editorials in *Coca-Cola Overseas* asserted, "In fact, the evidence is overwhelming that people are pretty much alike everywhere."[66] Therefore, "Every man, woman, and child, whether in a palace or a hut, of every nation, race, and faith, is a present or future customer of Coca-Cola."[67] This "universality" was then extrapolated into proof that Coca-Cola was metaphysically "good." Another article explained: "People like Coca-Cola. The amounting and necessary good will for the product stems, first of all, from the simple goodness of the drink. It is pure. It is wholesome. It provides a delicious and refreshing answer to the human problem of thirst. No product is so widely accepted everywhere as Coca-Cola."[68]

Drawing on this connection between "universality" and "goodness," Coca-Cola could suggest it improved the world by encouraging "hospitality" and "friendship." During the Second World War this idea was most fully developed in a series of magazine ads that showcased the international "good will" generated by Coca-Cola's operations with the American military. One of these advertisements explained:

> And everywhere your Yankee doughboy goes, it comes spontaneously from his heart in a good old home-town phrase, *Have a Coke*. That's the way he's letting our democratic allies know why he does the friendly things he does. Friendliness is bred in his bone, and to kindred spirits it bubbles out – like the bubbling goodness of Coca-Cola itself.[69]

Ultimately, the Coke Gospel implied, Coca-Cola brought out actual "goodness" in people. In 1950 *Coca-Cola Overseas* declared, "The business of producing and selling Coca-Cola is the greatest commercial adventure in friendship the world has ever seen."[70]

These attributes of Coca-Cola had unique ramifications when the Gospel of Refreshment was proclaimed in troubled postwar Germany. "As we look around our country," observed Max Keith in the early 1950s, "it is evident of the enterprises that are of great importance to our economy and the life of our people, that they all started small and developed from an idea that was put into action by able individuals. *The idea of 'Coca-Cola' is the idea of Refreshment, the idea of The*

Pause that Refreshes."[71] On a different occasion, Keith recalled, "While much fell in ruins [during the war], one thing could not be destroyed by bombs, hell, death and devil, and that was our belief in a new beginning, one that would one day be the fruit of our work and sacrifice." Rededicating the Coke bottling plant in Berlin, he asked, "May the spirit (*Geist*) never be lost that has animated this history of Coca-Cola's remarkable world-wide success, and may each who has been filled with this spirit . . . gain strength by drawing from its infinite well."[72]

In its own way Coca-Cola might help the new West German state, and individual Germans, transcend the Nazi legacy. To begin, the Coca-Cola business could help Germany rebuild, first its infrastructure and then its character. In the issue of *Coca-Cola Overseas* that reported to Cokemen worldwide that Coca-Cola was *wieder da* in Germany, editor Duke Ludwig observed:

> There are millions of people on this earth. We differ in looks, in language, in creed and wealth. Yet basically we are the same . . . It is the job of political and business leaders alike to provide opportunity for the industrious – to see to it that, with proper safeguards for the rights of all men, the man who works hardest and longest can enjoy the fruits of his labors. In short, we believe that the way to lasting peace, to a better, stronger world is to rebuild man's self-respect, his confidence that he can carve out his fortune with his own hands and his own brains.[73]

Two years later, Ludwig's successor at *Coca-Cola Overseas* reiterated, "Yes, we of 'Coca-Cola' may well be proud that ours is a business which helps so many others; one that builds up rather than tears down; one that brings happiness and friendship to all who bottle it – sell it and to all who drink it."[74]

During the 1950s "building up" Germany had significant ramifications. Most of Europe after the Second World War was in rubble and needed to be rebuilt, but the situation in Germany was unique. Germans were responsible for the war, and guilty of unprecedented crimes against humanity. As noted earlier, Germany needed not only reconstruction, it needed redemption. Nonetheless, the onset of the Cold War chill left the ambitious Allied plans for reforming German society unfinished. "By 1951," observed Thomas Schwartz, "the Americans had abandoned their search for justice against the Nazis." Without Allied pressure to confront the Nazi legacy, Germans appeared quick to forget the past and instead focus on building the future. "Although the United States could not force the Germans to come to a 'reckoning with the past,'" Schwartz continued, "American actions did contribute to Germany's national amnesia about Nazi war crimes."[75] Encouraging both Germans and Americans to overlook the troublesome past was the famous German work ethic. As one Coke T.O. remarked, "I couldn't teach myself to hate the Germans – they were so *industrious*."[76]

This hard work, and the *Wirtschaftswunder* it produced, facilitated the Federal Republic's claim of full political sovereignty in the Western community of nations. As Ralf Dahrendorf asserted in his classic study of *Society and Democracy in Germany*, "the qualitative economic miracle has furnished West German society with structures that are capable of supporting the constitution of liberty."[77] Coca-Cola GmbH was a conspicuous mainstay in this reconstruction. In the December 1951 *Coca-Cola Overseas,* Max Keith explained to fellow Cokemen worldwide, "Everywhere new life is growing out of the ruins and destruction of the war. Western Germany is rebuilding with tremendous efforts that which was destroyed, and the activity of 'Coca-Cola' bottlers is a part of this vast reconstruction and building program."[78] A later article, entitled "How Germany Rebuilt," continued, "It was seriously doubted whether there was any chance to rebuild some German cities such as Cologne and Dortmund . . . The many new factory buildings where 'Coca-Cola' is bottled . . . have helped in the rebuilding effort."[79] Speaking before the 1954 Coca-Cola GmbH convention, Keith made the connection most explicit: "the consumer goods industries of which 'Coca-Cola' is a part, with their rapid exchange of goods and money set the living standards and thereby the welfare of a nation."[80]

Beyond its economic ramifications, the reestablishment of Coca-Cola's presence in Germany helped demonstrate the Federal Republic's democratization and its rejection of war and fascism. After all, as an icon of America in the context of the Cold War, Coke signified "democracy." A placard at the international bottlers convention in 1948 had argued, "When we think of Nazis we think of the Swastika, when we think of the Japs we think of the Rising Sun (that set), and when we think of Communists we think of the Iron Curtain, BUT when THEY think of democracy they think of Coca-Cola."[81] One of the many *Coca-Cola Overseas* articles that made similar connections observed:

> Elections, of course, are not confined to the approval or disapproval of the candidates for public office, the political questions of the times. Businessmen, large and small, realize every day is election day, every business is a polling place . . . Wherever people gather to enjoy Coca-Cola, they are balloting with the coin of the realm for the delicious and refreshing, the pure and wholesome pleasure of the drink.[82]

In Germany, where during the 1930s the annual sales competitions between *Konzessionäre* had been framed with hunting or sports motives, and during the occupation Fanta promotions were illustrated with bricks, trowels, and construction workers, in 1950 the first postwar Coca-Cola GmbH sales competition was set up as an "election campaign." Getting into the "parliament of the successful" depended on "whether the thirsty (*erfrischungsbedürftige*) consumer . . . gives you his vote by buying a bottle of Coca-Cola."[83] While so co-opting the language of democracy to promote sales, the German Coca-Cola company also donated soft drinks to forums that fostered actual democratic discourse. "During discussion breaks," whether at the Essen International Club or the "Working-group for Political Questions" at Mainz University, "the chairman regularly suggested a trusted refreshing Pause with Coca-Cola."[84] "If in all our business activities we remain conscious of our community responsibilities," one German Coke executive reminded his colleagues in the early 1950s, "we can be sure that we are making a real contribution to the establishment of a new organic ordering of society."[85]

Such social consciousness manifested, Keith insisted, "the leitmotiv of our entire philosophy and business." In 1951 he greeted the foreign guests at Coca-Cola GmbH's annual convention, "through your visit, our slogan, 'Coca-Cola – a Symbol of Friendship in all the world' is granted visible expression."[86] Three years later, Franz Blücher, the Federal Republic's Vice-Chancellor, attended Coca-Cola GmbH's 25th-anniversary celebration. After taking the opportunity to assure the visiting members of Coke's international family that "Germany does not think of expansion at any other country's expense, the German people has had its lesson," Blücher gave his official endorsement to Coke's soft-drink diplomacy. "A new method of a successful economic co-operation between two counties, the United States and our own country, has been introduced by the 'Coca-Cola' Company. It appears to me to be one of the great examples worth to be followed." [*sic*][87] As Keith claimed, "We not only build attractive plants in Germany, but also we are helping those associated in business with us to become better citizens of the community in which they live."[88]

Thus, Coca-Cola and its Gospel of Refreshment helped make politically significant the hard work spent rebuilding the German Coca-Cola bottling network. Such examples of economic success also helped redefine how Germans saw themselves. Historian Michael Ermarth has argued:

> From its postwar ethos of hard work toward "success" in ways other than big-power politics, West Germany gained satisfaction and respect, as well as solace and refuge from a traumatic past ridden with catastrophic failures in power politics. West German "economism," . . . was not directed exclusively toward impressing the East or the West, indeed not primarily outward at all, but in a sense inward and also backward. A steady focus on the proximate practical future to be earned by individual effort offered Germans much relief and some reprieve from past ideological phantasms of grand destiny and their postwar pariah status – not only in the eyes of foreigners but in their own eyes.[89]

Ultimately, Coca-Cola's ability to "refresh" Germany transcended even the *Wirtschaftswunder* and the rehabilitation of West Germany's international image. As a product intended for mass consumption, Coca-Cola's Gospel of Refreshment could save individual Germans.

Mach mal Pause: The Call to be Born Again

Advertising-driven consumer capitalism is predicated on the idea that consumers will define themselves by the products they purchase. A recent article in the *International Journal of Advertising* noted that, "through the ever-growing plurality of consumer choice the individual is offered resources which may be used to achieve 'an ego-ideal which commands the respect of others and inspires self-love'."[90] As a successful international "power brand," Coca-Cola has mastered a "specialised discipline concerned with managing and maintaining a mix of factors, both tangible and intangible, that attract consumer loyalty."[91] Willi Bongard, a pioneer in the study of postwar German consumer culture, observed, "What's exceptional is the myth! Only that can explain the atrocious devotion to Coca-Cola . . . to such fetishized brand-named products one has an irrational, emotional relationship. The utility value is fully superseded by representative qualities. It is the image that the people consume, not the product."[92] This symbolic aspect of consumerism had a special significance for the new "consumer subjects" of the *Wirtschaftswunder*. "While previously and for so long consumption practices had involved making much out of little, now they meant learning to construct individuality out of the mass," observed the German historian Michael Wildt.[93]

Coca-Cola allowed individual Germans to "internalize," psychologically as well as physically, a symbol of postwar recovery and an icon of human fellowship. This, more than Coke's "American" qualities, underlay the soft drink's phenomenal postwar success. In fact, in the late 1950s per-capita Coca-Cola consumption in the former American zone of occupation (Bavaria and Hesse) was slightly lower than the West German average.[94] Moreover, whereas a 1958 statistic found that 45 percent of West Germans still found the American way of life "*Nicht so gut*" ("Not so good"), a survey three years earlier had suggested that more than 90 percent of them had tried Coca-Cola – and of these Coke consumers 44 percent drank it "often" and only 12 percent "seldom."[95] As one German explained in a recent oral history project, "Coca-Cola was one of the most sought after goods [during the *Wirtschaftswunder*]. Today, Coca-Cola is a company, in those days it was a *Weltanschauung*."[96]

That "worldview" was informed by a Gospel of Refreshment that offered more than economic recovery and political rehabilitation. From years of exposure to Coca-Cola advertising, Germans knew that Coke also promised something akin to metaphysical redemption, the vague and elusive transcendence of "*Erfrischung*." While at the national level the Coke Gospel's ability to facilitate socio-political rehabilitation was linked to Coca-Cola GmbH's successful economic recovery, on the more personal and cultural level Coca-Cola's iconic status invigorated the quest for a redeemed German national identity. This second dimension of Coca-Cola's "refreshment" was highlighted by the phenomenal popularity of Coca-Cola

GmbH's most famous advertising slogan, "*Mach mal Pause*" (roughly, "Take a break once in a while"). As Willi Bongard was already asserting in the 1960s, "The story of the rise and fall of this slogan mirrors the history of its time."[97]

Michael Wildt noted in his book on the origin of Germany's consumer society, "If there is one compact phrase that more-or-less contains the essence of the reordered and changing experience of work, consumption, and leisure during the 1950s, it is surely this slogan: *Mach mal Pause, Trink Coca-Cola.*"[98] (Figure 5.3) "Around the year 1955," Bongard observed, "the slogan was, as they say, in the air." Like an earlier famous aphorism, Karl Marx's "Workers of the world unite," the Coke advertisement "captured the spirit of its time." Moreover, continued the German cultural critic, "In one aspect '*Mach mal Pause*' was superior to the battle-cry of the proletariat: the [Coke] slogan caught on much faster, gaining popular currency considerably quicker."[99] "It was picked up immediately," recalled Hubert Strauf, Germany's "advertising pope" who coined the slogan, "It was simply catchy, it quickly transcended Coca-Cola and became as it were an autonomous sign of the times. Even to intellectuals, who normally reject advertisements as

Figure 5.3 *From Peter Zec,* Mythos aus der Flasche. Coca-Cola Culture im 20. Jahrhundert *(Essen: Design Zentrum Nordrhein Westfalen, 1994), p. 40.*

manipulation."[100] Acknowledged by scholars as the "absolute highpoint" of Coca-Cola's German marketing,[101] *Mach mal Pause* may well be "the best-known German ad slogan of the postwar years." In 1979, looking back on fifty years in Germany, Coca-Cola GmbH reflected, "That friendly invitation fitted exactly into those days when untiring work led to that rebuilding effort which all over the world became known as 'the German economic miracle'."[102]

Strauf derived *Mach mal Pause* from "The Pause that Refreshes," the classic American slogan that was first used in a *Saturday Evening Post* Coke advertisement in 1929, the same year that the soft drink was introduced in Germany. One of many familiar phrases coined by Coca-Cola's legendary ad-man Archie Lee, the slogan became the leitmotiv of one of the most successful advertising campaigns in history.[103] During the 1930s the German Coke subsidiary mimicked the American standard with a variety of phrases (e.g. "*Erfrischungspause*," "*Erfrisch Dich*," and, "*Das erfrischende Pause*") that sought to emphasize the soft drink's fundamental quality as "*köstlich -- erfrischend*" ("Delicious and Refreshing," Coca-Cola's original slogan from 1886). This trend continued during the Second World War with Coca-Cola GmbH's introduction of Fanta, which was marketed with the tagline, "*Das erfrischende Getränk*" ("The refreshing drink"). Following the reintroduction of The Real Thing in 1949, Coke's German advertising text returned to these familiar fundamentals. "No special advertising was necessary," noted Rudolf Brandes, Coca-Cola GmbH's advertising director. "We said simply, '*Coca-Cola ist wieder da*' and that was enough to get the people to come running." Preoccupied with rebuilding its production capacity and distribution network, the German Coke subsidiary had no need to generate more consumer demand. "But one day we could again obtain the desired amount of sugar and other ingredients for the Coca-Cola concentrate," remembered Brandes. "Once again, the word of the day was, turnover, turnover, turnover! That again placed a real demand on advertising."[104]

Max Keith once claimed that the *Mach mal Pause* campaign was a product of "exhaustive study, careful market analysis, and a great wealth of ideas." [105] Hubert Strauf told a different story. "For two years I tried unsuccessfully to sell the slogan to the Coca-Cola people," he reminisced. "There are these high-paid attorneys in Atlanta, and also here in Essen, they turned it down at the time. First because it was an imperative and second because it was such a colloquial phrase" [from the Ruhr region's working-class milieu.][106] Unlike in the United States, where colorful slang was already common in ad copy, "solemn, refined language was still considered the epitome of good advertising style" in postwar Germany.[107] Nonetheless, Strauf helped "Americanize" Germany's public sphere with a stream of famous slogans, including "*Pril entspannt das Wasser*" ("Pril dish-soap relaxes water") and the Christian Democrats' famous campaign slogan from 1957, "*Keine Experimente!*" ("No experiments!")

Although he had been affiliated with Coca-Cola GmbH since its start in 1929, Strauf had to sneak *Mach mal Pause* into the company's marketing portfolio. As he recalled the occasion, "one day [in 1954] Dr. Brandes came to me and said, 'We need a little advertising leaflet right away." The company had been granted the concession to supply the rest areas on the Cologne to Frankfurt Autobahn. "I thought about it a little, and then I remembered what I had on reserve." *Mach mal Pause* became the title of a rest-area map-brochure that suggested drivers "take a break" every two hours. "The lawyers didn't even notice that I set them up to eat crow," recounted Strauf. "That's a hit! That's certainly a hit," Keith reportedly exclaimed when he saw the Autobahn leaflet. He was right. For over a decade the slogan fueled Coca-Cola's skyrocketing German sales figures.

Advertising and communications scholars have sought to explain the slogan's phenomenal success. Dirk Schindelbeck, Rainer Gries, and Volker Ilgen at the Cultural and Advertising History Archive in Freiburg (KWAF), suggested that the use of the word "*mal*" (suggesting a brief inconsequential occurrence) helped mitigate both the slogan's imperative character and the subsequent stigma of indulgence. "The slogan's remarkable effectiveness was due to its considerate accommodation to the dominant 1950s mentality. It is the performed work itself that quasi calls for the *Pause*, not any inappropriate willful impertinence on the part of the individual that could be construed as contrary to the spirit of responsible workers' camaraderie."[108] One American with insight into the German character concurred, "They weren't asking to make a huge departure from their legendary work ethic (i.e. the only German virtue left to them after the horrible war)."[109] Other analysts have highlighted the phrase's alliteration.[110] On a similar note, Willi Bongard drew attention to the campaign's radio and television ads. Accompanying the slogan was a "four syllable . . . catchy acoustic 'poster'" created by Strauf's colleague from Berlin radio, Willi Köhler: "The melody was not simply composed, but instead so to speak picked up from the streets. It echoed familiar calls from street venders, '*hei-ße Würst-chen*' or '*Il-lu-strier-te*'" ("hot sausages" or "newspapers").[111]

In 1955 Köhler's distinctive four-tone *Pfiff* (whistle) began to sound on West German radios. Like a factory whistle or school bell, it announced that it was time to *Mach mal Pause*. The advertising jingles that followed suggested it be a Pause that Refreshes. For example,

> There once was a man in a hurry
> He knew neither peace nor rest,
> His wife told him, my dear husband,
> Take a break, now and then
> The husband carefully considered
> These words his wife had said.

Now he is no longer looking to break records
But rather, he now and again recalls the call to Pause:
Take a Break! Coca-Cola

He who doesn't take a break,
And only hurries on,
He won't get too far,
Take a Break, Take a Break,
Give yourself some time for a change!

Drink Coca-Cola.[112]

This advice, however "common" the original slogan, was soon echoed in pronouncements by Germany's scholarly elite. According to news reports in the mid-1950s, the Federal Republic's "miraculous" economic recovery was producing unwelcome side-effects, workaholism and stress, the so-called "managerial disease." A director from the Max-Planck Institute, Dr. Günther Lehmann, recommended "the introduction of organized short-breaks, for example five minutes for every fifty-five minutes of work." This, he claimed, would lead to greater productivity. "Therefore true *Pausen* were not a waste of time."[113] Coca-Cola GmbH capitalized on this apparent new social problem to further promote its soft drink. Not only did the company's press department induce countless journalists who covered the story to consider Strauf's advertising slogan a clever headline, Coke's regional *Konzessionäre* persuaded factories and offices across the country to install one of Coca-Cola's new vending machines. By the end of the decade, no respectable cafeteria was complete without one of these "silent salesmen" and its embossed reminder, "*Mach mal Pause, trink Coca-Cola und immer heiter weiter*" ("Take a break, drink Coca-Cola and go happily on your way.")

However, by the early 1960s the *Mach mal Pause* campaign had run its course. West Germans were able to feel more secure and confident, even self-satisfied. The erection of the Berlin Wall in August 1961 unexpectedly led to a quieting of Cold War tensions, at least over Germany. Meanwhile, domestically, the Federal Republic's democratic trappings were becoming as comfortable as the Levi's that were popular with the "baby boom" generation that was moving through the education system. Politically, the Social Democrats had formally jettisoned their rhetoric of Marxist revolution at Bad Godesberg in 1959, and the ruling coalition of Christian Democrats and Liberals was poised to outgrow the autocratic "chancellor democracy" under which the West German state had come of age. Although the *Spiegel* affair would rock the West German establishment at the end of 1962, the ultimate vindication of the free press demonstrated the vigor of the new state's democratic values. Economically, the establishment of full employment in 1960 engendered higher wages and a more demanding work force. In this climate it is not surprising that when showing Max Keith around one of his factories the managing director of Volkswagen, Heinrich Nordhoff, pointed to the batteries of Coke machines and complained, "Look, everywhere it says, '*Mach mal Pause*.' What do you think that does to the work-ethic?" Back in Essen, Keith called on the company's famous ad man, "Strauf, get rid of '*Mach mal Pause*.' We need something new, think of something."[114] Coca-Cola GmbH's famous slogan, Bongard later quipped, "no longer made sense in a time when it was the Pause that was interrupted by work."[115]

Contextualized with the Gospel of Refreshment, more can be read out of the rise and fall of *Mach mal Pause* than the assertion that hard-working Germans were anxious to enjoy the spoils of their *Wirtschaftswunder*. At the same time that the *Mach mal Pause* campaign first began suggesting that Germans deserved a break, the Federal Republic was beginning to call men back into uniform. Under the terms of treaties negotiated between Adenauer and the Western Allies during the autumn of 1954, the formal occupation of West Germany ended and the Federal Republic became a fully sovereign state. Nonetheless, as one diplomatic historian, Frank Ninkovich, noted, "the Federal Republic's status was not transformed overnight by signatures on pieces of paper."[116] Although they had regained their place in the (armed) fellowship of nations, Germany's *Vergangenheitsbewältigung*, or "mastering" of the Nazi past, remained an ongoing endeavor.

It is here, however, that the Gospel of Refreshment makes sense of Coca-Cola's phenomenal popularity in Germany during the 1950s. In her provocative history of postwar German consumerism, historian Erica Carter summarized: "the economy is seen to have become at this point a major focus of national pride among West Germans . . . a fantasy object for collective identification." In this redefinition of German identity, "consumerism [became] the source of core values for the nation."[117] Ninkovich concurred, "A fetishism of commodities was understandable for a generation that had suffered through postwar deprivation." Nonetheless, the nascent West German society was, in his words, "devoid of any positive spiritual appeal, offering in place of ideals a shallow commitment to naked material values."[118] Coca-Cola, however, was more than just another materialist *Wirtschaftswunder* consumer product. Informed by the Gospel of Refreshment, Coke complemented hollow economic success and questionable political rehabilitation with the effervescence of metaphysical "refreshment."

In this light, the unprecedented postwar sales figures of Coca-Cola GmbH manifested a West German quest for new spiritual values, for a new flavor of German identity. Slurring nostalgia for Coke's German roots with the soft drink's new accent on American-style freedom and international fellowship, Germans "creolized" Coca-Cola and its Gospel of Refreshment in order to recreate themselves as "consumer-democrats" in the new West-orientated German state. To borrow Rob Kroes' creolization metaphor, Germans were, "not unlike beach-combers . . . scavenging along the tide line of [the Cokempire], appropriating its flotsam and jetsam. They [felt] free to rearrange the order and meaning of what they collect[ed] . . . Syntax, semantics, and grammar become jumbled. At the same time, however, in their selective appropriation [they created] their own environment, doing so under their own auspices."[119] "A key element of nation building," noted Carter, "was the elaboration of specifically West German modes and forms of popular consumption."[120]

While the idea of becoming "Americanized" would remain problematic, post-war West Germans embraced being "Coca-Colonized." By adapting a hybrid cultural image of Coca-Cola to their own immediate needs, they were glad to be Born Again in the Gospel of Refreshment. In the postmodern church that consumer capitalism has made the market place, the *Mach mal Pause* whistle reminded them that with a small donation to Coca-Cola GmbH they could self-administer another dose of "refreshing" redemption. In the globalized world of post-national identity, where postindustrial corporations convey humanity from the materialist past into a semiotic future, millions of thirsty West Germans seeking "refreshment" make historical sense.

Notes

1. "'Fascination Coca-Cola': Insight into a Legend," Coca-Cola GmbH Press Release, Essen/Bonn, May 16, 2002. The exhibition ran from June 13 to August 4.

2. "Nearly 50,000 visitors to exhibition in Bonn," Coca-Cola GmbH Press Release, Essen/Bonn, August 5, 2002.

3. Noted by Stefan Domke, "Das erfolgreichste Erfrischungsgetränk ist reif fürs Museum," WDR.de Panorama, June 12, 2002. For scholarly reviews of the Coca-Cola Company's flagship venture into museum culture, the World of Coke museum in Atlanta, Georgia, see Neil Harris, "The World of Coke," *Journal of American History*, 82, June 1995, pp. 154–8, and Ted Friedman, "The World of *The World of Coke*," *Communication Research*, 19, October 1992, pp. 642–62. For analysis of such commercialization of public history, see Mike Wallace, *Mickey Mouse History and Other Essays on American History* (Philadelphia: Temple University Press, 1996).

4. Haus der Geschichte der Bundesrepublik Deutschland (Hg.), *Erlebnis Geschichte: Deutschland vom Zweiten Weltkrieg bis Heute*. 2nd edn (Bonn: Gustav Lübbe, 2000), p. 132.

5. "Crowd-Puller fascinates over 1000 visitors daily," Coca-Cola GmbH Press Release, Essen/Bonn, July 15, 2002.

6. These examples of German "Cokelore" were listed in a review of the Haus der Geschichte exhibit. See Anja Rützel, "Wer spuckt da in die Brause?," *Stuttgarter Zeitung*, June 15, 2002 (URL: http://www.stuttgarter-nachrichten.de/stn/page/detail.php/192461/stn_artikel_bildlinks_druck).

For scholarly discussions of similar folklore, see Paul Smith, "Contemporary Legends and Popular Culture: "It's the Real Thing," *Contemporary Legend*, 1, 1991, pp. 123–52, and Gary Alan Fine, "Cokelore and Coke Law: Urban Belief Tales and the Problem of Multiple Origins," *Journal of American Folklore*, 92, 1979, pp. 477–82.

7. This legitimate Cokelore can be found in most popular histories of Coca-Cola. See Chris H. Beyer, *Coca-Cola Girls: An Advertising History* (Portland: Collectors, 2000); Mark Pendergrast, *For God, Country and Coca-Cola: The Definitive History of the Great American Soft Drink and the Company that Makes It*, 2nd edn (New York: Basic, 2000); Frederick Allen, *Secret Formula: How Brilliant Marketing and Relentless Salesmanship Made Coca-Cola the Best-Known Product in the World* (New York: HarperBusiness, 1994); and Pat Watters, *Coca-Cola: An Illustrated History* (Garden City, NY: Doubleday, 1978). In German, see the 1995 translations of Pendergrast and Allen, as well as Botho G. Wagner, *Coca-Cola Collectibles: Vom Werbeartikel zum begehrten Sammlerobject* (Munich: Wilhelm Heyne, 1998); Thomas Jeier and Hans-Georg Fischer, *Das Coca-Cola Kultbuch: 100 Jahre Coke* (Munich: Wilhelm Heyne, 1986); and Ulf Biedermann, *Ein amerikanischer Traum. Coca-Cola: Die Unglaubliche Geschichte eines 100 jährigen Erfolges* (Hamburg: Rasch und Röhring, 1985).

8. As claimed in an advertising slogan from 1943. Coca-Cola's Second World War transformation has been highlighted by Mark Weiner, "Consumer Culture and Participatory Democracy: The Story of Coca-Cola during World War II," *Food and Foodways*, 6(2), 1996, pp. 109–29, and V. Dennis Wrynn, *Coke Goes to War* (Missoula: Pictoral Histories, 1996).

9. J.F. Curtis, "The Overseas Story," *Coca-Cola Overseas*, June 1948, p. 5.

10. "The Sun never sets on Cacoola," *Time,* May 15, 1950, p. 28.

11. Pendergrast, *For God, Country and Coca-Cola*, p. 38.

12. "Italian Invasion," *Time*, August 22, 1949, p. 71.

13. Reproduced in the *Schweizer Brauerei-Rundschau*, 60, December 1949, p. 208.

14. Robert Escarpit, "Mourir pour le Coca-Cola," *Le Monde*, March 29, 1950, p. 1.

15. Alexander Abusch, "Die geistige Coca-Kolonisierung – und der Frieden," *Sonntag: Wochenzeitung für Kultur, Politik und Unterhaltung*, January 22, 1950, p. 2.

16. "The Pause That Arouses," *Time*, March 13, 1950, p. 30.

17. Cited in Richard Kuisel, *Seducing the French: The Dilemma of Americanization* (Berkeley: University of California Press, 1993), p. 64. Kuisel devoted a chapter to the French Coca-Colonization controversy.

18. "La Société Coca-Cola pourra-t-elle librement développer ses ventes en France," *Le Monde,* December 30, 1949, p. 8, cited by Kuisel, *Seducing the French*, p. 65.

19. Robert Escarpit, "Coca-colonisation," *Le Monde,* November 23, 1949, p. 1. See also "Colonization by Coke," *Newsweek*, December 12, 1949, p. 31.

20. For a colorful account of the infamous "German thirst" for alcohol, see Regina Hübner and Manfred Hübner, *Der deutsche Durst: Illustriere Kultur- und Sozialgeschichte* (Leipzig: Edition Leipzig, 1994).

21. Technically the second French "anti-Coca-Cola bill" only granted the Ministry of Public Health authority to draw up new regulations for harmful non-alcoholic beverages. Nonetheless, not until December 1953 was Coca-Cola free of the law's entanglements.

22. The Bundestag's Coca-Cola consumption was mentioned during debate on the "taxation of stimulating drinks," *Deutscher Bundestag, Verhandlungen: Stenographische Berichte, 1. Wahlperiode, 1949–1953* (86 Sitzung, Bonn, September 15, 1950), p. 3233.

23. "Sonderbericht aus Bonn. Fanta im Bundeshaus," *Coca-Cola Nachrichten*, November 1949, p. 23.

24. Dr. Decker, transcribed in *Verhandlungen* (86 Sitzung, September 15, 1950), pp. 3236–7.

25. Domke, "erfolgreichste Erfrischungsgetränk," WDR.de Panorama, June 12, 2002.

26. Mary Nolan, "America in the German Imagination," in Heide Fehrenbach and Uta G. Poiger, eds., *Transactions, Transgressions, Transformations: American Culture in Western Europe and Japan* (New York: Berghahn, 2000), pp. 3–25, p. 18.

27. "Growth Company Business from 1929 to 1937," p. 423, and "German Coca-Cola Business (1938)," p. 425, in Roy D. Stubbs, ed., *Germany: A Compilation for The Coca-Cola Company* (1945), a binder held at the The Coca-Cola Company Archives in Atlanta.

28. See for example the newspaper clipping of a "public retraction of a slanderous assertion from the year 1936," contained in the 1993 *Diplomarbeit* of Olaf Krietemeyer, "Die Marketingpolitik bei der Einführung von Coca-Cola auf dem Deutschen Markt," Universität Regensburg, Wirtschaftswissenschaftliche Fakultät, p. 29.

29. *10 Jahre Aufbau: Sonderausgabe der Coca-Cola Nachrichten* (Essen: Coca-Cola GmbH, 1939).

30. H.B. Nicholson, *"Host to Thirsty Main Street"* (New York: Newcomen Society in North America, 1953), p. 18.

31. The author examines this "Germanization" of Coca-Cola in his forthcoming dissertation for Georgetown University, "Coca-Colonization, 'Refreshing' Americanization, or Nazi *Volksgetränk*? The History of Coca-Cola in Germany, 1929–1961." Also, Coca-Cola's role in German history has been addressed briefly by Ralph Willett, *The Americanization of Germany, 1945–1949* (New York: Routledge, 1989), pp. 99–106. The cow metaphor can be found in "'Coca-Cola' – Vertrauen aus Dienst und Verantwortung," an article from the *Industriekurier* republished in *Coca-Cola Nachrichten*, Nr. 11/12, 1962, pp. 4–7.

32. Coca-Cola advertisements with these texts can be found in such Third Reich periodicals as the *Berliner Illustriete Zeitung, Illustrierter Beobachter,* and the *Deutsche Illustrierten Zeitung*, as well as the German Army magazine, *Die Wehrmacht*, and the infamous anti-Semitic *Stürmer*. For a controversial analysis suggesting that Coca-Cola helped provide a state-free sphere of *Resistenz* against the Nazis, see Hans Dieter Schäfer, *Das gespaltene Bewußtsein: Deutsche Kultur und Lebenswirklichkeit, 1933–1945* (Munich: Carl Hanser Verlag, 1981). For a broader analysis of the Third Reich's perception of America, see Philipp Gassert, *Amerika im Dritten Reich: Ideologie, Propaganda und Volksmeinung, 1933–1945* (Stuttgart: Franz Steiner Verlag, 1997). For more on advertising in Nazi Germany, see Uwe Westphal, *Werbung im Dritten Reich* (Berlin: Transit, 1989).

33. Max Keith, "An alle unsere Konzessionäre und Mitarbeiter!," *Coca-Cola Nachrichten*, September 15, 1939.

34. For an overview of how the Nazis handled American companies, see Stephan H. Lindner, *Der Reichskommissariat für die Behandlung feindlichen Vermögens im Zweiten Weltkrieg* (Stuttgart: Franz Steiner Verlag, 1991).

35. Fanta's marketing strategy was presented in the company publications, "Wir werben für Fanta" (August 1940) and "Mal was Anderes!" (January 1942).

36. "History of Coca-Cola in Germany: Interview with Max Keith – June 29/30, 1966," a 23-page typed transcript of an interview with Hunter Bell, The Coca-Cola Company's in-house historian, available at the Coca-Cola Company Archives. During the 1970s the interview was translated and published as a pamphlet, *Wie war das damals als Sie anfingen . . . Ein Interview mit Max Keith* (Essen: Coca-Cola GmbH).

37. Ibid. Wartime sales figures calculated from records from the Reichskommissar für die Behandlung feindlichen Vermögens held at the Bundesarchiv in Berlin, Bestand R87/1627, specifically a letter from Max Keith to Reichskommissar Hagemann, dated October 7, 1944 (721/554/66, pp. 249–250), and the 28-page report on Coca-Cola GmbH prepared by Dr. Ohrtmann, dated February 16, 1946 (721/554/68, pp. 254–81).

38. Pendergrast, *God, Country and Coca-Cola*, p. 224.

39. Keith speech, November 27, 1963, included in the dual-language publication, *Max Keith: 30 Jahre mit Coca-Cola* (Essen: Coca-Cola GmbH, *c*. 1963).

40. Coke's alias "The Real Thing" was first used in American ads in 1942.

41. Henry Morgenthau, Jr., *Germany is our Problem* (New York: Harper & Brothers, 1943), inside front cover.

42. Cited in Diane Shaver Clemens, *Yalta* (New York: Oxford University Press, 1970), p. 296.

43. JCS 1067 is excerpted in Jean Edward Smith, *Lucius D. Clay: An American Life* (New York: Henry Holt, 1990), pp. 688–689.

44. Ansel Morrison, "Stuttgart, Germany – August 21 1945," *T.O. Digest*, 1(8), *c*. November 1945, p. 6.

45. "Weltmacht Coca-Cola," *Der Spiegel*, August 18, 1965, p. 44.

46. Keith Norton, "Home Away from Home: A Report from the American Zone of Occupation in Germany," *Coca-Cola Overseas*, April 1949, p. 21.

47. Reinhold Wagnleitner, *Coca-Colonization and the Cold War: The Cultural Mission of the United States in Austria after the Second World War* (Chapel Hill: University of North Carolina Press, 1994), p. 227. Despite his book's title, Wagnleitner has little to say about Coca-Cola. Instead, for Coke's history in Austria, see Irene Bandhauer-Schöffmann, "Die Amerikanisierung des Geschmacks: Coca-Cola in Österreich," *Historicum*, Fall 1995, pp. 22–8.

48. *Bilanz der Marke* (Essen: Die Werbe GmbH, 1949), cited by Rudolf Seyffert, *Werbelehre: Theorie und Praxis der Werbung*. Vol. 2 (Stuttgart: C.E. Poeschel, 1966), p. 555, and Willi Bongard, *Fetische des Konsums: Portraits klassischer Markenartikel* (Hamburg: Nannen, 1964), pp. 81–2.

49. Wagner, *Coca-Cola Collectibles*, p. 64.

50. See for example Bernhard Lilienthal, "Wie wir (wieder) Freunde wurden – Anmerkungen zur Berlin-Blockade," *Dollars & Träume*, 10, 1984, pp. 7–29.

51. Thomas Alan Schwartz, *America's Germany: John J. McCloy and the Federal Republic of Germany* (Cambridge MA: Harvard University Press, 1991), p. 308.

52. Memo on the "Freigabe von Coca-Cola-Syrup aus US Armeebestaenden" from the Bipartite Control Office Food, Agriculture and Forestry Group, Frankfurt, dated June 23, 1949, among the "Historical Documents" in "Die Anfangsjahre von Coca-Cola in Deutschland," a binder compiled in 1991 by Christine Rettemeier and Stefan Horn at Coca-Cola GmbH, Essen.

53. Michael Kriegeskorte, *Werbung in Deutschland 1945–1965: Die Nachkriegszeit im Spiegel ihrer Anzeigen* (Cologne: DuMont, 1992), p. 10.

54. Willett, *Americanization*, p. 15.

55. Michael Geyer, "America in Germany: Power and the Pursuit of Americanization," in Frank Trommler and Elliott Shore, eds., *The German-American Encounter: Conflict and Cooperation between Two Cultures, 1800–2000* (New York: Berghahn, 2001), pp. 121–144 here, p. 124. For an example of such sentiments directed against Coca-Cola, see Kurt Lochmüller, "Cola-Getränke: Eine heiter-kritische Betrachtung mit dem ernsten Vorsatz, objectiv zu bleiben," *Mineralwasser-Zeitung*, 4(38), September 19, 1951, pp. 405–6.

56. "Feuchte Stimme Amerikas," *Der Spiegel,* July 13, 1950, pp. 28–30.

57. Coke sales reported in the aforementioned 1966 Keith-Bell interview, "History of Coca-Cola," and Max Keith, "Die Festansprache," *Coca-Cola Nachrichten: Essener Tagen 1956*, Nr. 5/6, 1956, p. 20. German Gross National Product figures from V.R. Berghahn, *Modern Germany: Society, Economy and Politics in the Twentieth Century*, 2nd edn (New York: Cambridge University Press, 1987), p. 202.

58. Michael Wildt, *Am Beginn der "Konsumgesellschaft": Mangelerfahrung, Lebenshaltung, Wohlstandshoffnung in Westdeutschland in der fünfziger Jahren* (Hamburg: Ergebnisse Verlag, 1994), p. 105.

59. The average West German in 1964 consumed about 44 liters of mineral water and other soft drinks, 12 liters of which were contained in the 36 bottles of Coke. Of the DM 2 billion soft-drink industry, Coke's turnover was about DM 600 million. "An der Wasserfront," *Der Spiegel,* August 18, 1965, pp. 40–6.

60. Germany was ranked Coca-Cola's fifth-largest national market in 2001. Coca-Cola GmbH then controlled 14 percent of the domestic soft-drink market and German per capita consumption of Coca-Cola products was 45.7 liters, or 193 eight-ounce servings. See the company's web site, www.coca-cola-gmbh.de, and The Coca-Cola Company's 2001 Annual Report, also available on-line.

61. Richard F. Kuisel, "The French Cinema and Hollywood: A Case Study of Americanization," pp. 208–23, in Fehrenbach and Poiger, *Transactions, Transgressions, Transformations*, p. 208.

62. "Bottlers' Convention in Atlantic City," *Coca-Cola Overseas*, June 1948, p. 10.

63. ". . . A Unique Business," *Coca-Cola Overseas*, December 1952, p. 1.

64. Pendergrast, *God, Country and Coca-Cola*, p. 442.

65. "Intended for everyone overseas, from native truckmen to division managers," Coke's new "aristocrat of house organs" was a "concrete step toward building international peace and understanding through trade channels," reported Victor J. Dallaire, "International House Organ to Build World Understanding Through Trade," *Printers' Ink*, June 25, 1948, p. 30.

66. ". . . first citizens," *Coca-Cola Overseas*, June 1949, p. 1.

67. "... understanding," *Coca-Cola Overseas*, April 1950, p. 1.

68. "... good will," *Coca-Cola Overseas*, December 1948, p. 1.

69. For reproductions of these "Have a 'Coke' = The global high-sign" ads, see Wrynn, *Coke Goes to War*, pp. 51–77, here p. 72.

70. "... an adventure in friendship," *Coca-Cola Overseas,* December 1950, p. 1.

71. Max Keith, "Festansprache," *Coca-Cola Nachrichten: Essener Tagen 1954*, Nr. 5/6, 1954, p. 11. [original italics]

72. "Der Ehrenring war in Berlin," *Coca-Cola Nachrichten,* Nr. 11/12, 1953, pp. 20, 22.

73. "... the dignity of man," Coca-*Cola Overseas*, February 1950, p. 1.

74. "... A Unique Business," *Coca-Cola Overseas,* December 1952, p. 1.

75. Schwartz, *America's Germany*, p. 308.

76. Pendergrast, *God, Country and Coca-Cola*, p. 225.

77. Ralf Dahrendorf, *Society and Democracy in Germany* (New York: Doubleday/ Anchor, 1969; German original, 1965), p. 419.

78. Max Keith, "Coca-Cola Popular Again in Western Germany," *Coca-Cola Overseas*, December 1951, p. 20.

79. Rudolf Brandes, "How Germany Rebuilt," *Coca-Cola Overseas*, June 1955, pp. 16–19, 29.

80. Max Keith, "Opening Address," *Essener Tage 1954: Special English Edition of Coca-Cola Nachrichten*, Nr. 5/6, 1954, p. 18.

81. E.J. Kahn, Jr., *The Big Drink: The Story of Coca-Cola* (New York: Random House, 1950), p. 164. For a more formal elaboration of similar sentiments, see Edward S. Rogers, "Democracy and Trade-Marks," *Coca-Cola Overseas,* June 1948, pp. 7, 22–4.

82. "... concerning elections," *Coca-Cola Overseas,* August 1948, p. 1.

83. "Wettbewerb," *Coca-Cola Nachrichten,* November 1950, pp. 9–10.

84. "'Coca-Cola' im International Club," *Coca-Cola Nachrichten*, Nr. 3/4, 1954, p. 27, and "Nobis, Mainzer Studentenzeitung," *Coca-Cola Nachrichten,* Nr. 1/2, 1954, p. 22.

85. Dr. Ernst Bion, "Das Unternehmen, ein Teil der Gemeinschaft," *Coca-Cola Nachrichten: Essener Tage 1952,* Nr. 3/4/5, 1952, p. 30.

86. Max Keith, "Die Konzeption unseres Geschäftes," *Coca-Cola Nachrichten,* Nr. 4/5, 1951, pp. 5–6.

87. "Addresses by Honorary Guests," *Essener Tage 1954: Anniversary Convention – Special English Edition of Coca-Cola Nachrichten,* Nr. 5/6, 1954, p. 24.

88. "New Plants in Frankfurt and Nürnberg," *Coca-Cola Overseas,* February 1953, p. 14.

89. "Introduction," to Michael Ermarth, ed., *America and the Shaping of German Society, 1945–1955* (Providence: Berg, 1993), p. 14.

90. Richard Elliott and Kritsadarat Wattanasuwan, "Brands as symbolic resources for the construction of identity," *International Journal of Advertising,* 17(2), 1998, p. 131.

91. "Introduction," to Paul Stobart, ed., *Brand Power* (New York: New York University Press, 1994), p. 4. Former Coca-Cola CEO Donald Keough discusses Coke's brand power in the book's first chapter.

92. Helmut Fritz, *Das Evangelium der Erfrischung: Coca-Colas Weltmission* (Reinbek: Rowohlt Taschenbuch, 1985), pp. 114–15.

93. Michael Wildt, "Plurality of Taste: Food and Consumption in West Germany during the 1950s," *History Workshop Journal*, 39, 1995, p. 38.

94. Bongard, *Fetische des Konsums*, p. 82.

95. For the survey on the popularity of "die amerikanische Art und das Wesen des Amerikaners," see Elisabeth Noelle and Erich Peter Neumann, *Jahrbuch der Öffentlichen Meinung, 1958–1964* (Bonn: Verlag für Demoskopie, 1965), p. 549. The figures on German Coke consumption came from a marketing survey of 200 Kassel residents in 1955 that is recounted by Seyffert, *Werbelehre*, pp. 1438–40.

96. Maria Höhn, *GIs and Frauleins: The German-American Encounter in 1950s West Germany* (Chapel Hill: University of North Carolina Press, 2002), p. 79.

97. Bongard, *Fetische des Konsums*, p. 91. For a compilation profiling German advertising slogans, including *Mach mal Pause*, see Wolfgang Hars, *Lexikon der Werbespruche: 500 bekannte deutsche Werbeslogans und ihre Geschichte* (Frankfurt: Eichborn, 1999).

98. Wildt, *Am Beginn der Konsumgesellschaft,* p. 106.

99. Bongard, *Fetische des Konsums*, pp. 80–1.

100. Fritz, *Evangelium der Erfrischung*, pp. 76–7. For more on Strauf , see "Magische Formeln. 'Mach mal Pause' – 'Keine Experimente!': Zeitgeschichte im Werbeslogan," pp. 92–105, in Rainer Gries, Volker Ilgen, and Dirk Schindelbeck, *"Ins Gehirn der Masse kriechen!" Werbung und Mentalitätsgeschichte* (Darmstadt: Wissenschaftliche Buchgesellschaft, 1995); Martin Merkel, *Vorbilder: 12 Kreative, die das Bild der Werbung bestimmt haben* (Munich: Siegmund, 1988), pp. 28–39; Willi Bongard, *Männer machen Märkte: Mythos und Wirklichkeit der Werbung*, which contains much of the same material on Coke contained in *Fetische des Konsums* (Frankfurt: Ullstein, 1963), pp. 161–7; and "Hubert Strauf – 70 Jahre," *Coca-Cola Nachrichten,* Nr. 2/3, 1974, p. 53.

101. Christa Murken-Altrogge, *Coca-Cola Art: Konsum, Kult, Kunst* (Munich: Klinkart und Biermann, 1991), p. 31.

102. Alfons J.W. Hilgers, ed., *Fifty years in Germany* (Essen: Coca-Cola GmbH, 1979), p. 16.

103. *Advertising Age* ranked it the second-best ad campaign and third-best slogan of "The Advertising Century." Also among the top hundred campaigns were "It's the Real Thing" (1970), at place 53, and "Always" (1993) at place 86. Bob Garfield, "The Top 100 Advertising Campaigns," *Advertising Age* 70(13), 1999, pp. 18–41, with Robyn Griggs, "Coca-Cola slogan gives pause," as a sidebar, p. 36. See also, Julian Lewis Watkins, *The 100 Greatest Advertisements: Who Wrote Them and What They Did* (New York: Dover Press, 1949/1959), pp. 138–9.

104. Letter to Herr Schiffmann, 1 May 1986, from the collection of materials on Strauf collected by Dirk Schindelbeck at the Kultur- und Werbegeschichtliche Archiv Freiburg (KWAF).

105. "Ansprache von Max Keith ," *Coca-Cola Nachrichten,* Nr. 3/4, 1955, p. 15.

106. Transcript of an interview conducted by Schindelbeck of the KWAF, December 27–29, 1988.

107. R. Roth quoted by Harm G. Schröter, "Die Amerikanisierung der Werbung in der Bundesrepublik Deutschland," *Jahrbuch für Wirtschaftsgeschichte* (1997), p. 102. See also the articles compiled by Peter Nusser, ed., *Anzeigenwerbung: Ein Reader für Studenten und*

Lehrer der deutschen Sprache und Literatur (Munich: Wilhelm Fink Verlag, 1975), especially Leo Spritzer, "Amerikanische Werbung als Volkskunst," pp. 180–205.

108. Gries, et al., "Magische Formeln," *Ins Gehirn der Masse kriechen*, p. 97.

109. June Tierney, correspondence with the author, October 2, 2002.

110. Werner Betz, "Sprachkritik und Werbesprache," *Mauthner Gesellschaft* (August 25, 2001). URL: http://www.mauthner-gesellschaft.de/mauthner/intro/betz1.html

111. Bongard, *Fetische des Konsums*, p. 82.

112. Fritz, *Evangelium der Erfrischung*, p. 96. The original German:

Es war einmal ein Mann von Hast
Der kannte weder Ruh noch Rast,
Da sprach die Frau, mein lieber Mann,
mach doch mal Pause dann und wann
Der Mann, der hörte sehr genau
Auf diese Worte seiner Frau,
Nun denkt er nicht mehr an Rekord,
Nein, ab und zu ans Pausewort:
Mach mal Pause, Coca-Cola!

Wer nicht rastet,
Wer nur hastet,
Der kommt nicht sehr weit,
Mach mal Pause
Mach mal Pause, Hab mal für Dich selber Zeit!

113. "Mach mal Pause," *Coca-Cola Nachrichten*, Nr. 7/8, 1957, p. 32.

114. Gries, et al., "Magische Formeln," *Ins Gehirn der Masse kriechen*, p. 99.

115. Bongard, *Fetische des Konsums*, p. 91.

116. Frank Ninkovich, *Germany and the United States: The Transformation of the German Question Since 1945*. Updated edn (New York: Twayne, 1995), p. 103.

117. Erica Carter, *How German Is She? Postwar West German Reconstruction and the Consuming Woman* (Ann Arbor: University of Michigan Press, 1997), pp. 21 and 5.

118. Ninkovich, *Germany and the United States*, p. 103.

119. Rob Kroes, *If You've Seen One, You've Seen the Mall: Europeans and American Mass Culture* (Urbana: University of Illinois Press, 1996), p. 164.

120. Carter, *How German Is She?* p. 5.

6

Miracles for Sale: Consumer Displays and Advertising in Postwar West Germany

S. Jonathan Wiesen

Until recently, scholars and laypeople have accepted at face value the concept of the "Economic Miracle."[1] The narrative of the *Wirtschaftswunder* is by now familiar: after years of privation during the Second World War and under Allied occupation, West Germany, fueled by its expanding exports, rose astonishingly from the ashes of defeat to become a model democracy, bolstered by a healthy market economy. The Federal Republic grew into a Western-oriented, anticommunist nation that enjoyed full employment by the 1960s, a strong measure of social equality, and renewed international respect.

There is, to be sure, an overarching truth to this success story. In the 1950s West Germany did indeed experience a rapid recovery, with the help of the Marshall Plan, the Korean War boom, and the ruling Christian Democratic Union's (CDU) pro-market policies. As with many national myths, however, the *Wirtschaftswunder* was not just a slogan that entered effortlessly into the public lexicon during a time of economic resurgence. Instead Germans themselves actively imagined, scripted, and promoted the story of economic revival and the attending ideal of the "social market economy." As recent scholarship has revealed, "selling" the Economic Miracle was a political and ideological project that prepared West Germans for a postwar, Cold War, consumer citizenship.[2] This chapter expands upon this insight about the politics of consumption[3] by analyzing the cultural work of the *Wirtschaftswunder*. It argues that the Economic Miracle was itself a consumer product of sorts – dreamed up, marketed, and acquired by a public hungry for images of personal and national abundance. In particular, it suggests that visual displays of material goods were central to the promotion of the Economic Miracle. Through two media – trade fairs and advertisements – writers, politicians, businessmen, and advertisers disseminated a distinct narrative of West Germany's economic success. Visual displays of material abundance gave the Economic Miracle force during the 1950s and 1960s. Rather than offering a content analysis of specific products and advertisements, this chapter will explore the institutional and ideological underpinnings of postwar consumption. It will argue that these displays had a long history, drawing upon earlier tropes of past economic success and national glory. By displaying their visions of material well-being both at the "traditional" or "German" trade fair and through the more "modern" or "American" form of advertising, citizens of the Federal Republic were able to merge a long-standing philosophy of quality production with a new ethos of mass consumption.[4]

Creating a National Slogan

If one subscribes to a foundational myth of the FRG, the introduction of the Deutschmark in June 1948 marked the beginning of the Economic Miracle, when empty shelves were suddenly stocked with plentiful goods.[5] The economic assistance of the Americans, and the need for raw materials and armaments during the Korean War, solidified the country's economic comeback and inaugurated a new, democratic Germany. During these early years of the FRG, there appeared a spate of books and articles that documented this seemingly magical rebirth of the German economy. Photos of bombed-out cityscapes from 1944 and 1945 were juxtaposed with images of shiny factories and smiling workers, leading the country toward renewed prosperity.[6]

Yet 1948 was not so much the moment when the Miracle took off as the time when the work of *creating* the Miracle began. In the early FRG, political and economic elites carefully recast preexisting language about economic renewal – indeed language about "miracles" that had been present fifteen years earlier when the military-driven Nazi economy rebounded in the 1930s[7] – as a means of distancing the country from the recent past and enlisting the public in the project of national recovery. Even as they drew on this older "miracles" discourse, elites hoped to demonstrate that the former, morally compromised Germany was dead, and a new country was being born, washed clean of the stain of war crimes and capitalism's own complicity in them.[8] Ludwig Erhard bound his notion of a socially relevant economy to the promise of "Prosperity for All," (*Wohlstand für alle*), an idea eventually fleshed out during the CDU's 1957 campaign and Erhard's book bearing the same name.[9] If in 1948 few Germans could boast of true prosperity, the ultimate measure of the Economic Miracle's success would be a realization of this goal. "Prosperity for All" and the Economic Miracle became twin slogans that permeated the political and public culture of Adenauer's Germany.

The omnipresence of the miracle theme during the first decade of the FRG was due in great measure to the publicity efforts of businessmen and politicians.

Industrial organizations and local chambers of industry and commerce distributed to their workers and member firms books bearing titles like *The German Miracle*, which reflected the tone of wonder and self-congratulation that would persist into the 1960s.[10] Business leaders solicited companies for inspiring success stories and colorful pictures that could attest to the remarkable nature of industrial recovery, and the assurance of workers' own future gains as a byproduct.[11] Now familiar wordplays like "Wirtschaftswunderland" (land of the Economic Miracle) and "Wirtschaftswunderkinder" (children of the Economic Miracle) appeared throughout the media, lending the economy an almost mythical quality during the Adenauer years.[12]

The Economic Miracle noticeably preoccupied religious leaders, as theologians and conservative members of the CDU attempted to reconcile West Germany's economic success story with some of the ethical precepts and anti-materialist tenets of Christianity.[13] Hanover's Protestant Bishop and publisher Hanns Lilje used his newspaper the *Sonntagsblatt* as a vehicle in which to weigh the pros and cons of material wealth,[14] while articles in *Priester und Arbeit* (Priests and Labor), reflected on the meaning of the Economic Miracle for the Catholic workers' movement.[15] The Catholic Church and the CDU-sponsored Association for the Furtherance of Social Compromise (otherwise known as *Die Waage* – the Scale) published advertisements in 1952 with the simple motto, "Das Deutsche Wunder." These ads were part of a broader campaign to tie the market economy to the ideals of a "Christian" West.[16] Meanwhile, the Social Democratic Party (SPD), through its official periodicals, tried to understand in more worldly terms the moral and practical implications of this bustling economy for ordinary Germans.[17]

No sooner had the Economic Miracle become a popular phrase than critics began challenging its accuracy and utility from a number of different directions. Leftist mainstays such as *Die Weltbühne* questioned whether this "much quoted word 'Wirtschaftswunder'" masked an essentially shaky economy based on the speculation of "high financiers," rather than on the solid foundation of a true, widespread wealth.[18] Articles and books with titles such as "The German Miracle was No Miracle,"[19] or "Is the Economy a "Miracle?,"[20] or "The Economy without Miracles,"[21] made a different kind of claim by asserting, for example, that miracles could only come from God,[22] and the economic successes of West Germany were due not to some supernatural force but rather to the blood, sweat, and tears of the Germans themselves. In his article, "A Hundred-year Economic Miracle," Kiel economics professor Fritz Baade argued in a different vein that there was nothing new about the German *Wunder*; it was merely a moment in a remarkable process initiated a century earlier, when Germany, though still essentially an agrarian country, was soon to undergo a rapid phase of industrialization.[23] And *Der Monat* admonished its readers to remember that the German Economic Miracle was really a wider European phenomenon.[24]

But even as they were disavowing the miraculous nature of economic recovery and its uniqueness to the Federal Republic, critics were perpetuating the idea that there was something indeed extraordinary about the economic recuperation of the nation, whether its origins were supernatural or earthly. Ironically, the more that Germans debated and questioned the idea of a miracle, the more it took hold as a defining feature of West Germany's self-understanding. And the more the Miracle became the watchword of the era, the more that average Germans demanded evidence that they would benefit from it.

Displaying the Economic Miracle: The Trade Fair

These debates about the meaning of miracles would have been empty without some proof of sustained economic expansion. While the indicators were indeed impressive – from 1950 to 1960, the country's GNP tripled and wages grew 5 percent annually[25] – it was the *display* of industrial and consumer goods that gave life to the idea that the Economic Miracle was both real and, indeed, vital to the survival of capitalism and the personal welfare of German families.[26] Not just in popular booklets, but also in visual media, West Germans received the message that if they worked hard enough, they would simultaneously satisfy material desires and strike a blow to the communist enemy. Elites had to make the case that the Economic Miracle was not just about increased exports, business profits, and favorable spreadsheets. It would need to have a profoundly populist component, bringing together the business executive and the "man on the street."

A brief look at an analogous American example illuminates the centrality of visual display during periods of economic upheaval and transition. In his study of World's Fairs and international exhibitions, Robert W. Rydell has demonstrated how, during the height of the Great Depression in the United States, Americans came out in droves to visit the 1933–1934 Chicago Century of Progress Exhibition, as well as later expositions throughout the 1930s. According to Rydell, it was during times of crisis, not prosperity, that fairs "were designed to restore faith in the vitality of the nation's economic and political system," and imbue political, economic, and cultural elites with the power "to lead the country out of the depression to a new . . . promised land of material abundance."[27]

If the Great Depression sparked the consumerist fantasies of Americans during a period of privation, an even more dramatic process was played out in post Second World War Germany. At a time when the country was still reeling from wartime devastation, the loss of family members, and the ethical and judicial legacy of Nazi crimes, the marketing of the Economic Miracle became, to borrow Rydell's words, "an exercise in cultural and ideological repair."[28] Even before they were able to experience prosperity on an individual and familial level, West Germans flocked to trade fairs and industrial exhibitions to get a glimpse of the consumer products they hoped to someday possess and that in the meantime would serve as proof of national economic renewal.

Significantly, the trade fair was part of a long and proud German tradition, from the 600-year-old *Messe* in Leipzig to the varied celebrations of national strength, German ingenuity, and dutiful labor during the Hitler years.[29] Relatively soon after the Second World War, cities like Hanover began to compete with Leipzig, now lying in the Soviet Zone, for symbolic dominance in the still weakened consumer and manufacturing sectors.[30] Much of these early postwar exhibitions centered less on consumer goods than on industrial machinery, which served as symbols of West Germany's rapid recovery and its superiority over the Soviet economic model. These Cold War aims remained a consistent element of the trade fairs throughout the 1950s and 1960s.[31] One of the first major exhibits of West German products served a specifically anticommunist, pro-Western purpose. In the spring of 1949, the Allied Military Government in West Germany, in cooperation with the Joint Export-Import Administration, sponsored an exhibition of West German industrial products at the Museum of Science and Industry in New York City. The goal was to shore up American support for a technologically vital, export-based, anti-communist Western Germany.[32] Exhibited in the RCA Building in Rockefeller Plaza, the "Germany 49" exhibition represented West Germany's reinitiation into the world of industrial democracies. Half a year before it became a country, West Germany sent to New York its newest machinery produced in its revived factories, accompanied by a buyer's catalogue for American businessmen. The United States, eager to showcase West Germany as a productive, democratic nation, promoted the image of a once-defeated country now in the midst of an astonishing comeback.

A year and a half later, the FRG sponsored its own celebration of West German industrial recovery and ingenuity by inaugurating the annual German Industry Exhibition in West Berlin. Over the course of the 1950s and 1960s, the *Deutsche Industrieaustellung* (DIA) put the Economic Miracle on display. Millions of visitors from the FRG and the GDR (until the Berlin Wall cut off East–West traffic in 1961), as well as tourists and exhibitors from abroad, traveled to Berlin to wander through huge pavilions displaying heavy industrial goods and consumer merchandise, from tractors to typewriters to toys of all kinds. At the DIA, displays of kitchen appliances and fur coats stood next to demonstrations on the latest mining, engineering, and construction technologies. Over a million visitors gazed at electrical products and household appliances, and wound their way into rooms filled with the newest paints and dyes used in commercial production and in the home. They were greeted with displays of leather products, shoes, and textiles, as well as graphic design, office supplies, precious metals, glasswork, porcelain, furniture, building supplies, and machine tools.[33]

The Berlin exhibition was one of dozens of trade fairs that West Germans established or revived after the Second World War. Next to the DIA, Berlin also hosted the annual "Green Week" Agricultural Exhibition and the Great Art Exhibition; Frankfurt relaunched the world's largest book fair and the International Bakers' Exhibition; Düsseldorf sponsored the annual Candy Trade Fair; and Munich was the site of an annual Show for Secondhand Motor Cars. Cologne hosted, among its many shows, the International Trade Fair of Sporting Goods, Camping Equipment, and Garden Furniture; Nuremberg sponsored a toy fair and the German and International Inventions and Novelties Show; and by 1962 several of Germany's eight official *Messestädte* (trade fair cities) sponsored ladies' apparel displays, fur fairs, and men's-fashion shows.[34]

These displays were the visual manifestations of an emerging consumer society. A country that prided itself on its high quality and innovative production techniques was now, in fits and starts, trying to make room for a relatively new social type: the consumer, primarily the *Hausfrau*, who did the shopping and maintained the house while the father was at work in a factory.[35] In tracing the emergence of consumerism in the Federal Republic, however, one must not forget that West Germans were still very much in a survival mode during much of the 1950s, unable to go on the wild spending sprees that the increasingly lavish trade fairs seemed to entice. According to Arnold Sywottek, a true West German "consumer society" was realized during the years from 1957 to 1967. The prior years, from 1948 to 1957, represented a period of "reconstruction and modification," when people were still rebuilding a "collapsed society" that emerged from the rubble of war-defeated Germany.[36] This was a time when Germans went through an "eating wave," spending all of their money on food, transportation, and clothing, rather than on luxury items.[37] During this period, then, trade fairs were more acts of creation and embellishment than they were reflections of the actual purchasing habits or possibilities of the average German. At this point, what consumer displays offered were anticipatory visions of mass consumption.

Displays of television sets provide an illustrative case in point. So central to images of the conservative and complacent 1950s, both in Germany and the United States, the "television age" did not in fact begin in the FRG until the 1960s. In 1951, the DIA displayed its first television, almost a decade before this new technological arrival truly became a widespread and affordable item of consumption in West Germany. Over a million and a quarter visitors watched the RCA television demonstrations, although in 1951 the cost of the televisions themselves ranged from a prohibitive 1,000 to 1,500 DM, equivalent to $250 to $375 in that year.[38] Moreover, it would take another three years before West Germans could actually tune in to their first broadcast network, ARD, which remained their only television station until a second was added in 1963.[39]

Interestingly, exhibition organizers of the early 1950s implicitly and sometimes explicitly acknowledged that the Economic Miracle, so ubiquitous in the national vocabulary, was more about the promise of future material comforts than about the tangible reality of personal wealth.[40] Particularly in the early part of the decade, one finds a large gulf between the soaring language of economic resurrection that accompanied discussions of the economy *writ large* and the more modestly titled displays and literature at trade fairs. While the colorful, product-filled pavilions themselves attested to Germany's burgeoning consumer sector, the pamphlets and speeches accompanying many exhibits conceded that hard work lay ahead before Germany would in fact resemble a full-fledged consumer society. For example, at the DIA in 1951, the Rationalization Committee of the German Economy (RKW) distributed a brochure on "Better Living," which promised that American-style consumer comforts could eventually reach the German public if the country adopted "progressive" work models.[41] This message was echoed in the Regional Federation of Employer Associations' publication *Wir alle können besser leben* (*We Can All Live Better*),[42] which the organization distributed to professionals and business leaders in the hopes that they would pass on the pro-market message of the government and propagate its signature vision of socially engaged capitalism. In 1952, Agfa produced a color film for that year's DIA titled *Wir bauen ein besseres Leben* (literally, "we're building a better life" – translated loosely in correspondences as "Toward a Better Life").[43] And a 1953 Düsseldorf Exhibition on economic rationalization centered on a display of product packaging called "Everyone should live better." This exhibition highlighted not commodities themselves, but the containers and the wrapping that covered them – bottles, jars, paper, and tin foil. [44] Colorful packages tantalized the future consumer though the power of suggestion, holding out the promise of a household filled with convenient items that would make everyday life easier. It was as if the organizers were conceding that the empty receptacles of the consumer economy had yet to be filled with the actual substance of material abundance. In this broad literature about a "better life," the messages oscillated between the desire for a more affluent future and the actual ability to create it. They attested to the combination of cautious hope and confidence that still marked a period of lingering hardship and to a gradual shift in the grammar of the Economic Miracle – from we "*should* live better" to we "*can* live better," and ultimately to "we are *already* building a new life for Germans."

From the perspective of the exhibit organizers – politicians, manufacturers, economic journalists, and labor leaders – the stimulation of consumerist desires at trade fairs helped advance shared economic and social goals: the revival of international commerce and the increase of German exports; the promotion of local and regional business and culture; the encouragement of West German tourism; the creation and protection of jobs; and the defense of the nuclear family, with its strict division of labor. But these economic and social aims were always intertwined with Cold War tensions. Just a year after the founding of the FRG, Germans were boasting that Hanover was the biggest *Messe* in both Germanies, surpassing the

Leipzig fair in floor space by almost 60 percent.[45] More than the Hanover Fair, however, the DIA was recognized as the premier site where the West could combat communism through displays of merchandise and industrial ingenuity. Berlin served as the barometer of the East–West tensions throughout much of the Cold War, and it is perhaps not surprising that most public events in the divided city took on an ideological purpose. When West German president Theodor Heuss referred to the DIA as having both an "economic and a moral-political significance,"[46] he was speaking for a number of politicians and industrialists who sat on the planning boards or who displayed their merchandise at the exhibition. The international trade resulting from this event, Ludwig Erhard argued, would ensure "peace in the world" and "the triumph of mankind."[47]

In delivering such exalted rhetoric, planners never lost sight of the products themselves. For it was the *presentation* of these objects – the visitor's visual and tactile contact with the stuff of economic prosperity – that justified an industrial exhibit in the first place. West German trade fairs revealed not simply the ideological urgency that lay behind economic recovery, but also the political importance of manifesting this abundance to the world, and specifically to the Communist East, in the 1950s.[48] Wrote Ludwig Erhard in the catalogue to the second DIA in 1951:

> This exhibition has the character of a window display (*Schaufenster*) for the East. May our German brothers . . . living in Bolshevist bondage take from their visit to this exhibition the confidence that a happier fate awaits them if they reunite with us to live in peace and freedom. May the colorfulness and diversity of the products on display dispel the deceptive phrases of Eastern propaganda . . . and demonstrate what a free people are capable of achieving . . . in a free economic order.[49]

Indeed it is not accidental that during the 1950s, when West Germany was cautiously welcoming mass consumption into a traditionally producerist economy, the DIA advertised itself as a gigantic window display (*Schaufenster*). Through the repetition of this word *Schaufenster* (the *Schaufenster* "of the economy";[50] the *Schaufenster* "of the West";[51] the *Schaufenster* "of the World"[52]), politicians and industrialists were acknowledging the power of conspicuous consumption, and literally window-shopping, as a motivating ideal not only, or even primarily, for oppressed East Germans (notwithstanding the rhetoric) but actually for *West* Germans.[53] At a time when workers in the FRG were demanding broader participation in company decisions, and employers were resisting these demands for codetermination, Erhard and other leaders saw consumer goods as a means of schooling the public in the advantages of market economics. Industrialists themselves also hoped the promise of a consumerist future would calm some of the demands for economic democracy – to wipe away lingering "class war" rhetoric.[54]

On the fair grounds of Berlin, Eastern and Western Germans mingled together, both taking home dreams of conspicuous consumption and lofty messages about economic freedom.

This imperative to work and consume in the name of freedom was not without its problems. Many West German elites, from religious leaders to businessmen, saw mass consumption as potentially threatening to the country's spiritual values.[55] Yet some of these same people also recognized that consumerism was indispensable to economic recovery and Germany's own credentials as a democratic nation. Recent studies have documented this deep ambivalence about mass consumption – and its conflicted associations with the United States –during the early Adenauer years.[56] Yet they have paid less attention to the rhetorical strategies which elites – whether conservative or progressive – used to dampen their own uneasiness about a new, unfamiliar Germany populated by shoppers.[57] This discomfort with mass consumption was redressed by appeals to a more long-standing and indigenous symbol of economic power: the "Made in Germany" tradition. The DIA and other trade fairs were not simply spectacles of abundance designed to stimulate consumer spending. They were also places where West Germans could rediscover and promote the ideals of quality work and technical superiority, key components of national pride since the nineteenth century that were closely linked to an earlier ethic of industrial production and notably distinct from the mechanized crimes of the more recent past.[58]

While originally a term of opprobrium in late Victorian England, "Made in Germany" had, by the turn of the century, become a badge of pride, worn by industrialists and politicians, who reveled in the high international respect for German goods – whether cannons, automobiles, porcelain, or clocks.[59] After both world wars, Germans expressed concerns about maintaining this reputation for quality during a time when many politicians and social commentators feared the encroachments of mass democracy and mass tastes.[60] It is revealing that in 1951 West Berlin mayor Ernst Reuter welcomed visitors to the second DIA with the declaration that "only with quality labor and quality products can the German economy win back its share of the world market . . ."[61] In *Berlin Export*, a publication accompanying the 1950 DIA, Mayor Reuter gave thanks "to Berlin's skilled labor, proved to be of renowned quality."[62] In the official catalogue of the exhibit, Hans Böckler, the head of the German Trade Union Federation (DGB), likewise celebrated the work of the skilled worker, who took pride in the product of his toils.[63] This message of quality persisted throughout the almost two and a half decades of the DIA, culminating in 1968's theme "Quality through Research and Production."[64]

Reuter's and Böckler's words reflected a cautious optimism that the "Made in Germany" slogan could be salvaged from the wreckage of National Socialism as the country revitalized itself economically. But behind this invocation of the quality ethos lay an almost mournful nostalgia. From the trade fair catalogues in the 1950s, one gets the image of Germany as an enfeebled giant – a once-mighty economic powerhouse, recently reduced to rubble but struggling to rebuild. The "Made in Germany" slogan evoked memories of a bygone, "innocent" era, when the country was associated with quality, culture, and ingenuity – not with war machinery and crimes against humanity. Simultaneously, the slogan seemed to imply that Germany would not abandon its commitment to the production of high-quality goods, even in the midst of a burgeoning consumer-driven economy.

Consumer displays, rather than merely being enticements toward mass markets, were thus the site of this deeper struggle betweens Germany's traditions, its recent compromised past, and its imagined future. At almost every DIA, the objects of mass consumption were marketed not simply as items for convenience and comfort, but also as powerful embodiments of the German tradition of quality, which had been misused by Hitler but would now be salvaged for the good of the German population and the West. The Economic Miracle had its origins not in 1948, but in the longer tradition of fine German workmanship. And for many years the question of whether mass consumption could be combined with Germany's indigenous economic customs remained provisional.

Complicating these reflections was the presence of the United States at the trade fairs. In the 1950s, America offered both a vision of a prosperous future and the countermodel upon which skeptics of mass consumption could focus their anxieties.[65] On the heels of the "Germany 49" exhibition, the United States made special efforts to display German goods in America and to sell the American economic model at international industrial and trade fairs. At the first DIA in 1950, the United States unveiled the George C. Marshall Pavilion, which housed exhibits on American democracy, economics, and society. Much like the "America Houses" that were sprouting up all around the FRG in order to educate Germans in the features of American society, the Marshall Pavilion was built in order to teach Germans not only about political and social institutions, but also about successful business practices. The German-American Trade Promotion Office (GATPO) stationed workers at the pavilion to offer German businessmen information about sales possibilities in the United States. Visitors could learn how to find a distributor in the United States, how to gauge American buying habits, and how to understand competition, taxes, credit, brand-name protection, pricing, advertising, and public relations in the United States.[66] Other workers handed out the GATPOs "Better Living" brochure (see above), in which the authors promised that "because America was once fertilized by European culture and science," the United States, as the "country with the highest productivity and manufacturing" would return the favor to Europe and Germany through its technological assistance and its model of progressive work methods.[67] The message of the exhibit was that the "better lives" that Americans enjoyed was not their exclusive birthright. West Germans would soon live well if they followed America's model in producing more goods at a faster rate.

To impart this message, the United States, often under the aegis of the US Information Agency,[68] sponsored a different theme every year in the DIA's Marshall Pavilion, from the wonders of space travel and technology in 1956, to 1958's "Eine Mittelstadt im Mittelwest – Leben und Arbeit in Kalamazoo, USA" ("A Mid-sized City in the Midwest – Life and Work in Kalamazoo"). At this latter exhibit, visitors could learn about the daily life of the average American in Middle America while listening to the music of "hillbilly singer" Remberg Wall, "an actual resident of Kalamazoo."[69] The Americans hoped that such exhibits, which highlighted both industry and culture, would serve the explicit purpose of fighting communism and selling the benefits of a consumer economy; they would bind the citizens of the FRG more closely to the democratic West through a celebration of industrial ingenuity, material acquisition, and an exchange of knowledge and transatlantic good will.

Bringing the Miracle Home: Advertising as Display

The trade fair, particularly the DIA, served a host of political, ideological, and economic goals in the early 1950s by inviting Germans to envision future prosperity. It was of course not the only site of consumer display. From the corner shop, to exhibits at local chambers of commerce, to larger department stores, Germans during the *Wirtschaftswunderjahre* had immediate access to images of economic success. Yet the trade fair brought together the actual products and the well-honed message that everyone would soon be able to experience affluence. For many, this promise was realized as the 1950s drew to a close. By the last third of the decade West Germans were finally beginning to realize the Economic Miracle in their own lives. "Private consumption" became more widespread in the FRG, as disposable income grew, and the amount and diversity of products increased greatly.[70] The class leveling that many cultural conservatives had feared since the early years of the FRG was becoming more of a reality.

Not surprisingly, at the very moment that the Economic Miracle was losing its mythical quality, the original ideological force of the trade fair was diminishing. Its organizers no longer had to prove to the public the benefits of a social market economy. Consumption now came to people in the form of actual merchandise, and the spectacle of the trade fair – still teeming with visitors – no longer offered ephemeral escapes into abundance. If according to 1953's DIA program, the fair grounds were where "all one's wishes are fulfilled," by the end of the decade, the home took over this function. Germans therefore no longer traveled to consumer displays in search of a temporary respite from the hard work of economic reconstruction.[71] The public dreamscape of the fair – as the embodiment of the

Economic Miracle – gave way to the lasting reality of personal consumption. The trade fair still offered splendid tableaus of merchandise and product innovation, but its symbolic function had changed. It was now a place of carefree browsing where West Germans could applaud themselves for having landed on their feet. Increasingly, product displays would find more accessible terrain in magazines and newspapers, on films and on television, as an ever-expanding and lucrative advertising industry responded to the new consumerism in the FRG. By the late 1950s, advertising had replaced the trade fair as the primary medium through which Germans could spin out their fantasies of convenience and luxury.[72]

Of course, advertising did not "come to Germany" only in the late 1950s. As in any modern economy, Germans had witnessed a continuous stream of product, political, and public-event advertisements, from the *Reklame* (posters, exhibits, and handbills) of the nineteenth century to the more stylized ads and product films of the Weimar, Nazi, and early Adenauer Years. Indeed during the Third Reich, when consumer demand was limited by the regime's rearmament priorities, companies such as Henkel, the manufacturer of Persil soaps and detergents, produced innovative and graphically sophisticated ads.[73] While the Nazis' advertising organization, the Werberat der Deutschen Wirtschaft, attempted to regulate tightly advertisements in Nazi Germany, companies still had the latitude to produce colorful and often alluring product placements.[74]

During the early years of the FRG, advertisements, like trade fairs, were aimed at shoring up the market economy and creating images of plenty. Yet they too were limited by the reality of an economy still on the mend. For example, a 1949 advertisement for "Texas" brand cigarettes subordinated an illustration of a dapper, square-jawed smoker to lengthy copy about the company's inability to meet demand for their product and German cigarettes more generally (American cigarettes being too luxurious an item). "What's the point of being the best cigarette, when they are so hard to come by?" asked the ad provocatively. The answer offered was that while they could never entirely meet demand, the Brinkmann cigarette company was doubling the number of cigarettes produced. "Texas is sold-out," a familiar sign at kiosks, was an indication not only that production was lagging behind consumer demand for inexpensive German tobacco, but also that the economic condition of the FRG remained compromised, even in the throes of an Economic Miracle.[75]

Much as in the 1920s and 1930s, early postwar advertising was bound up with perceptions of American business practices, and what was deemed exportable to a producer-oriented economy.[76] While brand names such as "Texas" evoked the freedom of the American west, Germans struggled with the question of whether American advertising – based on mass distribution and seemingly aggressive and psychologically manipulative methods – would actually be effective in the FRG, a smaller country with a narrower customer base. One company that saw West

Germany as prime territory for modern advertising was the J. Walter Thompson Company, the world's largest ad agency. Founded in 1864, J. Walter Thompson had first come to Germany in 1928, when it opened an office in Berlin. Five years later, when the Nazis came to power, the company was purchased, renamed, and eventually closed, as all ad agencies were synchronized under the Nazis' *Werberat*. In 1952, J. Walter Thompson returned to Germany, this time setting up its headquarters in Frankfurt am Main. JWT Frankfurt, still a major advertising force today, held the accounts for international and German companies such as Lever, Kodak, Pan American Airlines, Pepsi-Cola, Kellogg's, Kraft, and Warner-Lambert. By 1962, the Frankfurt office had 450 employees – ranging in expertise from public relations to graphic design to text writing – and represented fifty-two clients and more than seventy products.[77] The company boasted a media-relations department, a film, radio, and television division, and a marketing research team.[78] Although an American firm, the office employed predominantly Germans, and the language of all internal meetings was German.

In the 1950s and 1960s, the managers at JWT Frankfurt saw themselves as presiding over the introduction of modern advertising to a country they felt had no genuine advertising tradition. In a 1979 interview, Denis Lanigan, the joint manager of the JWT Frankfurt in the 1960s, described the mood in West Germany upon his arrival in 1957:

> The initial period was particularly exciting, because it was the time of the Wirtschaftswunder, the economic miracle. Germany ended the War more or less like a medieval colony – each city existed on what could be grown around the city . . . And by 1957 they had gotten to the state where they had disposable income for the first time. So for anyone in advertising and marketing it was really an extraordinary [*sic*] exciting time. Patterns were forming and patterns were changing.[79]

Despite a longer history of advertising in Germany, JWT Frankfurt saw itself as bringing to the country practices "that previously did not exist."[80] "Advertising: U.S. Techniques Reach Europe," proclaimed the *New York Times* in a 1962 story about the recent arrival of dozens of ad agencies on the Continent.[81] But what *were* these putatively American techniques?[82] According to the *Times*, in Europe "advertising is imaginative from an esthetic standpoint, but the copy tends to be vague and the sales pitch 'soft.'" American advertising, in contrast, put its emphasis on the "hard sell." A JWT Frankfurt office profile elaborated on the difference, noting that American advertisers paid closer attention to market trends than Germans. "Research and critical analysis" were present at every step. American ad agencies, in contrast to their German counterparts, conducted motivational research and studied the "characteristics of the product and its competitor; the nature of the consumer and his desires."[83]

In order to disseminate this American brand of advertising, JWT Frankfurt paid particular attention to training. It sponsored special seminars, sent its employees to advertising congresses around the world, and established a "Monday School," at which JWT clients, along with retailers and wholesalers, listened to evening talks on advertising-related themes.[84] In keeping with the trend toward aggressive advertising, agencies found new outlets for their advertising in the drug store chains and large supermarkets that were increasingly supplanting the " mom and pop" store during this period.

American ad companies prided themselves on introducing Germans to a world of leisure and luxury. But forcing Germans to think like consumers was a difficult task, not the least because income distribution was still wide when American companies first arrived in Germany. As psychological compensation for their inability to purchase luxury goods, many Germans fell back upon their pride in the "made in Germany" label. J. Walter Thompson's internal correspondences in 1954 describe a country still wedded to its ethos of well-made goods produced for an elite minority. In a meeting about the marketing of Kodak products, JWT executives discussed the difficulty of selling a product in a country where people apparently still fancied themselves scrupulous judges of quality. West German camera dealers offered an explanation to JWT managers: "Germans were different [from Americans] – they were most interested in the *technical* side of photography! But now the German manufacturers in their advertisements are saying to the consumer, "Don't lose any of your precious moments – take a picture."[85] West Germans, from the perspective of industrialists and advertisers, would need to reconsider the camera as an object of mass leisure, not as a photographer's instrument.

By the late 1950s and early 1960s, advertising in Germany was undergoing a renaissance. With the explosion of new firms, ad agencies came together to form the Gesellschaft Werbeagenturen, a professional organization representing the entire industry in Germany. Advertising agencies also established the Aktion Gemeinsinn, a charity initiative modeled directly after the Advertising Council in the United States. It depended upon the donations and volunteer work of advertisers to conduct socially conscious ad campaigns – from the first year's (1959) urgings to "Help the Housewife" ("Helft der Hausfrau") to 1961's drive to make the public more sensitive to its oldest members ("Das Alter darf nicht abseits stehen").[86]

German and international ad agencies clearly reveled in their newfound business successes in the *Wirtschaftswunderland*, and they toasted each other at the industry's first "Advertising Ball" in Munich in 1963.[87] Yet just as the industry was taking off in the late 1950s, advertisers began to face increasing criticism that their trade was a dangerous import, bent on deceiving the public. With the rising income of Germans, and the omnipresence of consumer goods, came mounting criticism that the Economic Miracle, so heralded ten years earlier, had produced a mass society run amok – marked by "consumption terror."[88] As long as trade fairs and industrial exhibitions had been the chief means of demonstrating new products, indeed ones that most Germans could not afford, the population was protected from the deleterious effects of mass manipulation. At a trade fair, one could see the product close-up – stare at it, hold it, judge it for its quality. If a product was to be an item of mass consumption, one could at least judge it initially on its visible merits – through demonstrations and sales pitches. But advertising was a calculated form of *indirect* display; it ostensibly caught the consumer unaware, at home or in a waiting room or on the highway. Eyes flitted over the page or caught a glimpse of a billboard, all the while prone to "hidden messages" and subliminal exhortations to buy. Trade fairs, then, seemed to be tied to a producerist ideal so familiar to Germans, while advertising, according to its critics, abandoned the discriminating craftsman's ethos for an "American," mass-consumerist ideal.

Much of the literature critical of advertising was inspired by Vance Packard's 1957 classic *The Hidden Persuaders,* the translation of which became a bestseller in Germany and the subject of endless articles and private business conversations within the FRG. Packard's dire warning that the "shock troops of the advertising world are subtly charting your inner thoughts, fears, and dreams so that they can influence your daily living" resonated with Germans worried about the effects of mass tastes and social uniformity.[89] While the seeming dangers of advertising were a transatlantic obsession, in the FRG anxieties about advertising were symptomatic of a certain disillusionment with prosperity. At the end of the 1950s, it was now the years of reconstruction, according to Arnold Sywottek, that became the object of considerable nostalgia. These had been "lovely times of need,"[90] when the goal of future prosperity motivated Germans to hard work. But by the early 1960s, suggested one commentator at the time, people themselves had become walking advertisements – for themselves, for consumer goods, and for the market economy.[91] Germany had become populated by a mass of atomized human advertisements for consumption.[92] In the early 1950s, when he was actively promoting the idea of the social market economy, Economics Minister Ludwig Erhard had delivered rousing speeches to audiences of delighted advertisers. Advertising, he declared favorably in 1952, made the market transparent. It was an essential part of any free economy, revealing to consumers the "colorful fullness of life's possibilities."[93] By 1961, however, politicians like Erhard were more wary. At national advertising conferences, they admonished their listeners to heed the words of Packard and avoid dishonest practices and mass manipulation.[94] While in 1957 Erhard successfully led the CDU to reject the anti-materialist sentiments of its early party leaders, politicians still expressed concern over the social implications of the consumerism they were promoting. Advertising, lamented one frustrated defender of the industry, had become the public's favorite "whipping boy."[95]

Ironically, what ultimately helped to stem the tide of Packard-inspired punditry was the creation of a positive philosophical foundation for advertising that spoke directly to West Germans and the concerns of the day: the fear of totalitarianism and the desire to protect one's material well-being. According to its proponents, advertising achieved precisely the opposite of what its critics claimed. Rather than promoting social conformity, it engendered self-awareness and a sense of status, individuality, and freedom of choice. If, according to critics, advertising created false needs, in the minds of the image-makers, the goal was to bolster self-worth through the fulfillment of *actual* desires. Through consumption, a person discovered him- or herself as a free agent – one who could obtain goods that held the key to self-esteem. Advertising, in a typical formulation, was the very means by which the housewife discovered the magic of the washing machine, which in turn freed up time for her to be with her children.[96] Advertising was all about the freedom to choose – from 400 models of cars to scores of different refrigerators and sewing machines. It was the very lack of choice in communist states, argued some, that was the real threat to humanity. Under communism, so went a familiar joke, "the person buying a car can have any color he wants, as long as it is black." Ultimately, advertising, as Ludwig Erhard himself had argued in 1952, was a form of political and economic freedom that would help lead to the collapse of the Soviet Bloc.[97] These appeals to individual self-worth successfully played into much larger discussions about the fate of the West and its struggle for spiritual survival in the age of mass consumption. Advertising, if produced honestly, was considered a true form of democratic expression. But these appeals were lost on the industry's staunchest critics. As one observer of clothing ads sarcastically mused, the consumer could now discover his or her "personality through underwear."[98]

It is difficult to gauge the effects of this social criticism on the actual spread of advertising throughout the Federal Republic. By the late 1960s and early 1970s, most people accepted advertising as a permanent feature of West German society, and both the attacks and the justifications grew less intense in the pages of national and trade publications. All the while, advertising in the FRG had grown into a hugely lucrative business, bringing together specialists from around the world and serving as a key form of transatlantic communication. Advertisers and marketers associated with major German retailers such as Kaufhof did apprenticeships abroad – working, for example, in New York's Macy's Department Store by day and taking courses on copyright law and advertising at night.[99] Delegations of Levi's executives made trips to Germany to find ad agencies that would promote the hipness and modernity of blue jeans to the country's youth. Such business contacts indicate, in Harm Schröter's assessment, not just the explosive growth of German advertising, but its "Americanization."[100] By the late 1960s, most business leaders and politicians, whatever they felt about this "American" import, came to understand the indispensability of advertising in a modern capitalist society. As the

Economic Miracle came to fruition, advertising successfully asserted itself as a permanent and indispensable feature of the German economic and cultural landscape.

Conclusion: The Dynamics of Display

The rise of a consumer society in West Germany begs a number of questions about the nature and meaning of postwar economic recovery. While historians have effectively questioned whether the FRG was singularly "miraculous" in its rates of growth or in its ability to produce social equality, one must still ask whether there *was* something unique about the visual displays that gave life to the Economic Miracle. In many respects, these consumer displays were very familiar in form and function. Barbara Kirshenblatt-Gimblett, in her study of world's fairs, ethnographic museums, and heritage exhibits, has located several constants in the multiple sites of modern display. She has argued, for one, that there is necessarily a "foreignness" of objects within their particular national contexts. People come to displays to see the new and the strange, whether it is the much-touted "missing link" at a Berlin exhibition in 1894, or the sites and sounds of a circus or a colonial exhibition.[101] During the early years of the Economic Miracle, West Germans paid an entrance fee to see items that were at once familiar and foreign. While many remembered the luxuries enjoyed before war and defeat, they would not again have access to these items until *after* – sometimes many years after – they saw them on display. In this respect we come full circle to the notion of "miracles," which are by definition unexpected, strange, and bewildering. Germans, in effect, witnessed the economic recovery of the 1950s as something unknown and unforeseen.

Kirschenblatt-Gimblett has also drawn attention to what she has called the "agency of display," and the "political economy of showing."[102] Again with respect to the FRG, we find that business leaders, politicians, labor leaders, and advertisers knew the political advantages of showcasing economic success. While they themselves were caught off guard by the rapidity of economic recovery, they were nonetheless well aware that visual images of abundance would serve both practical and ideological purposes – stimulating consumption, creating jobs, fighting communism, and fostering international respect. Even if they did not identify themselves as "Hidden Persuaders," West German elites detected very early the value of public display in the creation of wants and needs. And when the FRG had attained the levels of prosperity that would constitute a consumer society, Germans still responded positively to the visions of the exotic – often coded as American – from a newer, faster car to a cigarette evoking images of the "Wild West."

To be sure, notwithstanding the Cold War context, the trade fairs and advertisements that accompanied economic growth in postwar Germany were familiar features of modern society. Exemplified by feats such as the unveiling of the Krupp cannon at the London Crystal Palace exhibit of 1851[103] or the introduction of new product lines today, public display has been the hallmark of market economics for centuries. But while one may detect universal modes of capitalist spectatorship in the FRG, one must not lose sight of what *was* unique about consumer displays in West Germany. During the Adenauer years, the Federal Republic was still very much a *postwar* society.[104] This was a society born from the ashes of dictatorship and total war, during which the multiple objects of German ingenuity had been marshaled in support of murderous aims. The FRG, writes Frank Biess, was "compelled to cope with the direct social, moral, and psychological consequences of the racial war of destruction well into the second half of the 1950s."[105] In this respect, the consumer displays of postwar Germany took on a uniquely powerful meaning. They were not just about celebrating the return of the German economy or the anticipation of material abundance. They responded directly to West Germans' sense of "injured citizenship," in which Germans, accustomed to a sense of privilege in Nazi-dominated Europe, had been shocked by defeat and the material hardships that followed.[106] Over the course of the 1950s, "the imagined-community" [107] of the social market economy defined consumption as central to a new, post-Hitler conception of citizenship.

Consumer displays and advertisements were highly selective sites of German memory. Meditating on the country's compromised economic position, Germans made little room for reflection as to the causes of their own misery – Adolf Hitler, their own support of a dictatorship, and Nazi crimes. But through the exhibitions and ads of the 1950s and early 1960s, the average German citizen was able to recuperate a form of nationalism, as diminished as it was after the war. Wandering the pavilion grounds or reading an advertisement, West Germans discovered their own economic patriotism. The industrialist was able to take pride in the creations of his company; and the worker was able to rediscover his own subjectivity through the universal appreciation of his or her own handiwork. The popularity of visual displays ultimately reflected West Germans' desire to experience a "dream-world" of consumption, where the imagery of abundance fed into fantasies of both personal wealth and national rehabilitation.[108]

Germans today tend to celebrate the first decade of the FRG as the "golden fifties," perhaps due to the energetic optimism that accompanied the country's emergence from the miserable war years and immediate postwar years. Product and industrial displays, and the language of miracles, aided in this process of rebuilding, by promoting and consolidating a consumerist national identity that transcended the bad memories and horrible realities of a genocidal war. Trade fairs and advertisements served as orchestrated moments of forgetting. At an exhibition or in an advertisement, the everyday objects of consumption were transformed into powerful symbols of renewal. Through visual and tactile interactions with both necessities and luxury items, observers were overwhelmed with the promise of individual prosperity, and in turn, were bound to an ideal of a resurrected Germany – an anticommunist, market-driven country that would provide for future material gratification after the lean years of war and occupation.[109]

Trade fairs ultimately served as a transitional form of spectatorship, helping West Germans to navigate the shift from a producer-centered economy to a consumer society. They appealed to prewar logics about German quality that were familiar and coherent, but they also presented "American" forms of consumption to visitors. Arguably, then, by the late 1950s, when advertising supplanted the trade fair as the chief site of consumer display, Germans, still clinging to traditional ideals, were also prepared for the mass production and mass consumption that came to define their economy.

"The postwar years are over!" declared Chancellor Ludwig Erhard in November of 1965.[110] Two decades after the end of the Second World War, the former Economics Minister saw fit to declare West Germany at a crossroads – between a period of hardship and rebuilding and a new era of full employment, low inflation, economic well being, and "prosperity for all." While as Axel Schildt has pointed out, there were still "stepchildren of the Economic Miracle"[111] – those who fell through the mesh of the safety net and depended on the state for survival – the majority of Germans had come a long way. This was undoubtedly a success story. Yet, whether it was a miracle or not remains debated. Diethelm Prowe has argued that the true German miracle was political, not economic; the fact that West Germany could transition so quickly from fascism to democracy had not at all been a given when surveying the moral wreckage of 1945.[112] For good or ill, West Germany had become the consumer society that some of the loudest proponents of consumption had secretly feared. But it had also become a political democracy.

Although Germany had become a wealthy consumer society by the early 1960s, the adherence to a producerist national identity persisted, thus situating this newfound prosperity within a much longer historical narrative. Despite – or perhaps because of – the country's successes, the Economic Miracle remained an omnipresent catchphrase to define the changes the FRG had undergone. Yet the expression itself became more and more of a cliché, and often found more jaundiced expressions. A 1960 German film *Mein Mann, das Wirtschaftswunder* (My Husband, the Economic Miracle) treated audiences to a farce about a nanny's attempts to coax love out of a businessman.[113] Had Germany's striving for economic success, the movie seemed to ask, shut down the country's emotional side? And a joke also made the rounds in the early 1960s that the "Economic Miracle" could only refer to the Austrians. "For the Germans, it's hardly a miracle; they actually work!" Whatever one was to make of the *Wirtschaftswunder*, it had coincided with, and indeed engendered, a rapid social and economic transformation in the FRG. In the end, concluded a J. Walter Thompson employee in 1962, "It doesn't matter what the change in Germany is called. The fact remains that the Germans are enjoying a better life."[114]

Notes

1. Recent scholarship has turned a critical eye to several aspects of this purported miracle, including the question of whether swift recovery would have taken place regardless of the influx of American financial aid. See a summary of these arguments in Henry Burke Wend, *Recovery and Restoration: U.S. Foreign Policy and the Politics of Reconstruction of West Germany's Shipbuilding Industry, 1945–1955* (Westport, CT: Praeger, 2001), pp. xxi-xxii; for a broader discussion about the economic realities of the 1950s, see Axel Schildt and Arnold Sywottek, "'Reconstruction' and 'Modernization': West German Social History during the 1950s," in Robert G. Moeller, ed., *West Germany under Construction: Politics, Society, and Culture in the Adenauer Era* (Ann Arbor: University of Michigan Press, 1997), pp. 413–43.

2. On party politics and the use of polling to promote the market economy, see Mark E. Spicka, "Selling the Economic Miracle: Public-Opinion Research, Economic Reconstruction and Politics in West Germany, 1949–1957," *German Politics and Society*, 20(1), Spring 2002, pp. 49–57.

3. This term is drawn from Martin Daunton and Matthew Hilton, *The Politics of Consumption: Material Culture and Citizenship in Europe and America* (Oxford and New York: Berg, 2001).

4. For a history of the concept of "consumption" in Germany, see Ulrich Wyrwa, "Consumption, Konsum, Konsumgesellschaft. Ein Beitrag zur Begriffsgeschichte," in Hannes Siegrist, Hartmut Kaelble, Jürgen Kocka, eds., *Europäische Konsumgeschichte: Zur Gesellschafts- und Kulturgeschichte des Konsums (18. bis 20. Jahrhundert)* (Frankfurt: Campus, 1997), pp. 747–62. On consumerism in West Germany, see Michael Wildt, "Changes in Consumption as Social Practice in West Germany During the 1950s," in Susan Strasser, Charles McGovern, and Matthias Judt, *eds., Getting and Spending: European and American Consumer Societies in the Twentieth Century* (Washington D.C.: German Historical Institute/Cambridge University Press, 1998). On consumption and consumerism in Europe and the United States more generally, see Daunton and Hilton, *The Politics of Consumption*; and Gary Cross, *Time and Money: The Making of Consumer Culture* (London and New York: Routledge, 1993).

5. On the memories and mythology of the currency reform, see Frank Grube and Gerhard Richter, *Das Wirtschaftswunder: Unser Weg in den Wohlstand* (Hamburg: Hofmann und Campe, 1983); and Christoph Buchheim, "Die Währungsreform 1948 in Westdeutschland," *Vierteljahrshefte für Zeitgeschichte,* 36, 1988, pp. 189–231. Some Germans placed the beginning of the Miracle at the "zero hour," when in 1945 Germans, especially the "rubble

women," took charge of the clean-up effort in bombed out cities; see Elisabeth Heinemann, "The Hour of the Woman: Memories of Germany's 'Crisis Years' and West German National Identity," *American Historical Review*, 101(2), April 1996, pp. 354–95. Other West Germans saw the Economic Miracle as a continuation of the recovery of the 1930s. See Ulrich Herbert, "Good Times, Bad Times, Memories of the Third Reich," in Richard Bessel, ed., *Life in the Third Reich* (Oxford: Oxford University Press, 1987), pp. 97–110.

6. See e.g. Heinrich Hauser, *Unser Schickal: Die Deutsche Industrie* (Munich: Steinebach, 1952).

7. Germans during the mid–1930s often spoke of the country's economic comeback as unbelievable or miraculous. See e.g. Hans E. Priester, *Das deutsche Wirtschaftswunder* (Amsterdam: Querido Verlag, 1936).

8. On the legacy of business crimes, see S. Jonathan Wiesen, *West German Industry and the Challenge of the Nazi Past, 1945–1955* (Chapel Hill and London: University of North Carolina Press, 2001).

9. Ludwig Erhard, *Wohlstand für alle* (Düsseldorf: Econ, 1957).

10. *Das Deutsche Wunder* (Munich: Co-Presse Europäische Hefte, 1953).

11. See Wiesen, *West German Industry*, pp. 195–6.

12. These terms can be found in a 1961 retrospective article on the economy of 1950s: "Die Wende nach dem 'Wirtschaftswunder,'" *Schlesische Rundschau*, 13, 1961, pp. 1–2.

13. On Christian anti-materialism during the Adenauer years, see Maria Mitchell, "Materialism and Secularism: CDU Politicians and National Socialism, 1945–1955," *Journal of Modern History*, 67(2), June 1995, pp. 278–308.

14. For an article about the "economic miracle" in Lilje's newspaper, see Ferdinand Fried, "Das Deutsche Wirtschaftswunder," *Sonntagsblatt*, 5(8), 1952, p. 8.

15. Theodor Hüpgens, "Das Wirtschaftswunder," *Priester und Arbeiter*, 6, 1956, pp. 259–64. See also "Ist die Wirtschaft unser Schicksal? Deutsche Wirtschaftsführer in Loccum," *Evangelische Welt*, 7, 1953, pp. 742–3.

16. On *Die Waage*, and the CDU's attempts to promote consumerism more generally, see Mark E. Spicka, "Gender, Political Discourse, and the CDU/CSU Vision of the Economic Miracle, 1949–1957," *German Studies Review*, 25(2), May 2002, pp. 305–32; and A.J. Nicholls, *Freedom with Responsibility: The Social Market Economy in Germany, 1918–1963* (Oxford: Clarendon Press, 1994), p. 296. On ideas about the Christian West, see Mitchell, "Materialism and Secularism"; and Heide Fehrenbach, *Cinema in Democratizing Germany: Reconstructing National Identity after Hitler* (Chapel Hill and London: University of North Carolina Press, 1995), chapter 4.

17. See e.g. "Das 'deutsche Wirtschaftswunder,'" *Jahrbuch der Sozialdemokratischen Partei Deutschlands*, 1952–53, pp. 318–20.

18. "Man wundert sich nur über ein Wunder," the article continues, in a play on words. Hans W. Aust, "Das Wirtschaftswunder geht vorüber," *Die Weltbühne*, 10, 1955, pp. 455–9.

19. Johann Gottfried Frey, "Das deutsche Wunder war kein Wunder," *Christ und Welt*, 6(6), 1953, p. 4.

20. Friedrich J. Lucas, "Ist die Wirtschaft ein 'Wunder'?" *Der Lehrrundbrief: Monatsschrift für Lehrerfortbildung und Schulpraxis*, 14, 1959, pp. 493–6.

21. A. Hunold, ed., *Wirtschaft ohne Wunder* (Erlenbach-Zurich: E. Rentsch, 1953).

22. Hüpgens, "Das Wirtschaftswunder."

23. Fritz Baade, "100 Jahre Wirtschaftswunder," *VDI-Zeitschrift,* 99(28), October 1, 1957, pp. 362–70.

24. Solomon Wolff, "Das Europäische Wirtschaftswunder. Ist unsere Prosperität schon vorbei," *Der Monat,* 9(101), 1957, pp. 3–9.

25. See Axel Schildt and Arnold Sywottek, "'Reconstruction' and 'Modernization.'" For these statistics, see pp. 420, 427.

26. On West German families and the Economic Miracle, see G. Robert Moeller, *Protecting Motherhood: Women and the Family in the Politics of Postwar West Germany* (Berkeley and Los Angeles: University of California Press, 1993), pp. 212–13.

27. Robert W. Rydell, *World of Fairs: The Century-of-Progress Expositions* (Chicago and London: University of Chicago Press, 1993), p. 9. The ellipses in the quotation stand in for "racially exclusive" – a key aspect of Rydell's argument regarding American society.

28. Ibid., p. 10.

29. There is a vast literature on German trade fairs, particularly in the early modern period. For a brief introduction to German trade fairs, see Philip Glouchevitch, *Juggernaut: the Keys to German Business Success* (New York: Touchstone, 1993): pp. 46–51. A 1939 exhibition in Düsseldorf, "Schaffendes Volk," highlighted products of the Nazi economy and celebrated the country's workers. See E.W. Maiwald, *Reichsausstellung Schaffendes Volk – Düsseldorf 1937: Ein Bericht* (Düsseldorf: A. Bagel, 1939).

30. On these two fairs, and their significance for East German women, see the contribution of Katherine Pence in Chapter 2 of this volume.

31. On the Cold War and exhibitions from the American perspective, see Walter L. Hixson, *Parting the Curtain: Propaganda, Culture, and the Cold War, 1945–1961* (New York: St. Martin's, 1997); and Robert H. Haddow, *Pavilions of Plenty: Exhibiting American Culture Abroad in the 1950s* (Washington and London: Smithsonian Institution Press, 1997).

32. On "Germany 49," see summaries of the exhibit and its sponsors, Rockefeller Center Archives, New York City. I thank Jim Reed for this information. On Jewish protests against this exhibit, see Peter Novick, *The Holocaust in American Life* (Boston: Houghton Mifflin, 1999), pp. 96–7.

33. On the 1950 DIA, see Deutsche Industrie Ausstellung, Berlin, October 1–15, 1950, Press Information Materials, A1019, Landesarchiv Berlin (hereafter LAB).

34. For a list of all the annual fairs in Germany in 1962, see Lars Akerblom, Marketing Department of the J. Walter Thompson Company, Frankfurt Office, to C.D. Dulley, J. Walter Thompson Company, São Paulo Office, 22 January 1962, folder "Intl. 62 January–December, A–Z," Box 1, Peter Gilow Papers, General Correspondences, in John W. Hartman Center for Sales, Advertising, and Marketing History, J. Walter Thompson Company Archives, Frankfurt Office Records, Duke University, Durham, NC (hereafter "JWT/Duke").

35. On women, gender, and consumption in West Germany, see Erica Carter, *How German is She? Postwar West German Reconstruction and the Consuming Woman* (Ann Arbor: University of Michigan Press, 1997); Jennifer A. Loehlin, *From Rugs to Riches:*

Housework, Consumption and Modernity in Germany (Oxford and New York: Berg, 1999); Katherine Pence, "Labours of Consumption: Gendered Consumers in Post-War East and West German Reconstruction," in Lynn Abrams and Elizabeth Harvey, eds. *Gender Relations in German History: Power, Agency and Experience from the Sixteenth to the Twentieth Century* (London: UCL Press, 1996), pp. 211–38. On gender and consumption more broadly, see Victoria de Grazia with Ellen Furlough, eds., *The Sex of Things: Gender and Consumption in Historical Perspective* (Berkeley and Los Angeles: University of California Press, 1996).

36. Arnold Sywottek, "From Starvation to Excess? Trends in the Consumer Society from the 1940s to the 1970s," in Hanna Schissler, ed., *The Miracle Years: A Cultural History of West Germany, 1949–1968* (Princeton and Oxford: Princeton University Press, 2001), pp. 341–58.

37. Interview of Denis Lanigan, October 19, 1979, Colin Dawkins Papers, Box 17, JWT/Duke.

38. *JWT Company News,* 6(38), September 17, 1951, p. 4, in International Branch Notebooks, Box 1, James Webb Young Papers. See also the special insert "Where Television Grows" in *JWT Company News*, 6(33), December 31, 1951 in the same collection, JWT/Duke.

39. On television in the early FRG, see Sywottek, "From Starvation to Excess?" p. 348. Also Schildt and Sywottek, "'Reconstruction' and 'Modernization,'" p. 435.

40. Erhard declared in 1953 that the "luxuries of today" could "only become the general consumer goods of tomorrow . . ., if we accept that in an initial phase, they will only be available to a small group with elevated incomes who will have the purchasing power to obtain these goods." Quote from Schildt and Sywottek, "'Reconstruction' and 'Modernization,'" p. 429.

41. *Besser Leben,* brochure in files of Deutsche Industrieausstellung Berlin 1951, October 6–21, A1019, LAB.

42. Ludwig Reiner, *Wir alle können besser leben* (Munich: Wilhelm Steinberg, 1953).

43. See "Abschrift: The Foreign Service of the United States of America," film branch (Munich), sent from George Templeton to German-American Trade Promotion Company, Zweigstelle München, May 22, 1953, collection B140, file 120 [B140/120], Bundesarchiv, Koblenz (hereafter BAK).

44. "Alle sollen besser leben" was displayed in Düsseldorf from July 18 to August 16, 1953. See undated memo for Herrn Dr. Dehne, in German-American Trade Promotion Office Files, B140/272, BAK.

45. *Der Spiegel,* 4(19), May 11, 1950, p. 22.

46. Deutsche Industrieausstellung Berlin 1950: 1–15. Oktober, p. 9, A1019, LAB.

47. Ludwig Erhard, "Aktivere Berlin-Hilfe," in *Deutsche Industrieausstellung Berlin 1951: 6–21. Oktober*, pp. 17–19, A1019, LAB.

48. Raymond Stokes has referred to visits by East and West German engineers to rival fairs as "technological tourism" – as a way for specialists to learn about the economies of their ideological opponent. See Raymond G. Stokes, *Constructing Socialism: Technology and Change in East Germany, 1945–1990* (Baltimore and London: Johns Hopkins University Press, 2000), pp. 58–66.

49. Erhard, "Aktivere Berlin-Hilfe," LAB.

50. Ludwig Erhard, "Berlin – Schaufenster der Wirtschaft," *Deutsche Industrieausstellung Berlin 1950: 1–15. Oktober*, pp.11–13, A1019, LAB.

51. Passage in ibid.

52. *Berlin im Brennpunkt des Weltgeschehens* (1954) [#7 in series *Schaufenster der Welt*], Sig. Ser 30, LAB.

53. Critics of the West German economy also used the window-shopping motif as a way of exposing the "glassy" or "superficial" wealth of the country. See Fritz Diwok, "Wirtschaftswunder nur Schaufenstererfolg?" *Der Österreichische Volkswirt*, 44(18), 1958, p. 15. On the importance of window displays in nineteenth-century Germany, see Uwe Spiekermann, "Display Windows and Window Displays in German Cities of the Nineteenth Century: Towards the History of Commercial Breakthrough," in Clemens Wischermann and Elliott Shore, *Advertising in the European City: Historical Perspectives* (Aldershot: Ashgate, 2000).

54. On industrialists, class war, and "codetermination," see Wiesen, *West German Industry*, pp. 180–8.

55. On business leaders' fears of mass culture, see idem, "Mass Society, America, and the Decline of the West: Businessmen and Cultural Pessimism in Postwar West Germany," in Ursula Lehmkühl, and Michael Wala, eds., *Technology and Culture: Transatlantic Perceptions during Three Centuries* (Cologne: Böhlau Verlag, 2000), pp. 203–24.

56. See Uta G. Poiger, *Jazz, Rock and Rebels: Cold War Politics and American Culture in a Divided Germany* (Berkeley: University of California Press, 2000); Fehrenbach, *Cinema in Democratizing Germany*; and Maria Höhn, *GIs and Fräuleins: The German-American Encounter in 1950s West Germany* (Chapel Hill and London: University of North Carolina Press, 2002), esp. chapter 6.

57. This anxiety about mass consumption was already present during the Weimar years, when political and economic elites alternatively welcomed and questioned modernizing trends in an economically vibrant society. See Mary Nolan, *Visions of Modernity: American Business and the Modernization of Germany* (Oxford: Oxford University Press, 1994).

58. On Germans' belief in the superiority of their products, see Anita Kugler, "Vor der Werkstatt zum Fliessband: Etappen der frühen Automobilproduktion in Deutschland," *Geschichte und Gesellschaft*, 13(3), 1987, pp. 304–39; and Nolan, *Visions of Modernity*: pp. 58–82.

59. On the history of the term "made in Germany," see David Head, *'Made in Germany,' The Corporate Identity of a Nation* (London: Hodder & Stoughton, 1992); Jörg Kirchbaum, *Made in Germany: Tempo, Tesa, Teefix und 97 andere deutsche Markenprodukte* (Munich: Deutsche Taschenbuch Verlag, 1997); Gabriele Wölke, *Zum Image des Made in Germany: Beispiele aus Japan, Frankreich, und den Vereinigten Staaten* (Cologne: Deutscher Instituts-Verlag, 1985). For reflections on this phrase in the 1960s, see Erhard Hille, "Aus dem Blickwinkel der Werbung: Mit 'Made in Germany' hat es etwas Besonderes auf sich," *Der Erfolg*, 11(22), 1962, pp. 978–81.

60. On Germans' obsessions with "mass society" (not just "mass culture"), see as an introduction Axel Schildt, *Zwischen Abendland und Amerika: Studien zur Westdeutschen Ideenlandschaft der 50er Jahre* (Munich: Oldenbourg, 1999), pp. 90–100.

61. West Berlin mayor Ernst Reuter's welcome speech, *Deutsche Industrieausstellung Berlin: 1951 6–21. Oktober*: p. 24.

62. Reuter in Introduction to *Berlin Export* (1950), a book accompanying the first DIA, A1019, LAB.

63. Hans Böckler, "Der deutsche Facharbeiter," *Deutsche Industrie Ausstellung Berlin 1950: 1–15. Oktober*, p. 29, A1019, LAB.

64. *Qualität durch Forschung und Entwicklung* [title of the catalogue to the 1968 DIA], A1019, LAB.

65. There is a vast literature on Americanization in Germany. On recent debates and for bibliographical references, see Heide Fehrenbach and Uta G. Poiger, eds., *Transactions, Transgressions, Transformations: American Culture in Western Europe and Japan* (New York and Oxford: Berghahn, 2000).

66. "Deutsche Industrie Austellung Berlin, 6–21 October 1951," in B140/404, BAK.

67. *Besser Leben*, A1019, LAB.

68. For details on the USIA's relationship to German trade fairs, see "First semi-annual Report: President's Special International Program, July 1, 1956–December 31, 1956," Special Projects, International Offices and Special Assignments for Sam Meek, Box 9, Howard Henderson Papers, JWT/Duke.

69. Deutsche Industrieausstellung Berlin 1958. 13–28.9, A1019, LAB.

70. For statistics on "private consumption," see Michael Wildt, "Privater Konsum in Westdeutschland in den 50er Jahren," in Axel Schildt and Arnold Sywottek, eds., *Modernisierung im Wiederaufbau: Die Westdeutsche Gesellschaft der 50er Jahre* (Bonn: J.H.W. Dietz: 1993), pp. 275–89.

71. "Alle Wünsche werden erfüllt" is a subheading on a page from *Jährlich einmal in Berlin*, a publication accompanying the 1953 DIA–September 26 to October 11, 1953, A1019, LAB.

72. To this day, the trade fair remains an important source of tourism in German cities.

73. On advertising during the Hitler years, see Uwe Westphal, *Werbung im Dritten Reich* (Berlin: Transit, 1989); also Dirk Reinhardt, *Von der Reklame zum Marketing: Geschichte der Wirtschaftswerbung in Deutschland* (Berlin: Akademie, 1993), pp. 445–8; and Hartmut Berghoff, "Von der 'Reklame' zur Verbrauchslenkung. Werbung im nationalsozialistischen Deutschland," in idem, ed., *Konsumpolitik: Die Regulierung des privaten Verbrauchs in 20. Jahrhundert* (Göttingen: Vendenhoeck & Ruprecht, 1999). On Henkel and advertising during the Nazi years, see Wilfried Feldenkirchen and Susanne Hilger, *Menschen und Marken: 125 Jahre Henkel, 1876–2001* (Düsseldorf: Henkel, 2001), chapter 3.

74. For introductions to advertising in Modern Germany and Europe, see Reinhardt, *Von Reklame zum Marketing*; Peter Borscheid and Clemens Wischermann, eds., *Bilderwelt des Alltags: Werbung in der Konsumgesellschaft des 19. und 20. Jahrhunderts* (Stuttgart: Steiner, 1995); and Christine Lamberty, *Reklame in Deutschland, 1890–1914. Wahrnehmung, Professionalisierung und Kritik der Wirtschaftswerbung* (Berlin: Duncker & Humblot, 2000).

75. See Michael Kriegeskorte, *Werbung in Deutschland 1945–1965. Die Nachkriegszeit im Spiegel ihrer Anzeigen* (Cologne: Dumont Reise, 1992), p. 156.

76. For introductions to advertising in the FRG, see Harm G. Schröter, "Die Amerikanisierung der Werbung in der Bundesrepublik Deutschland," *Jahrbuch für*

Wirtschaftsgeschichte (1997): 93–115; Rainer Gries, Volker Ilgen, and Dirk Schindelbeck, *"Ins Gehirn der Masse kriechen!": Werbung und Mentalitätsgeschichte* (Darmstadt: Wissenschaftliche Buchgesellschaft: 1995).

77. "The J. Walter Thompson Company in Germany," folder "History (1962 English)," Box 1, Gilow Papers, JWT/Duke.

78. See profile of J. Walter Thompson Company, folder "History, 1959 (Germany)," Box 1, Gilow Papers, JWT/Duke.

79. Interview with Denis Lanigan, October 19, 1979, Dawkins Papers, Box 17, JWT/Duke.

80. Ibid.

81. "Advertising: U.S. Techniques Reach Europe," *New York Times*, October 7, 1962.

82. For introductions to the history of American advertising, see Stuart Ewan, *Captains of Consciousness: Advertising and the Social Roots of the Consumer Culture* (New York: McGraw-Hill, 1976); also Pamela Walker Laird, *Advertising Progress: American Business and the Rise of Consumer Marketing* (Baltimore: Johns Hopkins University Press, 1998).

83. "The J. Walter Thompson Company in Germany," folder "History File (1962 English)," Box 1, Gilow Papers, JWT/Duke.

84. Ibid.

85. Howard Henderson to Thomas Cannon of Eastman Kodak, 15 November 1954, Box 6, Henderson Papers, JWT/Duke.

86. For a collection of papers on Aktion Gemeinsinn, see "Organisations – Aktion Gemeinsinn, 1961 Jan – 1963 Dec, A–R," Box 12, Gilow Papers, JWT/Duke, as well as the specific campaign binders in the Aktion Gemeinsinn main office in Bonn. I thank the Aktion Gemeinsinn for access to their papers.

87. Allgemeine Korrespondenz files, Box 1, Gilow Papers, JWT/Duke.

88. Schildt and Sywottek, "West German Social History," p. 426.

89. From promotional blurbs on page I of Vance Packard, *The Hidden Persuaders* (1957) [16th edn] (New York: Pocket Books, 1961).

90. Lutz Niethammer, "Bürgerliche Wechseljahre – zur Konjunktur erinnerter Gefühle einer Klasse," in Lutz Niethammer et al., eds. *Bürgerliche Gesellschaft in Deutschland: Historische Einblicke, Fragen, Perspektiven* (Frankfurt: Fischer, 1990), pp. 533–48. Quoted in Sywottek "From Starvation to Excess?, p. 345.

91. Heinz Giebelhausen, "Der Mensch und die Werbung," *Der Lebenweiser,* 30(12), 1963, pp. 8–22.

92. For two examples of the many advertising-related articles that cited "mass society" literature, see Claus Borgeest, "Soll der Werber die Masse ansprechen?" *Wirtschaft und Werbung*, 11, 1957, pp. 319–20; and Karl Sacherl, "Kulturpsychologische Aspekte der Werbung," *Archiv für die gesamte Psychologie*, 16(3), 1964, pp. 299–310.

93. Ludwig Erhard, "Marktwirtschaft und Werbung gehören entrennbar zusammen," *Wirtschaft und Werbung,* 6(12), 1952, pp. 327–28.

94. Heinz Michaels, "Der gemachte Mensch: Objekt der Werbung," *Die Zeit*, June 2, 1961, p. 19.

95. Klaus J. Müller-Neuhaus, "Werbung: Prügelknabe der Öffentlichkeit," *Der Erfolg*, 10(18), 1961, pp. 832–4.

96. Ulrich Nussberger, "Fördert Werbung die Vermassung?" *Zeitungs-Verlag und Zeitschriften-Verlag*, 60, 1963, pp. 352–4.

97. These arguments about freedom and self-worth were found e.g. in Nussberger, "Fördert Werbung die Vermassung?" and in Walter Hollstein, "Die Werbung und der Mensch von Morgen," *Die Kommenden*, 18(6), 1964, pp. 25–6.

98. Engelbert Hofheinz, "Persönlichkeit – durch die Unterhose," *Wirtschaft und Werbung*, 1(3), 1957, pp. 70–71.

99. On the 1960 visit to Macy's, see the Kaufhof correspondences, in file "Other JWT Offices and Clients," folder "Clients, 1959–60, K–N," Box 2, Denis Lanigan Papers, JWT/Duke.

100. See Schröter, "Die Amerikanisierung der Werbung."

101. See Barbara Kirshenblatt-Gimblett, *Destination Culture: Tourism, Museums, and Heritage* (Berkeley and Los Angeles: University of California Press: 1998), p. 218.

102. Ibid., p. 1.

103. Barbara Wolbring, *Krupp und die Öffentlichkeit im 19. Jahrhundert: Selbstdarstellung, öffentliche Wahrnehmung und gesellschaftliche Kommunikation* (Munich: Beck, 2000), pp. 93–4.

104. Frank Biess, in his study of Second World War returnees, refers to "the nature of West German society specifically as a *postwar* society." Biess, "Survivors of Totalitarianism: Returning POWs and the Reconstruction of Masculine Citizenship in West Germany, 1945–1955," in Schissler, ed., *Miracle Years*, pp. 57–82.

105. Ibid., p. 57.

106. See Michael Geyer, "Cold War Angst: The Case of West-German Opposition to Rearmament and Nuclear Weapons," in Schissler, ed., *Miracle Years*, pp. 376–408.

107. On the application of Benedict Anderson's term to Germany, see Carter, *How German is She?*, p. 6; and David F. Crew, "Review Essay: Gender, Media, and Consumerism in Germany, 1920s–1950s," *Journal of Social History*, 32(2), Winter 1998, pp. 395–402.

108. Rosalind Williams, *Dream Worlds: Mass Consumption in Late Nineteenth-Century France* (Berkeley and Los Angeles: University of California Press, 1982).

109. Ironically, this mechanism bears a superficial similarity to how Germans had felt during the Nazi years, when the economy had recovered and people reveled in Hitler's ability to rearm the country back into prosperity. Indeed as Michael Geyer has pointed out, even into the early 1950s, public opinion polls indicated that 1937 was lodged in the collective memory as a "miracle" year, when the effects of the Great Depression were no longer experienced widely. See Geyer, "Cold War Angst."

110. Quoted in Schildt, "Materieller Wohlstand – pragmatische Politik – kulturelle Umbrüche. Die 60er Jahre in der Bundesrepublik," in Axel Schildt, Detlef Siegfried, and Karl Christian Lammers, eds., *Dynamische Zeiten: Die 60er Jahre in den beiden deutschen Gesellschaften* (Hamburg: Hans Christians, 2000): pp. 21–53, here p. 21).

111. Ibid., p. 26.

112. Diethelm Prowe, "The 'Miracle' of the Political-Culture Shift: Democratization Between Americanization and Conservative Reintegration," in Schissler, ed., *Miracle Years*, pp. 451–8.

113. *Mein Mann, das Wirtschaftswunder* (directed by Ulrich Erfurth, 1960).

114. Lars Akerblom to Norman Philip, 16 January 1962, Allgemeine Korrespondenz Files, Jan–Dec. 1962, Box 1, Gilow Papers, JWT/Duke.

7

Drugs, Consumption, and Internationalization in Hamburg, 1960–1968

Robert P. Stephens

Between 1964 and 1968, Germany experienced a rapid rise in drug consumption among its young citizens. Youth consumption of drugs was largely a product of two closely tied phenomena that emerged at the end of the 1950s and continued unabated throughout the 1960s: the creation of new youth-consumer markets and the internationalization of youth culture. Both of these trends arose from the success of economic expansion and globalization after the Second World War, and both had broad implications. If there was, as Arthur Marwick has argued, a "cultural revolution" between 1958 and 1974, then young people were the avant-garde of this revolution, and their attempts to break free from what they saw as the stifling conformity of the 1950s and the long shadow of the Third Reich led to broad changes throughout German society. In particular, this early period witnessed the emergence of a new international youth culture based around the consumption of illicit substances. Drug use may have represented only a part of larger social transformation in Germany and the Western world, but it was a central and quite conspicuous facet of these broad changes.

The focus of this chapter is "youth." For the purposes of my argument, I am interested in a small and fairly marginal group of youths, those who began using drugs before 1968, before the great "drug wave" of the early 1970s began in earnest. These young people were largely born during or directly after the war and saw themselves, by the mid-1960s, as a distinct group with interests – to paraphrase E.P. Thompson – different from and opposed to those of their parents' generation. This group, however, tells us much of the changes of the 1960s. They were, in many cases, the cultural vanguard and organized a transformation as important as the student movement. In this way, the focus on these young people allows us to view the origins of a larger cultural revolution that touched the lives of all young people by the early 1970s, whether they used drugs or not. The methodological problems involved in discussing specific young people and the broader category of "youth" are significant (the constructed nature of the category, the multivalent experience of youth, the gendered nature of the category, among others), but I have attempted to be cognizant of the specificities of my subjects and the constructed nature of the category and to be sensitive to the relationship between individual lives and the broader category. "Youth," during the period of study, was not merely a discursively constructed category, though it was certainly that; it was also a structure of feeling that gave meaning to people who understood their own experiences in terms of a larger "youth" revolt.

Besides the problem of "youth," the study of drug consumption raises some methodological questions that other consumerism topics do not face, largely due to the influence of international regimes of drug prohibition over the last century. The amount and types of source material available, particularly before the 1970s, limit the certainty with which historians may make conclusions. Patterns of distribution and consumption remain mostly speculative; the official documents are patchy at best and must be cobbled together from various, incomplete sources: local police estimates, national police reports, and United Nations documents. Other quite different evidence about the experience of drug consumption at particular historical moments can be gleaned from welfare and medical institutions charged with monitoring and "solving" drug abuse, though these documents tend to tell us more about the institutions themselves than about drug users. What is most often absent, however, is the voices of drug traffickers, dealers, and users themselves. The oral sources we do have tend to be generic and their stories illuminate the ways in which stories of drug abuse are told more than the actual experience of users. Therefore, recreating drug trades of the past require considerable reading "against the grain," questioning of sources and motivations, and confronting what is opaque or simply unknowable.

Despite these methodological problems, the study of drugs contributes to a more nuanced understanding of the transformation to global capitalism. At the same time, it reveals Western youths' broad rejection of the social values of the immediate postwar period and the emergence of a new culture of refusal. Young people throughout the industrial West adopted drug use because it was pleasurable, because it proved to be a potent symbol of rebellion against their parents' and grandparents' generations, and because they saw drug use as a means of refusing to follow well-worn paths to the adult world. Drug consumption threatened authority; more importantly it represented, perhaps more than any other phenomenon, a broad-based rejection of the rule of law. Simply by taking drugs, a substantial minority if not a majority of young people transgressed the legal boundaries of the state. Individuals who would never consider property crimes, for example, saw drug consumption as a private issue and therefore proved willing to not only break the law but often to flaunt their lawbreaking openly. Drug consumption and the related social problems that increasingly took center stage as the 1960s reached their close illustrate the complications of broad capitalist consumerism. Indeed, drugs represent the dark side of the consumerist ideal. This chapter explores the radical shift that took place at the intersection of consumption, internationalization, and the culture of refusal that lies at the root of the modern drug problem.

Illegal drug use in Germany in the 1960s grew within the context of rising affluence and changing patterns of consumption. At the end of the 1950s and the outset of the 1960s, West Germany saw a drastic change in what historian Victoria de Grazia has termed "consumption regimes" – the social process of consumption as well as ideas of what consumption meant. Throughout the decade of the 1950s, as historian Michael Wildt has convincingly shown, the fear of the hunger years haunted the generations that had lived through it. Since the war, this 'hunger mentality,' with its concomitant frugal consumption of goods, had praised the virtues of savings and economy.[1] Yet within a decade this pattern, which had held sway since at least the First World War, was replaced by a modern "consumer economy" focused on consumption as a social duty and the key to economic prosperity.[2] The shift in basic values of what consumption and goods meant was among the most rapid and most sweeping in history.[3] The generation that had lived through the war and rationing could not have imagined the pleasure of consuming anything as unproductive and ephemeral as drugs. The generation of 68ers, on the other hand, grew up with very different ideas about their role as consumers. Born at the end of the war or after it, their formative years fell well within the scope of Germany's economic miracle. Without the basic and drastic changes in fundamental patterns of consumption and in basic social attitudes, the spectacular increase in drug use in the late 1960s simply would not have occurred.

Although the economy of the Federal Republic showed unprecedented improvement in the 1950s, the benefits did not reach consumers until the end of the decade. Rising income was the most immediate effect of the German "*Wirtschaftswunder*" (economic miracle). In 1950, the average working-class family of four in Hamburg made only 343 DM a month; by 1963 this had almost tripled to 975 DM. Despite the rise in income, consumption patterns did not change rapidly. Through the entire period, the single most important category of expenditure remained food. At the beginning of the 1950s, families spent nearly half of their total income on food; by 1963, they still spent just over a third of their income on this basic need. It was not until 1958 that average Germans began shifting their expenditures away from necessities.

Though consumers were drawn to goods like televisions, automobiles, and household labor-saving devices, what people initially desired was *Genußmittel*. A German term that does not translate easily into English, *Genußmittel* literally means "articles of pleasure" and includes items physically consumed expressly for pleasure, as opposed to consumption of necessities such as food. Included among the *Genußmittel* are spices, coffee, tea, chocolate, alcohol and even narcotics such as opium. According to David Jacobson: "The word *Genußmittel* therefore also implies that these substances are luxuries for sybaritic enjoyment, means for creating Epicurean delights and, by extension, a state of sensual bliss."[4]

Between the founding of the republic and the middle of the 1960s rising consumption of *Genußmittel* far outstripped any other type of expenditure. During this period, expenditure on beer exceeded the rise in real income by a third.[5] In 1950, individuals spent over five million DM on alcohol and over four million DM on tobacco and consumed over thirty-eight liters of beer per capita. Consumption of these "luxuries" increased drastically in the late 1950s; by 1963, alcohol and tobacco purchases had risen more than threefold.[6] Three years later, alcohol consumption had reached the highest point in German history and, per person, Germans drank more alcohol than milk.[7] The rise in *Genußmittel* consumption signaled Germans' rising willingness to spend money to buy intoxicants a decade before the drug wave of the late 1960s. Increasing consumption of tobacco, coffee, chocolate, beer, and wine became a sign of growing affluence. Though these ephemeral consumables did not change the basic rhythms of life, as did the television set or the automobile, they made everyday life more enjoyable. Germans valued them not so much as status symbols, though this certainly occurred, but as something akin to a fundamental right.[8]

Though adults dramatically increased their own alcohol and tobacco use, they worried about their children's consumption habits. To parents, government authorities, and youth welfare experts alike, youth consumption represented a risk to the moral fiber of the country. They feared that the ability to purchase pleasure threatened to remove children from the guiding hand of tradition and thrust them into a commercial world they had neither the wisdom nor the self-restraint to overcome. Rather than preparing for a life of industry and hard work, the new "teenagers" appeared to be content to revel in their youth and newfound purchasing power.

During the 1950s, youth experts tended to conflate notions of consumption and addiction. Addiction was not a specific physical or psychological illness but rather any habit that threatened to confound or obscure the moral compass of young people, turning them into hedonistic consumers rather than cultured citizens. One "youth-protection" advocate warned that the consumerism of modern life threatened youth more than ever before and had specific consequences: ". . . They surrender themselves to the two greatest types of endangerment: all forms of addiction (eating sweets, tobacco, alcohol, light-weight reading, movies, dancing, pop music, games, etc.,) and all forms of aberrant sexual development (*geschlechtliche Fehlentwicklung*)."[9] Experts located youths' addiction on a spectrum based on their level of indulgence in consumer society. By preventing young people from entering into commercial relationships that endangered their development, youth-protection advocates believed they could prevent the slide into the colonization of everyday life by the free market.

The idea that unbridled consumption represented the greatest menace to youth was not new. Attempts to control youth consumption grew with the development of modern youth-welfare policy. As early as the Wilhelmine period, government officials and "youth savers" worried about the effects of industrialization on young unskilled workers between "primary school and the barracks," the period crucial in transforming young men into good citizens.[10] Often this meant guiding or controlling the behavior of young men with decidedly different ideas of propriety and thrift than those of reformers interested in curbing their youthful excesses. Indeed, middle-class reformers believed that young workers squandered their money on penny dreadfuls, movies, alcohol, cigarettes, and sex and used legislative action to attempt to impose their own set of values upon Germany's working-class youth.[11] As youth welfare expanded during the Weimar republic, social workers focused on two types of "problem behavior": consumption and (mostly young women's) sexuality. Frequently the two were, at least in the eyes of the authorities, directly connected. Under the Nazis, the scientific rationalist tendencies of the Weimar welfare system became explicitly racialized. The novelty of Nazi policy rested not in the understanding of the roots of problem youth; like the policy of the Weimar period, it relied on psychological models. The Nazis, however, saw outward deviance as a sign of genetic inferiority that should be purged from the body social.[12]

The collapse of the state at the end of the Second World War failed to lead to the reformation of youth welfare in the Western sectors. Though the occupation governments discarded certain laws, particularly those dealing with censorship, there was a marked continuity in youth-welfare policy and personnel.[13] After the war, the National Youth Welfare Law still stood in its Nazi form.[14] While many of the more coercive measures instituted under the Third Reich were abandoned in favor of progressive, therapeutic policies that harkened back to Weimar and favored preventative, consensual strategies,[15] the system retained the conservative ideology that placed "normal" and "deviant" youths in wholly separate categories. This meant that youth-welfare policy in the postwar period focused on maintaining an often artificial division between problem youth and their peers to police the boundaries between "normality" and "waywardness."

Although the public discourse about youth after the end of the war focused on controlling "criminal" youth spurred on by high unemployment, by the middle of the 1950s, the fears of mass unrest among the nation's youth rapidly gave way to a focus on "youth protection."[16] Indeed, by the late-1950s the youth-protection movement dominated debates on problem youth. With the founding of the national organization Action Youth Protection (*Aktion Jugendschutz*) in 1951, which published its own influential journal beginning in 1956, youth protection became a significant force in youth advocacy and became an integral part of most state welfare departments.[17]

During the 1950s, controlling consumerism became an increasingly significant priority for conservative youth-welfare and youth-protection advocates. They saw young consumers' habits as part of a spiritual decline dating back to industrialization, and wished to mold youth into a morality based in a "mythical Christian-patriarchal golden age, which they located at the beginning of the nineteenth century, before the onset of the age of iron."[18] Though the occupation governments had rejected the Nazi censorship law of 1935 and the youth-protection law of 1943, reconstituting these types of protections became a primary goal of conservative youth-welfare experts after the founding of the Federal Republic in 1949. In particular, conservative critics believed that the spread of consumer technologies such as radio, television, film, and phonographs threatened to destroy traditional social ties and leave young people morally adrift, bereft of spiritual guidance.[19]

By the early 1950s, conservative reformers had turned to legislation – just as their Weimar counterparts had – as a means to protect youth from the threat of the entertainment industry and perceived increases in youth crime and deviance. As early as 1949 the film industry, in order to ward off state intervention, began a voluntary system of self-censorship. Two years later the Law for the Protection of Youth in Public, the cornerstone of the youth-protection movement in the Federal Republic, went into effect. The new law regulated the acceptable ages for movie-going, dancing, drinking, smoking, and gambling, among other provisions. Then, in 1952 the Federal Republic passed a new law controlling objectionable literature that bore a striking resemblance to the 1926 law.[20] The purpose of these laws was to insulate youth from what critics saw as the penetration of the private sphere by the market economy. Rather than seeing capitalism as a boon to democratic citizenship, youth-protection advocates saw consumerism as a threat to the underpinnings of the social contract. Though adults should certainly participate in the market, youth deserved a space free of the force of modern consumer economy in which to grow not merely as economic actors but as moral individuals.

Despite the concerns and legislative efforts of youth-protection advocates, youth emerged as a distinct market for the first time at the end of the 1950s. New types of entertainment, new products, and new experiences beckoned and, by 1963, youth buying power had dramatically increased. According to market-survey estimates, the total purchasing power of youths was around twelve billion DM. Of young Germans, 72 percent owned their own bicycle, 44 percent a camera, and 29 percent a radio. The average university or high school student had a weekly disposable income of over ten DM, while young workers had over thirty-seven DM a week to spend as they saw fit.[21] Considering that the average adult male worker only earned around a thousand DM a month, this was a considerable sum.[22]

Much of this new disposable income went to small pleasures and *Genußmittel*. More than half of young men and 15 percent of young women smoked. A third of young men drank beer often, and nearly half of young women drank coffee frequently (a statistic which in itself raises interesting questions about the gendering of intoxication).[23] In the late 1950s, it was drinking and smoking that often provoked outrage from the youth-protection advocates. Otto Landt of Hamburg's State Office of Action Youth Protection (*Aktion Jugendschutz*) warned that, "alcohol and tobacco are much more dangerous than morphine or cocaine."[24] Indeed, the way experts wrote about cigarettes and alcohol foreshadowed the way they would talk about drugs a decade later:

> The first smoking experience is unpleasant and often arouses a strong defensive reaction from the body. Dependence takes place gradually. Yet soon – as with dependence on most alkaloids – a desire for another dose of nicotine begins. Without another dose of nicotine the body does not feel right. Out of this emerges a psychological addiction that only subsides after a couple of cigarettes. The youth needs nicotine. He has thus developed a real addiction that imperiously demands satisfaction. Pocket money is no longer enough; often other devious ways must be attempted. Thus the danger of sliding down the slippery slope has emerged.[25]

The moral was clear: smoking leads to addiction. Once addicted, the addict runs out of money to support his (in these stories it was always "his") addiction and is forced to turn to crime. This familiar progression, popularized first by nineteenth-century temperance movements, proved easily adaptable to most threatening forms of consumption. Philosophically grounded in the idea that "senseless" consumption signified moral failure, the theory of the "slippery-slope" came to dominate twentieth-century thinking about all substance abuse.

For authorities threatened by youth consumption, the principal response was repression. In Hamburg during the latter 1950s the state Youth Authority and the Women's police created a new form of youth policing. Youth Protection Patrols (*Jugendschutzstreifen*) made rounds to bars and public places where youth congregated, transporting those caught drinking or smoking home to their parents.[26] At the same time, however, authorities tried to co-opt youth rebellion, and force it into an institutional framework where, if they could not stop unwanted activities, they could at least tame them. In 1957, concerned about the growing popularity of "Rock 'n' Roll" dancing, Hamburg's Action Youth Protection (*Aktion Jugendschutz*), began holding dances with "modern dance music and modern dancing." Under the watchful eyes of adults, five hundred youths, "some of them so-called '*Halbstarken*',"[27] danced without the "intemperance" of the various commercial dance clubs.[28] Whether or not these efforts reformed their intended targets, they reflect the authorities' recognition of a new type of power wielded by youth: the power to consume as they chose.

A fundamental rise in expendable income, and changes in patterns of consumption, as well as in the ideas of what it meant to consume, provided the preconditions for the massive rise in drug use by Germany's youth in the late 1960s. People earned more, and near the end of the 1950s they began spending more. While adults continued to remember the hunger years, they nonetheless began to increase their consumption. Youths, unburdened by memories of the hard winters of 1947 and 1948, developed new ideas of what it meant to consume. They learned from the media and from each other that consumption could and should be pleasurable. Without this basic change in the way people saw their economic roles, the enormous spending on recreational pharmaceuticals would not have occurred.

Along with the growth of affluence and the welfare state in the industrial West, internationalization[29] was one of the defining trends of the postwar period. Internationalization occurred in any number of areas: business, transportation, military cooperation, international government, nuclear regulation, crime, and policing, among others. An under-appreciated aspect of this internationalization, though, was the unprecedented cooperation among youth beginning in the 1960s. The very success of capitalist economies in the industrial West opened the door for the formation of cross-cultural ties that brought youth from different national backgrounds closer together than ever before. Young people shared not only a cultural vocabulary dominated by rock 'n roll; they also had more individual contact with other nations due to massive increases in tourism and travel.[30] The identification of young people with a real or imagined international youth movement was not new. The Swing Kids of the Third Reich or the *Halbstarken* of the 1950s certainly saw themselves as part of a larger cultural movement. What was new in the 1960s was that while youths' interaction with cultural products became increasingly international as the youth market grew, young people also began to experience a new freedom of mobility. They began both to recognize and to exploit the contacts between like-minded people in other nations and used these connections to build international movements and markets.

The increasing number of youths traveling outside the borders of the Federal Republic, the emergence of new forms of international cultural production, the formation of youth groups that spanned borders and continents, as well as the explosion in the underground press created a new sense among young people that they could bridge the traditional boundaries of the nation and create new forms of politics and culture based on shared ideas.[31] The expansion of drug use cannot be fully understood without taking this new form of internationalism into account; without these international contacts and youthful entrepreneurialism, the drug trade could not have become so pervasive and persistent. Yet the ways in which the new consumerism and internationalism converged differed from place to place, and the drug scenes that developed also showed a remarkable amount of variation. The remainder of this chapter will trace how these processes merged in Hamburg in the 1960s, creating new forms of youth culture and consumption.

Youth drug consumption flourished in the context of international exchange. Between 1964 and 1968, young people on both sides of the Atlantic developed a fairly sophisticated international market in illicit drugs.[32] Along with this market grew a distinct drug culture, with new forms of expression based on the use of drugs. Young people developed new rituals and created a distinct language to describe their experiences. It was an international language, dominated by Anglo-American slang adapted to serve distinct scenes. Yet expanding drug use was at once an international and a distinctly local phenomenon. Over the course of a decade, most of Western Europe developed new and not necessarily homogenous patterns of drug consumption. Different cities developed distinct drug scenes, depending on location, supply, and local preferences.

The term "drug scene" deserves some clarification.[33] I have chosen to use that term to characterize the specific patterns of youth drug consumption that emerged in the 1960s. The word "scene" to describe the drug milieu was widespread in Germany by the end of the 1960s. Young drug users usually referred to the drug trade and the participants as the scene; journalists wrote about the scene, and even officials thought of the organization of drug distribution and consumption as a scene. A drug scene is not merely a place where drug transactions take place, though that is certainly a part of any drug scene. Rather, it is a set of social relationships that develop around a market in illicit drugs. For practical purposes, a drug scene usually is limited geographically to a city or urban area, since the majority of individuals involved in the drug market have little to do with the international or domestic distribution of drugs. One's relationship to the scene is a product of one's role in that scene (consumer, dealer, trafficker, etc.) and, more importantly, of one's contacts.[34] Though there has long been a certain amount of street dealing, especially in the last two decades, the illegal nature of the drug market has meant that drug dealers tend to prefer to transact business with people they know. Therefore, the number and quality of contacts often define one's role and status in the scene. The end result of this is that individuals more involved with the drug scene have better access to drugs, but they also carry greater risk of coming to the attention of the police.

"Drug culture," as opposed to the term drug scene, I take to mean the cultural manifestations that developed as a result of the spread of drug use. Drug use in the 1960s and early 1970s profoundly affected certain established forms of popular culture: it spawned the psychedelic rock movement; writers both new and established wrote about drug use; filmmakers began to use drug themes in their work; fashion turned to the psychedelic movement for inspiration; and graphic artists illustrated the influence of drugs, especially in poster art and comic books. At the same time, drug consumption created a market for new items, such as drug paraphernalia, which became, in many cases, art forms of their own. Concomitant with rising drug use was the introduction of new cultural forms that, though not directly a result of drug use, gained a certain popularity among drug users. These included a fascination with Eastern religions, macrobiotic cooking, and yoga, for example. As drug use expanded in the 1970s, entrepreneurs capitalized on the rising popularity of drug consumption and created a secondary licit market based on this youth culture. Head shops, ceramic bongs, psychedelic rock, posters, and T-shirts emblazoned with pot leaves or magic mushrooms arrived, at least in Germany, mostly after 1968. Indeed, many of the cultural forms associated with drug use formed the basis of an alternative culture that took on a life of its own over the course of the 1970s.

Despite the rapid rise in drug use throughout the industrial West, the development of local scenes was uneven, more rapid in some places than in others. Germany lagged behind the United States, England, Scandinavia, and the Netherlands in drug consumption. Yet Germans did not look directly to the United States for instruction and encouragement, as is often assumed. America and Americans were certainly a major influence. But the American influence on the drug scene in Hamburg was, more often than not, mediated through larger and richer scenes in London, Copenhagen, and Amsterdam. Hamburg's drug scene looked to America, but through a distinctly European lens.

Hamburg's own drug epidemic began quietly. In the mid-1960s, stock images of that decade's drug culture – youngsters clad in psychedelic clothing or black turtlenecks passing a joint or taking LSD – had yet to manifest themselves. In fact, hash and marijuana consumption came to Germany quite late. Instead, speed was the initial drug of choice in Hamburg.[35] Curious youths found it easy to buy diet pills and various stimulants, many of which were available over-the-counter. Taken as prescribed, these drugs did little; taken in large doses, they produced a sense of euphoria and excitement. Other widely prescribed stimulants such as Preludin, Rosimon, Ritalin and Captagon, popular with prostitutes for some time, proved easy to find. Students used these stimulants to stay awake and study for exams; athletes took them to improve their performance; but more and more frequently, small groups of youths popped uppers to go to clubs and dance all night.[36]

The drug culture in Hamburg during the early years revolved around the numerous beat clubs. These clubs featured rock 'n roll bands and gave young people a space relatively free of adult supervision. In the first few years of the 1960s certain clubs around the Reeperbahn (Hamburg's red-light district,) such as the Top Ten Club, the *Kaiserkeller* and the Star Club on Hamburg's notorious *Große Freiheit Straße* drew not only German beat bands, but bands from England and the United States as well. The Beatles spent their formative years in Hamburg's *Kaiserkeller* and Star Club before moving on to Liverpool's famous Cave Club. Many lesser-known Liverpool bands also spent time in Hamburg, where the work was plentiful.

The Star Club also brought in big-name touring shows. In the summer of 1963, for example, Ray Charles, Bill Haley and the Comets, The Searchers, and Chubby Checker all played the Star Club.[37] This constant flow of British and American bands into Hamburg kept the local scene abreast of the happenings in London and, to a certain extent, in North America. The music also drew young people from Scandinavia to Hamburg. The clubs acted as a catalyst to the internationalization of Hamburg's youth.

The use of stimulants by club-goers in these early years was identified not by the police, but rather by the policing arm of the Youth Authority, the so-called Youth-Protection Troops (*Jugendschutztruppe*). Originally formed as a joint venture between the Youth-Protection Department and the Women's Police, the Youth-Protection Troops patrolled the streets of Hamburg looking for "wayward" youth. The focus of their work was two-fold: they sought to control male youth consumption (smoking, drinking, and pornography), and youth sexuality ("protecting" the sexual purity of young women by keeping them from the sex trade, and guarding young men from homosexual "predators"). This meant that officers spent most of their time patrolling areas where youth congregated: parks, train stations, and especially bars and music clubs. Indeed, the clubs near the University and in St. Pauli proved to be the most intractable problems for the Youth-Protection Troops.

Several of the earliest cases of youth drug consumption that came to the attention of the authorities implicated one club in particular. Early in 1964, Palette – a downtown club on ABC Straße near Gänsemarkt and not far north of the city hall – became the popular hangout for the nascent youth drug scene.[38] One writer described Palette this way:

> The air in the bar was a stuffy haze of beer, hairspray, tobacco smoke and mothballs. The barmaid announced free rounds by ringing a ship's bell. In the room to the right of the entrance, a man momentarily stumbled over a half-empty *Green*, as bottles of a Hamburg export beer are called. In the niche at the entrance to the third room, called the *End*, the drop-outs slept. From time to time, the bartender came and talked to one or another of them. Then the drop-outs rummaged in their pockets and Captagon tablets, Prelus (Preludin) or Hash (marijuana cigarettes) changed hands."[39]

Palette received considerable attention from the police and the youth authorities alike because of this type of drug trade as well as its reputation as a gay hangout. It was shut down by 1967, but later reopened under the name Why not? and remained popular with drop-outs and young tourists.[40]

The case reports resulting from the Youth-Protection Troops are an invaluable resource in reconstructing the early drug scene in Hamburg. Their notes on the youth scene are the best direct evidence we have of the emergence of a drug scene in Hamburg until the "discovery" of drug consumption by the authorities at the end of the 1960s. For example, on April 13, 1964, during their normal rounds, Youth-Protection Troop officers discovered a 19-year-old Austrian named Sonja. Since she was apparently homeless and without means, the officers took her into custody. Under questioning at the police station, Sonja claimed that she was staying with a 22-year-old student named Lutz who worked at the Axel Springer publishing firm. She also admitted to having a "relationship" with a young Englishman named Mike. She was searched before being sent to a young women's hostel (*Mädchenheim*) and the investigators found a number of brown pills wrapped in blue paper and stuffed inside a matchbox. Sonja initially protested that she had no idea where the matchbox had come from, but under further questioning admitted that Mike had given it to her two days earlier.[41]

On the fifth of July, 1964 a young Swedish woman named Ingrid arrived in Hamburg. That night she went to Palette and met Lutz, the man Sonja had stayed with. He offered her a place to stay. Two days later, in the evening, Ingrid returned to the club to drink a few beers. After a time, a young man introduced himself and handed her ten small white pills. He told her that if she took all of them at once, she would feel wonderful. With little hesitation, Ingrid swallowed the bunch. Soon she became nauseous and bolted for the door. As she vomited violently outside the front door, Youth-Protection officers arrived. Before taking her to a doctor, they questioned a second girl, aged 17, who admitted to having been given two tablets of speed.[42]

In the middle of October, a Youth-Protection patrol (*Jugendschutztruppe*) picked up a 22-year-old named Gretchen. Gretchen had run away from home in December 1961. According to her statement, she and her mother had argued frequently because of Gretchen's regular visits to Palette. Gretchen's twin sister had long visited the club and had "gone downhill;" Gretchen's mother worried that she would do the same. Two months later Gretchen had reported to the young women's home at Schwanewik, though she only slept there. Sometimes she stayed with a friend. During the day, she hung out with other drop-outs at Palette or another club named *Kaffeeklappe*. She did not have a steady job, but she claimed the drop-outs looked out for each other, sharing money, or stealing money from other customers at Palette. According to her story, only once had she been involved with drugs. A young man named Mike had asked her for twenty DM. She gave him the money, and the two headed down to the Reeperbahn. At the corner of *Herbertstraße*, where prostitution was legal and regulated, they found a man who sold them 30 tablets of Preludin for 18 DM. They could not sell the pills, so they turned them over to another drop-out who claimed he could sell them. She never saw the man again and thought he had probably been arrested, since so many of the Palette regulars had been. "Those who 'drop out' too long all become criminals," Gretchen claimed, "and I don't want to."[43]

These reports and the others like them illustrate the international character of the scene and the ways in which cultural change was slowly transforming youth consumption by the mid-1960s, fully half a decade before the "drug problem" became a public issue. New commercial spaces and new forms of consumerism promoted a youth culture geographically and ideologically distinct from the adult world: this was the physical and cultural space in which the drug scene would emerge as a major cultural force by the 1970s.

These Youth Protection cases, however, only illuminate a portion of the emergent drug scene. By the mid-1960s, drug users came from several segments of society. Though the scene was not as diverse as it would become, members of several marginal groups came together in the clubs around the Reeperbahn: sailors, bohemians, prostitutes, students, and drop-outs.

One group that had always been prominent in the St. Pauli port district was sailors. Drug use and trade had long been part of the experience of the merchant seaman, and sailors from all over the world poured into Hamburg's notorious red light district. Calling at ports in Morocco, South Africa, India, and Asia where cannabis and opium consumption were the norm rather than the exception, many sailors smuggled drugs to the West for personal consumption and a quick profit.

Small circles of bohemians welcomed new experiences including drugs. Students at the Art College, intellectuals, writers, and journalists proved willing to experiment. These were young, educated children of the 1950s German middle-class milieu that was fascinated with French existentialism and modern jazz. Though small in number, these "Exis," as they were called, represented the Continental equivalent of the American beatniks. They borrowed from American and French intellectual currents, inhabiting loose groups that resented "their parents' material orientation, philistine lifestyles, and voluntary subjugation to stifling social norms."[44] It is difficult to gauge the extent of these groups or their effect on the emergence of more widespread drug consumption because they tended to keep to themselves and rarely came to the attention of the police.[45]

Speed use had long been a part of the sex trade in Hamburg. Pimps, bartenders, and porters in certain St. Pauli clubs carried on a lively trade selling speed to prostitutes, who routinely used the stimulants Captagon, Preludin, and Previtin. The large supply of speed used in these circles came from drugs diverted from pharmaceutical companies, usually through an inside contact, or from Scandinavians who brought the drug down from Stockholm's drug scene.[46]

University students had a more ambivalent attitude toward drug use. In the first few years, some student protesters used speed as a means to keep working long into the night. Yet the dominant Marxist bent of the German New Left viewed drug consumption with suspicion. Though there was some initial interest in the "consciousness expansion" of cannabis and LSD, most leftist students saw drugs as a diversion from the mission of overthrowing the political system. Drugs, so the argument went, were antirevolutionary; the way to an expanded consciousness lay not in chemical alteration but in overcoming an oppressive capitalist economic system.

The group of youths most involved in the early spread of drug use was the so-called *Gammler*, or "Drop-Outs." *Gammler*, a term with negative connotations, was a label placed on young bohemian types by the media, but a label that they adopted and translated into a badge of honor. Sporting long hair and flaunting their rejection of the bourgeois values of industriousness and thrift, these young drop-outs congregated in most of the large cities: near the Gedächtniskirche or on Kurfürstendamm in Berlin, on the Reeperbahn in Hamburg, on Nikolaiplatz in Munich. Seeing themselves as part of a larger international movement, many of these young people traveled to Paris, Stockholm, Rome, Amsterdam, and London.[47] Though it is impossible to accurately estimate the number of *Gammlers*, one historian estimates that at their high point, there were 200,000 full-time hippies in the United States and another 200,000 in Europe, and many more were sympathetic to the movement.[48] A contemporary journalist estimated only around 100,000 in Europe.[49]

In a 1966 cover article, *Der Spiegel* described the "typical" German *Gammler*:

> They move easily through the Old World and now and then also through the New World. With a sleeping bag under the arm, a few coins in the pocket, they hitch rides with the stream of tourist convoys and settle wherever the sun always shines or where they find companions who also proudly call themselves "*Wir Typen*." Like migratory birds they tend to go south in the autumn or settle down by their mother's hearth when winter gets near.[50]

Though the German drop-outs certainly remained cognizant of their "Germanness," many of them felt they had more in common with *Provos* in Amsterdam, the "heads" and "freaks" in London, *Raggare* in Stockholm, or the Hippies in San Francisco than with other groups in their own society.[51] Though these young people from various countries were often quite different, they shared a common core belief in the rejection of the values of their parents' generation, exacerbated in Germany by the rising awareness of the Nazi past.

Concomitant with the rejection of the past was a rejection of consumerism. The drop-outs and the nascent student movements were, in fact, two sides of a coin. Both rejected the idea of the affluent society based on mass consumption. Yet while the student movement, inspired by Marxism, saw the imminent collapse of capitalism under the weight of its own internal contradictions, the *Gammler* youth simply rejected capitalistic society altogether. In a sense, the drop-outs marked the culmination of the *Wirtschaftswunder*. They took the promise of affluence for all and rising leisure time and stood it on its head, rejecting affluence and reversing the traditional relationship of work to leisure. Rather than working in order to be able to enjoy some leisure, they made leisure a job in itself. As one drop-out on Hamburg's Reeperbahn put it: "It [dropping out] is a hard job."[52]

Drugs fit perfectly into the "anti-ideology" ideology of the *Gammler*. Taking drugs represented, at heart, the consumption of pleasure in a tangible form. At the same time, the drop-outs symbolically rejected traditional forms of consumption by smoking hashish, as opposed to their parents' ever-increasing consumption of alcohol. Rather than confronting the so-called "Alcohol Generation," though, they simply ignored it, which was all the more infuriating to adults.[53] These young people took drugs not because their parents disapproved, though this was certainly an added benefit; they took drugs because they wanted to, because it was fun, and because they just did not care what their parents' generation thought.

Parents worried that their children would "tune in, turn on, and drop out." Drugs presented a both real and imagined threat, as did the refusal of the drop-outs to pursue a "normal" lifestyle. Walter Becker saw the *Gammler* as the heart of the danger:

> An international phenomenon, most *Gammlers* here [in Germany] appear to be at risk. If we include other groups of youths under this heading, then most show signs of considerable instability. They rebel against the norms of middle-class society in indiscriminate ways but in a weak-willed manner, wishy-washy and feeble as it were. They are not true rebels who enthrall us and are able to lead to new destinations but rather tired mutineers more inclined to resignation than protest. In their circles they turn to marijuana cigarettes, small brown packets or – more recently – to LSD-25! The authorities must acknowledge and fight against this danger to our youth in a timely manner. *Due to the devastating effects of drugs, there can be no pardon.*[54]

Adults felt threatened by the drop-outs because this motley crew publicly flaunted what their critics most desired: an orderly society. Their appearance, their refusal to work, their obtrusive begging, and their drug use put a public face on a much larger conflict. Drug use appeared to be a threat because many adults saw drugs as leading to this kind of behavior, when, in fact, the opposite was probably the case.

Yet Becker was right in that *Gammlers* played an important role in the early drug trade in Hamburg. As the popularity of speed use, predominantly of Preludin, continued to spread between 1964 and 1966, police began to focus on these young drop-outs. On November 24, 1965, police arrested 18-year-old Marion K. at a bar in Harburg, south of the Elbe. She had recently run away from a youth home and, despite already having gone through a withdrawal treatment at a local hospital a year before, had begun using Preludin again. She admitted to purchasing 250 tablets, using some and selling the rest.[55] In February 1966, police caught a 19-year-old Swede named Klaus who had convinced a friend who worked in a doctor's office to steal a prescription book for him. He and his friend then carved a doctor's stamp. Klaus managed to fill two prescriptions for Preludin before being discovered.[56] In June, authorities uncovered a group of young men at Rahlstedt Youth Home conspiring to sell Preludin.[57] In September, the Youth Authorities questioned a drop-out named Adolf, who claimed to be "unenthusiastic" about continuing his life as a *Gammler* and asserted that Preludin use was becoming more and more popular with the drop-outs, many of whom were becoming addicts.[58]

The use of drugs in clubs spread after 1966 as the ranks of the long-time drop-outs were swelled by an influx of new drug consumers drawn by the increasing visibility of drug consumption both in the media and in the clubs. While in 1964 the number of clubs where drugs were prevalent was small, limited to Club 99 and a few of the clubs on the Reeperbahn, by 1968 drugs could be had in any number of clubs. The Youth-Protection Department considered nineteen clubs to be drug hangouts. Most were located within a twenty-block radius around the Reeperbahn. One block on Große Freiheit was home to three suspected clubs: Club 39, Salambo, and Imbißstube. Other St. Pauli clubs included Mambo-Schänke, Drei-Weisheiten, Rattenkeller, Top-ten, Past-Ten, as well as the Hotel Nobistor and the Sahara-Inn. Club 99, near the Dammtor train station and the University, remained a center of the drug trade, along with a club across from the main train station at first called Oblomoff but later changed to Augustenburg. Police found the spread of clubs to other parts of Hamburg more troubling. Authorities suspected the Casino Club in Harburg as well as Cleopatra on Bramfelder Chaussee north of Barmbeck of involvement in the drug trade. Even in the relatively middle-class western suburb of Groß Flottbek a club called Big Ranch across from the horse-racing track fell under suspicion.[59]

After the middle of the decade an international culture based on a rejection of industrial society, an interest in Eastern spiritualism, and a penchant for drug use began to coalesce. Americans came to Europe in increasing numbers, while Britons and Swedes began to travel to Morocco along with their American compatriots. For the next few years, Morocco was the focus of the European hash trade, because of both its close proximity and its exotic appeal.[60] The international fascination with Tangier, home in the 1950s to prominent writers and drug users such as William Burroughs and Paul Bowles, was rooted in the availability and cultural acceptance of cannabis. The rapid increase in arrests of young Americans and Europeans in both Morocco and Spain attested to a blossoming drug culture that crossed national boundaries.[61]

Cannabis increasingly found its way to West Germany in the mid-1960s. On March 3, 1965, police in Soltau arrested a young American man and a Swedish woman for stealing gasoline. Upon inspection of their car, the officers found slightly more than a kilogram of marijuana under the back seat. According to the report, these two had been employed by a drug-trafficking group in Stockholm to purchase the drugs in Tangier. After driving through West Germany, France, and Spain, they traded a Moroccan some clothing for the marijuana. On the trip back to Sweden, they delivered a small quantity of the drug to a jazz musician in Paris and to a Turk in Cologne. The American admitted that he had made the journey to Morocco a number of times and had sold the drug in both Spain and the United States.[62]

In the summer of 1966, Christian B., only 16 years old, stole 3,000 DM and various valuables from his parents. Christian planned to drive to Morocco and buy some marijuana with his 19-year-old friend Ulrich B., who happened to have a car. On the way, they met a Luis T., a 25-year-old from Peru. The three of them hit it off, so the Germans invited him to come along on their journey. Near Tetuan, Morocco, they purchased eight kilograms of marijuana for 800 German DM. They hid the contraband in the car and drove back across Spain and France. In Belgium they split 200 grams into small packages, which Luis tried to sell in several cities. Convinced London was the place to sell the hash, Luis attempted to cajole his new friends into the journey across the Channel. Christian and Ulrich wanted to go back to Germany instead and sell the stash there. Luis decided to part company with the Germans and went to stay with a friend in Antwerp. The two German teens then drove to Hamburg. Ulrich offered the marijuana to a porter at one of the clubs on the Reeperbahn for 20,000 DM. The police were tipped off about the deal and waited for Ulrich to return with the contraband. Not long after, Ulrich returned and the porter turned him down. The police followed Ulrich back to the car. Once he realized he was being followed, Ulrich ran for the car and tried to pull away. The police rammed the car to keep the young men from escaping. The arresting officers found 7.8 kilograms of marijuana hidden under the trunk.[63]

While young Europeans traveled to foreign lands in search of hashish, immigration from the developing world brought traditional forms of cannabis consumption to Europe: Algerians in France, Turks in Germany, West Africans and West Indians in Britain. Among the Algerian workers in France smoking *kif* – a North African cannabis product – was a matter of tradition. Some young Algerians, though, took part in the burgeoning international youth networks, introducing hashish to young people in much of Southern Europe, and supplying much of the demand of the American troops stationed in Southern Germany.[64] In Britain, Nigerians and other West Africans, as well as Jamaican immigrants, played a significant role in the trade.[65] In Germany, Munich and Frankfurt became the early centers of the marijuana trade, Munich because of its large number of Turkish guest workers, and Frankfurt because of its proximity to large numbers of American soldiers.[66] At the same time, Spaniards and Moroccans played an important part in the traffic, because of the increased interest in Moroccan hashish.[67]

As time wore on, young hippies began driving through the Balkans to Istanbul or Beirut, smuggling hashish back to Europe through Bulgaria, Yugoslavia, and

Austria.[68] Turks bringing small shipments into Southern Germany also traveled this route extensively. Occasionally Lebanese smugglers took advantage of this path, though they preferred to use shipping channels. In late March 1966, Mustafa Tantalkaya was returning from Turkey to his job in Munich when he was arrested in Yugoslavia with 150g of hashish. A month later, Yugoslavian customs arrested Saim Bacharanlar for trafficking eight kilograms to Germany. Six days later, officers discovered 3.75 kilograms of hashish in a false-bottomed suitcase belonging to Sezaj Boskurt, who claimed to be delivering the drugs to Mehmed Ozdemir in Munich.[69] In August 1968, Bulgarian police arrested a German, a South African, and a Malaysian trying to smuggle 19 kilograms of hash into the Federal Republic. Two months later, they arrested a young Englishman seeking to smuggle 18 kilograms from Afghanistan to Australia. A few days thereafter, 14 kilograms of hashish were discovered in the gas tank of an Iranian traveling to the Federal Republic.[70] As these cases exemplify, the traffic in hashish through the Balkans initially included both Europeans bringing drugs back from their travels, and Turks, Lebanese, and Iranians delivering drugs to the Federal Republic and Scandinavia; most of this trade remained relatively small-scale.

Around 1966, the hippies who had caused such a stir in Morocco began to migrate toward the Middle East and South Asia. Seeking "enlightenment" in Eastern mysticism and ample supplies of cannabis, young drop-outs headed down the hash trail. Richard Neville, one of those who traveled this long road during 1966 and 1967, described this motley band:

> Young Americans, Australians, British, Canadians, French, German, Dutch, Italians, Japanese, Scandinavians, and South Africans who dress, talk and travel the same language. New gypsies who flow across the world; congealing in communal crash pads, caves, camping grounds, Youth Hostels, YMCAs and hotels. Hundreds of them dream months and even years away in Moroccan and Spanish pot holes. Thousands more press eastwards from Istanbul through Ankara, Erzurum, Tabriz, Tehran, Mashed, Herat, Kandahar, Kabul, Peshawar, Lahore, Amritsar, Patna, Katmandu, Calcutta, Rangoon, Bangkok, Vientiane, Phnom Penh, and south through to Kuala Lumpur, Singapore, Indonesia and Australia . . . Nowhere is inaccessible . . .[71]

For the first few years, over half the number traveling the hash trail were young Americans, but Europeans made up most of the remainder; in the early 1970s this relationship was reversed. Many of those who made the trip did so in search of some "authentic experience" or to escape what they saw as the oppressiveness of the home countries. According to Lieschen Müller:

> you either stayed home and got into politics, the French Revolution of '68, the Vietnam demonstrations, Red Rudi Dutschke in Berlin, or you went East. A lot of people stayed

> for the politics, got disillusioned and then went East, because things hadn't changed overnight as expected."[72]

The trip East, however, was normally only a temporary escape. A few stayed for years; most returned to their homes and a more normal life.[73]

Between 1968 and 1971, what had been a trickle of hashish mainly from Morocco became a flood from the Near and Middle East and Central Asia.[74] Hashish smuggling, which had been a way to supply oneself and one's friends, became a way to finance a life on the margins. As a result, young Europeans and North Americans attempted to smuggle ever-larger caches of contraband. Many of them ended up serving lengthy prison sentences in wretched conditions in countries such as Turkey and Lebanon, Bulgaria and Yugoslavia.[75]

No one knows the number of young westerners who made this journey, though the Indian and Nepalese government tourism statistics recorded about 47,000 American visitors in 1966 and slightly fewer Europeans.[76] A much smaller estimate that probably gives a better idea of the traffic on the hippie trail counted two thousand hippies passing through Kabul in 1967 alone.[77] What was certain, however, was that more and more hippies were being arrested for trafficking hashish. In August 1967, for example, German police were on the trail of their first large-scale bust. Two British students sold ten kilograms of hashish in Munich and Frankfurt, after which they headed back toward the East. In December, they purchased eighty kilograms of hashish in Pakistan. The two then flew to Paris, rented a car and drove to Frankfurt. On New Year's Day 1968, Frankfurt police arrested them for attempting to sell the hashish.[78]

How did this broadly international increase in hashish smuggling affect Hamburg? For the first few years (1964–1966), Hamburg was simply a way station for the larger drug scenes in Stockholm and Copenhagen. Police repeatedly claimed Hamburg served mainly as a "trans-shipment center" (*Umschlagplatz*).[79] Despite the reluctance of police to admit that Hamburg also hosted a growing internal market, the number of hashish consumers grew rapidly in 1966 and 1967. On February 1, 1967 during the annual press conference on crime, Hamburg Senator Hans Ruhnau pointed for the first time to an alarming rise in drug consumption. In that year's annual narcotics summary to the Federal Criminal Office, the Hamburg police reported a rapid climb in the number of hashish cases: "The number of hashish/marijuana cases coming to light rose from 9 in 1966 to 70. Fifty-five of these were youth and teenagers (*Jugendliche und Heranwachsende*), including 8 foreigners."[80]

Hamburg's Youth-Protection Troops uncovered much of the new hashish consumption. In 1967, they detained forty-three teens between the ages of fifteen and twenty for drug possession. Young men made up the bulk of the detainees, averaging nineteen years of age. The young women caught with drugs were just seventeen, on average. Most came from so-called "orderly homes." Except for seven students attending a secondary modern school (*Realschule*), all attended a vocational school (*Volksschule*), implying that most came from working-class families. Most of the youths initially received drugs from friends, particularly from friends who were drop-outs. They usually bought drugs at clubs in St. Pauli, around the Reeperbahn and on Große Freiheit Straße, but they preferred to smoke their hash in small groups, either in someone's home or in one of the parks.[81]

What linked these teens more than their shared sociological characteristics was their experience of drug use. Smoking hashish was pleasant for most, though the experience varied. One respondent declared, "I felt transported to another world." Another claimed, "My spirit was carried off somewhere." Some had a less spiritual and more common reaction: "I suddenly had to laugh, and I couldn't stop laughing;" or "The music sounds entirely different. I could hear every mistake. If I haven't smoked any hashish, music isn't so important to me." At least one young man was not as convinced of the effects of hashish: "I couldn't feel anything."[82]

Along with hashish consumption, a market in LSD emerged in 1967. Though LSD had probably been available sporadically in Hamburg since 1966, Hamburg Police Criminal Director Herbert Hoyer claimed at the end of 1967 that not a single case of LSD consumption had come to the attention of the police.[83] Despite police claims to the contrary, it is fairly clear that LSD was available in Hamburg's clubs in 1967–1968. In a *Konkret* article that same month, Stefan Aust commented on the obliviousness exhibited by police to the rapid changes in drug consumption: "The naïveté of the official offices is simply fantastic. Everyone who doesn't look exactly like a police officer can buy LSD in every second beat club or hippie bar in the Federal Republic. In every big city, there are already several thousand young people taking LSD."[84] Aust was probably more correct than Hoyer, but the rapid spread of LSD, already a reality in American cities and in London, did not occur before 1969.

The data on the rise in drug consumption around 1968, however, tells us little about how these quantitative changes were experienced by young people. Until recently, the student movement has dominated the discussion of youth in the 1960s. Indeed, since the 1960s, the mythical year of 1968 has been seen as the pivotal moment in postwar history by both nostalgic 68ers and their critics. Although the political events of 1968 took center stage, other facets of youth culture grew substantially yet garnered less attention than the student protests. Drug use blossomed in 1968. What had been a fairly peripheral activity began to spread, as more and more young people experimented with drugs. This spread in drug use took place quietly; the authorities and the press were too busy dealing with the more explosive combination of war and protest to pay much attention to drug use. But, unlike the massive protests, drug consumption occurred on the scale of everyday life. The drug scene quietly grew without directly challenging the power of the state.

A report by an anonymous author, probably an undercover police officer or a paid informant, gives a certain insight into the everyday world of the drug scene. One of the members of the Hamburg Youth Department visited Club 99, on the Esplanade near city hall, and wrote a memorandum about his or her experiences. The report follows the format of an ethnography but often reads like the musings of a postmodern urban *flâneur*, fascinated and repulsed by a world that seemed completely foreign and threatening. This horrific captivation springs from the realization that the author has entered a completely foreign world within his or her own city, reminiscent of the *flâneurs* of "Outcast London" during the 1870s and 1880s.[85] The author opens the report with a foreboding description of the surroundings. "In the club the same atmosphere dominates the entire day. It turns out that the club is a long tunnel in which almost no daylight enters," the author claims. "The partial darkness is partially illuminated by dim lamps. This long crepuscular tunnel is confusingly arranged because of the many small niches, and because of this the youth can go about their pleasure undisturbed."[86] Behind the bar, Günther or Wolfgang, the two bartenders, handed out beers and cokes to the ragged teens planted on bar stools. Beyond the packed bar area, visitors passed into the claustrophobic back room. Even darker than the bar area and incessantly smoky, the back room consisted of numerous small niches. These tight spaces, most large enough for only two or three, were filled day and night with high school students skipping school, students from Hamburg's university, apprentices, hippies, street kids, and working-class toughs. Klatches of young men and women sat on benches or barstools or stood, smoking cigarettes and talking about philosophy, the state of the student protests, the drudgeries of high school, or sex. Much of the conversation, however, focused on drugs: someone's recent trip to Istanbul and the best way to smuggle hash back to Germany; the place to score in Amsterdam; whom to contact in London for "Blue God" LSD; how to dry banana peels in the oven for smoking; or about a friend of a friend who knew a nurse who could get pills.

The informant claimed that it was not difficult to buy drugs at Club 99, attesting that, "In the meantime, I have often asked after stuff and have received something every time."[87] The small alcoves, hidden from the view of prying eyes, and the filthy bathrooms at the back of the bar offered ample opportunity to transact business. Yet the bargains made at the Club 99 were not the kind of deals that particularly interested the police; this was all small-time trade: a gram of hashish, a few uppers, or some barbiturates. Someone might trade a joint for a few pills or trade a few grams of hash for a stolen radio.[88]

This kind of ethnographic detail, however, was only part of the report; much of the report was given over to telling horror stories and warning of the dangers – real or imagined – of this new milieu. In the middle of the report, the author tells the story of a young girl:

> One late afternoon as I came into the club, an approximately 16-year-old girl slept in a partially hidden niche. As she was awoken by the words of an older guest: She's taken too many birth control pills (*Antibabypillen*), she looks pretty wrecked . . . Talking between them was out of the question at first, because she was hardly in the shape to talk rationally. When she had regained some of her senses, she disappeared for a few minutes and then returned. Her acquaintance told her as they were leaving that she shouldn't take so many tablets at the same time in the future. Of course she could have some anytime she wanted."[89]

This and the other stories reported by the author repeatedly highlight the sexual danger of this milieu. The author concludes that the place itself is a threat and must be closed: the fault is not placed on the youths but on the milieu itself. These new social spaces breed corruption and must be stamped out so that youths can regain their senses.

Despite the fears of the author and the tone of fascinated horror, this ethnographic report gives us a glimpse into the everyday experience of the drug scene: young people sharing a joint, passing around a bottle of schnapps someone had shoplifted, or taking a few pills. Bars like Club 99 played midwife to an emerging drug culture. The culture of drug use emerged at the intersection of popular culture, consumption, and rebellion. It developed among groups of friends who shared a set of values gleaned from popular culture, a widespread discontent with the affluent society, and a longing for some kind of meaning outside of the traditional passage from school to work. They craved "authentic" experience and sought ways to escape what they saw as a mundane, bourgeois existence. Drugs offered a means to this end. Rather than being a form of resistance to market mechanisms beyond their control, or the result of youth being swindled by the machinations of the culture industry, youth drug use marked a very real triumph of postwar youth consumer culture. Young people rejected consumption through consumption. Though they believed smoking hashish or dropping acid could release them from the vulgar materialism of modern capitalism, they were actually promoting the development of a global capitalist market in drugs.

Walter Becker, director of the national Action Youth-Protection association and the most prominent voice warning of the dire consequences of rising drug consumption during the 1960s, saw drugs as a harbinger of things to come. "Addiction is the central problem of our times," Becker perceptively noted. "A universal addictive attitude is becoming, to a certain extent, the model of modern life and human needs."[90] Drug consumption was part and parcel of a larger revolution in consumption sweeping the Western world. People acquired things at an unprecedented rate. Particularly novel was the rising purchasing power of youth. During the 1960s, young people bought things they had never been able to: radios, records, magazines, books, bicycles. And they bought drugs. Over the course of the 1960s, young people became more and more disaffected with the society created by their elders. For many, discontent took the form of protests against the State, the war in Vietnam, control of the media, and the failing education system. Others simply rejected the status quo altogether. The flight into drugs was a flight from reality, but it was also a retreat from a society which many youths felt no longer served their needs.

Within this context, young people created a space for themselves, out of the reach of the adult world. The birth of a drug scene was an international phenomenon. Not only did it take place in most Western countries, it took place because large numbers of youths became more international in their influences and tastes. Though this emergence of an international youth culture took place most visibly in the world of popular culture, it also took place on the ground, with young people coming into direct contact with like-minded individuals from other countries.

Changes in consumption regimes and the internationalization of youth did not cause drug use. We cannot blame consumerism and travel for drug consumption; to do so not only would be crudely simplistic but also would parrot the laments of the 1960s as the decade of permissiveness that led to the inevitable and destructive decline in morality. New patterns of consumer practice, new forms of production to meet those desires, and an increasingly international economic structure fundamentally changed the social structures of the industrial West. The new consumerism and the unprecedented prosperity improved the lives of many. Yet the consequences were complicated and often unforeseeable. The new social realities and globalization created the preconditions for the boom in drug consumption in the last thirty years of the twentieth century. In this respect, drug consumption represents, ironically, the success of consumerism.

Notes

1. See Michael Wildt, "Plurality of Taste: Food and Consumption in West Germany during the 1950s," *History Workshop Journal* 39, 1995, pp. 24–6.
2. See Erica Carter, *How German is She? Postwar West German Reconstruction and the Consuming Woman* (Ann Arbor: University of Michigan Press, 1997).
3. See Wolfgang Schivelbusch's provocative book *Tastes of Paradise: A Social History of Spices, Stimulants, and Intoxicants* (New York: Pantheon Books, 1992), especially pp. 3–14.
4. Ibid., p. xiii.
5. "Bier: Sieg der Flasche," *Der Spiegel* 18(43), October 21, 1964, p. 54.
6. Norbert Mieck, "Entwicklung der Suchtgefahren," *30 Jahre der Hamburg Landesstelle gegen die Suchtgefahren* (Hamburg: n.p., 1978), p. 9.

7. "Wohlstand: Über alles in der Welt," *Der Spiegel,* 20(1/2), January 3, 1966, p. 23.

8. "Bier: Sieg der Flasche," p. 54.

9. Anton Strambowski, "Jugendgefährdung – ein Problem unserer Zeit," *Jugendschutz* 1(1), 1956, p. 4.

10. Derek S. Linton, *"Who Has the Youth Has the Future": The Campaign to Save Young Workers in Imperial Germany* (Cambridge: Cambridge University Press, 1991), p. 227.

11. Ibid., p. 44.

12. See Edward Dickinson, *The Politics of German Child Welfare from the Empire to the Federal Republic* (Cambridge: Cambridge University Press, 1996) and Detlev J.K. Peukert, *Inside Nazi Germany: Conformity, Opposition and Racism in Everyday Life*, trans. Richard Deveson (New York: Penguin, 1987), pp. 208–235.

13. Dickinson, *German Child Welfare*, pp. 244–5.

14. Ibid., p. 245.

15. Ibid., p. 252.

16. Schildt, *Moderne Zeiten: Freizeit, Massenmedien und "Zeitgeist" in der Bundesrepublik der 50er Jahre* (Hamburg: Christians, 1995), pp. 153–4.

17. For an admittedly biased review of the first ten years of Youth Protection work see Bundesarbeitstelle Aktion Jugendschutz, *Jugendschutz heute und morgen* (Hamm: Hoheneck-Verlag, 1961).

18. Dickinson, *German Child Welfare*, p. 265.

19. Ibid., p. 266.

20. Ibid., p. 267. See also Germany (West), *Bundesgesetze zum Schutz der Jugend in der Öffentlichkeit und über die Verbreitung jugendgefährdender Schriften* (Munich: Beck, 1954); Bundesarbeitstelle Aktion Jugendschutz, *Jugendschutz*; and Karl Hukeler, *Jugendschutz in öffentlich-rechtlicher Sicht* (Lucern: Fachgruppe Jugendschutz, Caritaszentrale, 1961).

21. "Jugendbericht: Oben sitzt einer," *Der Spiegel*, 19(28), July 7, 1965, pp. 22–3.

22. See *Statistisches Jahrbuch für Hamburg, 1968/1969*, p. 346.

23. "Jugendbericht: Oben sitzt einer," *Der Spiegel*, 19(28), July 7, 1965, pp. 22–3.

24. Otto Landt, "Das Sucht-Gespräch mit Jugendlichen," *Jugendschutz,* 3(6), 1958, p. 15.

25. Gerhard Hüffmann, "Süchte bedrohen die Jugend" *Jugendschutz* 1(2), 1956, p. 8.

26. Paula Karpinski, "Jugendschutz in einer Welt- und Hafenstadt" *Jugendschutz*, 6, 1961, pp. 33–5.

27. On Halbstarken see Thomas Grotum, *Die Halbstarken: zur Geschichte einer Jugendkultur der 50er Jahre* (New York: Campus, 1994).

28. "'Treffpunkt Jugend' mit Rock 'n Roll" *Jugendschutz* 2(6), 1957, p. 23. See also Walter Becker, "Jugendtanz – eine Frage der Erziehung und des Jugendschutzes," *Jugendschutz*, 7, 1962, pp. 11–15.

29. The term "globalization" has gained a certain amount of cachet in the 1990s as an explanatory concept for these types of issue. In the 1960s, however, "internationalization" is probably much more accurate. Most of the innovations were limited to the industrial West and Japan, with the rest of the "undeveloped" world being a victim of internationalization

rather than a participant. There is a new terminology emerging out of the rejection of Americanization. See Axel Schildt, "Beyond the 60s – Finally Arrived in the West? Notes on the Americanization of Culture in West Germany," and Anselm Doering-Manteuffel, "Transatlantic Exchange and Interaction – The Concept of Westernization," both papers given at The American Impact on Western Europe: Americanization and Westernization in Transatlantic Perspective conference at the German Historical Institute, March 25–27, 1999.

30. On the increase in tourism in Germany see Hasso Spode, ed., *Goldstrand und Teutonengrill: Kultur- und Sozialgeschichte des Tourismus in Deutschland 1945 bis 1989* (Berlin: W. Moser, Verlag für universitäre Kommunikation, 1996), especially the contribution of Rainer Schönhammer, "Unabhängiger Jugendtourismus in der Nachkriegszeit", pp. 117–128. For the 1950s see Schildt, *Moderne Zeiten*, pp. 180–208, and Alon Confino, "Traveling as a Culture of Remembrance," *History and Memory*, 12, 2000, pp. 92–121.

31. For a more substantial discussion of these issues see my dissertation, Robert Stephens, "The Drug Wave: Youth and the State in Hamburg, Germany, 1945–1975" (Ph.D. diss., University of Texas at Austin, 2001), pp. 84–94.

32. This statement needs some qualification. Not all the people involved in the drug scene were young, though most were. The distribution of drugs often rested in the hands of older individuals and groups. But in Germany, unlike in the United States, there were very few organized criminal syndicates intent on dominating the distribution of drugs until the early 1970s, when the bulk trade was taken over by international syndicates.

33. During the 1970s, scholars, particularly at the Birmingham Center for Contemporary Cultural Studies, developed an elaborate critique of youth cultures. Influenced by a New Left reading of Marx, these scholars looked to youth "subcultures" for signs of resistance to capitalist oppression. They saw subcultures – hippies, mods, teds, bikers, punks, etc. – as both tied to a hegemonic "parent" culture and as a force capable of subverting the dominant culture, at least in part. By the 1980s, however, much of the initial promise of subcultural studies had been spent. According to Dick Hebdige, one of the most prominent Birmingham school theorists, the premise of subcultural studies – that youth could be an avant-garde of cultural subversion – had hit head-on the reality of the Reagan-Thatcher years. "The idea of subculture-as-negation," Hebdige argues in *Hiding in the Light*, "grew up alongside punk, remained inextricably linked to it and died when it died." Perhaps more damning to subcultural studies, however, has been the more general move away from Marxist theory in the intervening years. The idea of looking for anticapitalist subversion within youth consumption after the fall of the Berlin Wall, especially with the enormous expansion of the youth consumer market in the last thirty years, seems at best naive. Drug use, particularly chronic hard-drug use, may indeed be subversive of the dominant culture but certainly not in any way that subcultural theorists would find comforting. For these reasons, I have shied away from using the term or the idea of subculture in relation to drugs. See for example Dick Hebdige, *Subculture, the Meaning of Style* (London : Methuen, 1979), and *Hiding in the Light: On Images and Things* (London and New York: Routledge, 1988), as well as Stuart Hall and Tony Jefferson, *Resistance through Rituals: Youth Subcultures in Post-war Britain* (London: Hutchinson, 1976).

34. Anthropologists and epidemiologists have shown that drug markets often act like kinship systems with certain groups tied to other groups through loose contacts, often dealers. See Martin A. Plant, *Drug Users in an English Town* (London: Tavistock, 1975).

35. Arthur Marwick argues the progression from speed to grass was also true of London, *The Sixties Cultural Revolution in Britain, France, Italy, and the United States, c. 1958–c. 1974* (Oxford: Oxford University Press, 1998), p. 78.

36. Arthur Kreuzer *Drogen und Delinquenz: eine jugendkriminologisch-empirische Untersuchung der Erscheinungsformen und Zusammenhänge* (Wiesbaden: Akademische Verlagsgesellschaft, 1975), p. 8. On the history of Preludin see Werner Pieper (ed.), Nazis on Speed: *Drogen im 3. Reich*, Vol. 1 (Berlin: Aufbau Verlag, 2002), and "Preludin: Bomben auf St. Pauli," *Der Spiegel*, 20(8), February 14, 1966, p. 58.

37. See Rüdger Articus, *Die Beatles in Harburg* (Hamburg: Hamburger Museum für Archäologie und die Geschichte Harburgs, 1996), pp. 20–1.

38. Palette was the subject of an important modernist novel by Hubert Fichte, *Die Palette: Roman* (Reinbeck bei Hamburg: Rowohlt, 1968).

39. Margret Kosel, *Gammler Beatniks Provos: Die schleichende Revolution* (Frankfurt am Main: Verlag Bärmeier & Nikel, 1967), p. 84.

40. Ibid., pp. 84–5.

41. StAH, 354–5 II, Jugendbehörde II, Abl. 11.11.1992, 356-04.04 Band 1, Report from Jugendschutztruppe -A-, April 14, 1964.

42. StAH, 354–5 II, Jugendbehörde II, Abl. 11.11.1992, 356-04.04 Band 1, Report from Jugendschutztruppe -C-, July 8, 1964.

43. StAH, 354–5 II, Jugendbehörde II, Abl. 11.11.1992, 356-04.04 Band 1, Report from Jugendschutztruppe, October 16, 1964. Walter Becker, a senior official in the Hamburg Youth Authority, used these three examples in his 1967 article "Die neue Rauschgiftwelle," *Zentralblatt für Jugendrecht und Jugendwohlfahrt*, 54, 1967, p. 362. He misrepresents the cases as recent.

44. Sabina von Dirke, *All Power to the Imagination!: the West German Counterculture from the Student Movement to the Greens* (Lincoln: University of Nebraska Press, 1997), p. 23.

45. Kreuzer, *Drogen* p. 138.

46. Ibid., p. 138–9.

47. Ibid., pp. 139, 226–8. See also Kosel, *Gammler Beatniks Provos*, pp. 9–15, 55–117.

48. Marwick, *The Sixties*, p. 480.

49. The author broke down the figure of more than 100,000 in the following manner: twenty thousand in Holland, thirty thousand in Scandinavia, twelve hundred in Switzerland, twenty-five hundred in Austria, seven thousand in Italy, six thousand in West Germany, two thousand in East Germany, twenty-six thousand in France, eighteen thousand in England, three thousand in Czechoslovakia, six thousand in the Soviet Union, three thousand in Belgium, and only three in Liechtenstein. Walter Hollstein, "Gammler und Provos," *Frankfurter Hefte*, 22, 1967, p. 410.

50. "Gammler: Schalom aleichem," *Der Spiegel*, 20(39), September 19, 1966, p. 72.

51. See Kosel, *Gammler Beatniks Provos*, pp. 53–80; Marwick, *The Sixties*, pp. 479–98. See also Walter Hollstein, "Hippies im Wandel," *Frankfurter Hefte,* 23, 1968, p. 641 and Hollstein, "Gammler und Provos," pp. 409–10.

52. "Gammler: Schalom aleichem," p. 76.

53. "Jugend: Übertriebene Generation," *Der Spiegel*, 21(41), October 2, 1967, p. 168.

54. Walter Becker, "Die neue Rauschgiftwelle," p. 361.

55. StAH, 354–5 II, Jugendbehörde II, Abl. 11.11.1992 356-04.04 Band 1, KM Tullius, Report, November 29, 1965.

56. StAH, 354–5 II, Jugendbehörde II, Abl. 11.11.1992 356-04.04 Band 1, KK 1 B 2, Report, March 18, 1966.

57. StAH, 354–5 II, Jugendbehörde II, Abl. 11.11.1992 356-04.04 Band 1, Amt für Jugendbeförderung, "Verkauf von Preludin-Tabletten im Jugendheim Rahlstedt," June 1, 1966.

58. StAH, 354–5 II, Jugendbehörde II, Abl. 11.11.1992 356-04.04 Band 1, Gehrcke, "Preludin," September 20, 1966.

59. StAH, 354–5 II, Jugendbehörde II, Abl. 11.11.1992 356-04.04 Band 2, Regierungsoberinspektor Hinsch, "Abgabe von Rauschgiften in Gaststätten," July 23, 1968; StAH, 354–5 II, Jugendbehörde II, Abl. 11.11.1992 356-04.04 Band 2, Herman Brandt, "Bekämpfung von Rauschgiftgebrauch," December 5, 1968.

60. For examples see UN Secretary General. "Summary of reports on illicit transactions and seizures of narcotic drugs and psychotropic substances, received by the Secretary-General." 1963: E/NS.1963/Summary 12, p. 11. United Nations documents will be subsequently given in their abbreviated form, as follows: E/NS.1964/Summary 3, pp. 8–9; E/NS.1964/Summary 4, pp. 10–11; E/NS.1964/Summary 12, pp. 6–7; E/NS.1966/Summary 8, p. 15; E/NS.1966/Summary 9, p. 8; E/NS.1966/Summary 10, p. 8; E/NS.1967/Summary 5, p. 9; E/NS.1967/Summary 6, p. 11. See also Richard Neville, *Play Power: Exploring the International Underground* (New York: Random House, 1970), pp. 232–6.

61. E/NS.1965/Summary 4, p. 9; E/NS.1965/Summary 5, pp. 10–11.

62. E/NS.1966/Summary 5, p. 10.

63. StAH, 354–5 II, Jugendbehörde II, Abl. 11.11.1992 356-04.04 Band 1, "Jahresbericht für die Rauschgiftkommission des Wirtschafts- und Sozialrates der Vereinten Nationen," January 19, 1967, BfIH, Rgd. KK Westfal, Report, 1966; StAH, 354–5 II, Jugendbehörde II, Abl. 11.11.1992 356-04.04 Band 1, KM Rytlewski, Report, July 28, 1966; StAH, 354–5 II, Jugendbehörde II, Abl. 11.11.1992 356-04.04 Band 1, KM Rytlewski, "Vernehmung," July 28, 1966.

64. See Kreuzer, 139, 212–213. E/NS.1964/Summary 3, 6–8; E/NS.1965/Summary 4, p. 8; E/NS.1966/Summary 9, p. 10; E/NS.1968/Summary 2, p. 13; E/IT/1966/21; E/IT/1967/74.

65. See E/NS.1964/Summary 4, p. 10; E/NS.1966/Summary 5, p. 15.

66. See E/NS.1965/Summary 5, p. 12; E/NS.1966/Summary 5, p. 10; E/NS.1968/Summary 2, p. 12.

67. See E/NS.1965/Summary 5, p. 12; E/NS.1966/Summary 5, pp. 10, 14; E/NS.1967/Summary 10, p. 15.

68. See E/NS.1965/Summary 5, pp. 11, 14; E/NS.1966/Summary 7, pp. 11–13; E/NS.1966/Summary 8, p. 15; E/NS.196/Summary 8, pp. 22–3; E/NS.1967/Summary 10, p. 10; E/NS.1968/Summary pp. 2, 13.

69. E/NS.1967/Summary 8, pp. 22–3.

70. E/NS.1968/Summary 3, p. 8.

71. Neville, *Play Power*, p. 207.

72. Lieschen Müller quoted in David Tomory, A *Season in Heaven: True Tales from the Road to Kathmandu* (London: Lonely Planet Publications, 1998), p. 25.

73. See Tomory, *A Season in Heaven*, and Jonathon Green, *All Dressed Up. The Sixties and the Counter-Culture* (London: Jonathan Cape, 1998), 224–236. For a more critical view of hippies in the East see Vera Vuckovacki, *Endstation Kathmandu* (Blick + Bild Verlag, 1972).

74. See Neville, *Play Power*, pp. 203–50. On Kabul see also Suzanne Labin, *Hippies, Drogues et Sexe* (Paris: La Table Ronde, 1970), pp. 112–19.

75. This story received considerable press in both Europe and the United States. The book *Midnight Express* by Billy Hayes (New York: Dutton, 1977) was made into a memorable film of the same name the next year. Directed by Alan Parker from a screenplay by Oliver Stone it starred Brad Davis as Billy Hayes, John Hurt as the effete British heroin addict Max, and Randy Quaid as the manic American Jimmy Booth. The movie demonstrates the international breadth of 1960s and 1970s drug tourism. The main four characters are American, British and Swedish.

76. Tomory, *A Season in Heaven*, p. 16.

77. Neville, *Play Power*, p. 207.

78. E/NS.1968/Summary, pp. 1, 3.

79. See "Das Rauschgift Angebot in Hamburg wächst," *Die Welt*, December 27, 1967; Ulrich Mackensen, "Rauschgift am 'Tor zur Freude': Erfolgreiche Razzia der Hamburger Polizei," *Vorwärts*, November 15, 1967, in StAH, 354–5 II, Jugendbehörde II, Abl. 11.11.1992 356-04.04 Band 1. Helmut Locher, "Rauschgift kommt: Bundesrepublik wird Tummelplatz der Banden," *Vorwärts* 20 April 1967, in StAH, 354–5 II, Jugendbehörde II, Abl. 11.11.1992 356-04.04 Band 1.

80. BfIH, Rgd, "Jahresbericht für die Rauschgiftkommission des Wirtschafts- und Sozialrates der Vereinten Nationen," January 17, 1968.

81. StAH, 354–5 II, Jugendbehörde II, Abl. 11.11.1992, 356-04.04 Band 1, Brandt, "Rauschgift unter Jugendlichen in Hamburg," October 12, 1967.

82. Ibid.

83. "Das Rauschgift-Angebot in Hamburg wächst," *Die Welt*, December 27, 1967.

84. Stefan Aust, "LSD in Deutschland," *Konkret*, December 1967, p. 18.

85. See Judith Walkowitz, *City of Dreadful Delight: Narratives of Sexual Danger in Late-Victorian London* (Chicago: University of Chigaco Press, 1992), especially pp. 15–39.

86. StAH, 354–5 II, Jugendbehörde II, Abl. 11.11.1992 356-04.04 Band 2. "Club 99," March 1, 1968.

87. Ibid.

88. Ibid.

89. Ibid.

90. Becker, "Die neue Rauschgiftwelle," p. 363.

Index